RED SAPPHIRE

RED SAPPHIRE

The Woman Who Beat the Blacklist

JULIA BRICKLIN

LYONS
PRESS

Essex, Connecticut

An imprint of Globe Pequot, the trade division of
The Rowman & Littlefield Publishing Group, Inc.
4501 Forbes Blvd., Ste. 200
Lanham, MD 20706
www.rowman.com

Distributed by NATIONAL BOOK NETWORK

British Library Cataloguing in Publication Information available

Library of Congress Cataloging-in-Publication Data
Names: Bricklin, Julia, 1970–
Title: Red sapphire : the woman who beat the blacklist / Julia Bricklin.
Description: Essex, Connecticut : Lyons Press, [2023] | Includes bibliographical references and
    index.
Identifiers: LCCN 2023008022 (print) | LCCN 2023008023 (ebook) | ISBN 9781493061877
    (cloth) | ISBN 9781493078516 (epub)
Subjects: LCSH: Weinstein, Hannah, 1911–1984. | Women journalists—United States—
    Biography. | Women political activists—United States—Biography. | Women television
    producers and directors—Great Britain—Biography. | Women motion picture producers and
    directors—Great Britain—Biography. | Sapphire Films Ltd.—History.
Classification: LCC PN4874.W375 B B55 2023 (print) | LCC PN4874.W375 (ebook) | DDC
    070.92 [B]—dc23/eng/20230320
LC record available at https://lccn.loc.gov/2023008022
LC ebook record available at https://lccn.loc.gov/2023008023

♾™ The paper used in this publication meets the minimum requirements of American National
Standard for Information Sciences—Permanence of Paper for Printed Library Materials, ANSI/
NISO Z39.48-1992.

For my daughter Jane

CONTENTS

Author's Notes

- In her earlier career, Hannah Weinstein often used her maiden name, Dorner. I use only her married name for continuity's sake.
- For the most complete list (thus far) of pseudonyms and their owners for the scripts used for *The Adventures of Robin Hood* and Weinstein's other television productions, please see Steve Neale, "Swashbuckling, Sapphire, and Salt," Chapter 12, in *"Un-American" Hollywood: Politics and Film in the Blacklist Era*, edited by Frank Krutnik, Steve Neale, Brian Neve, and Peter Stanfield (New Jersey: Rutgers University Press, 2007).
- There is no relationship between the family depicted in this book and that of the infamous movie producer of the same name.

Introduction

ONE OF THE FIRST THINGS I DID WHEN I BEGAN TO DO RESEARCH FOR this book was to write a Freedom of Information (FOIA) request to the FBI for Hannah Weinstein's files. As is sometimes the case with public figures, hers had already been sent to the National Archives. Some nice archivists tracked them down and sent them to me. Frustratingly, many names, places, and comments were redacted, but there was enough there to get a clear picture of the enormous number of resources spent surveilling Weinstein. An equal if not greater amount was spent surveilling her better-known writer/producer/actor friends like Ring Lardner Jr., Lillian Hellman, John Howard Lawson, Lester Cole, and Howard Koch, to name just a few.

Weinstein's CIA file was an entirely different hurdle. I sent an FOIA request to the agency thinking I'd receive it within a few months. Indeed, I got a response that said I could expect it by the end of that year. December came and went. When I followed up, the agency gave me a new expected fulfillment date for the following spring. When that date came and went, I followed up, only to be given a deadline six months later. COVID-19 hit, so I understood when I followed up and its public information people blandly told me that someone was working on my request. Deadlines moved substantially every time I followed up. Finally, I decided to hire an attorney.

This was difficult, too. My need for Weinstein's CIA files to write a book was not a big enough case for most lawyers to take on, even those who deal with First Amendment issues. Frankly, I didn't have the money to pay someone, either. But I was angry. What could possibly be in seventy-year-old files that required three years of vetting? Probably nothing, but that begged another question: Why do we have to pay for such lumbering bureaucracies that have seemingly no accountability to American taxpayers? I would never have heard from the CIA again were it not for some dogged follow-up.

Finally, one lawyer took my case and wrote a demand letter to the agency, thinking this would spur them to provide the information or at least tell me why they could not, as prescribed by transparency laws. But the CIA did not respond. Subsequently, that attorney had to move on to bigger cases, and once again, I fished around for another to take pity on me. Thankfully, a lawyer in San Francisco referred me to a colleague named Daniel Stotter.

A specialist in public records access and FOIA, Stotter thought that my request of the agency rose to the level of the public's right to know and decided to help me file suit against the agency. After some more pro forma sparring, the CIA finally provided its paperwork on Weinstein, in dribs and drabs.[1]

If Weinstein were alive, she likely wouldn't have batted an eyelash at this obstruction. Her thoughts about the American agencies that had dogged her and her family and friends for years are apparent in advertising copy she helped write for the Committee for Public Justice:

Go ahead, figure it out. You work part time for the government. If you're like most of us, you work 2 to 3 days a week [just] to pay your taxes. Some of those taxes fund the FBI, the CIA and other government "intelligence" agencies.

What's so intelligent about them? Well, for starters, they've used your money to do things in your name that you would never approve of. Things like:

Illegal wiretapping
Burglaries
Spying
Assassination plots.

The American public found out about these abuses after they hap-pened—long afterwards. Isn't it about time someone began keeping an eye on the Justice Department and the CIA?[2]

Weinstein would probably not have been surprised in the least to learn what agencies were putting in their files about her, at a time when no one thought anyone but a few bureaucrats would read them—statecraft such as, "There is a story about her (definitely not authenticated) that some years ago when she (unmarried) had a baby and was asked who the father was she said, 'The Communist Party.'"[3]

Ring Lardner Jr. spoke of his friend Hannah fondly yet reverently at her funeral in 1984. "The Times obit called her an activist, and I don't think the word has ever been used more aptly." He continued, "Most of us—when we read or hear what's going on in the world—react with approval or disapproval or detachment, and go back to daily living. Han-nah's reaction was more likely to be, 'What can I do about it?' and then 'Who can help?' and 'What approach will get the best results?'" Wein-stein's response to events, Lardner said, was to create counter events, and they were always "bigger and broader than anyone else thought they could be."[4]

***

I am not a Cold War historian. I have little background in the Red Scare and could not possibly keep up with the many PhDs, authors, and other experts out there who have studied it for decades and will always be twenty steps ahead of me in the era's intellectual and political ramifications and rabbit holes. The sheer number of people involved in just Weinstein's European story was staggering. I culled just a hundred or so of the most pertinent people from perhaps more than a thousand potential sources, among them children and grandchildren, nieces, and nephews of people from Weinstein's extensive professional sphere. I am sure there are hundreds more we will never know about, given that their work and communication had to be clandestine, as was the case with informants and politicos.

This last obfuscation applies to Weinstein, too. In her professional and private life, by necessity, she did not share information with people who did not specifically need it. Because this is an unauthorized biography, I did not have the luxury of knowing the personal events and education of her formative years that motivated her to pursue the career that linked her brilliance in activism with her media prowess. It's my sincere hope that someday those who were close to her might choose to fill in those gaps. It's also my sincere hope that someday MI6 and other British intelligence agencies will make their coverage of Weinstein available. My request to those agencies turned up nothing, but we know that US intelligence overseas had to work in tandem with them at times. MI6 and the Home Office, for example, kept watch on blacklisted actor and director (and colleague of Weinstein) Sam Wanamaker throughout the 1950s. One agent wrote, "I am always interested in anyone who works for HANNAH WEINSTEIN and her Sapphire Films Co. which is a nest for 'un-Americans' or Communist Americans."[5]

I re-tread a lot of ground, sourcing works by Paul Buhle, Dave Wagner, Jim and Tony Kahn, Rebecca Prime, Larry Ceplair, Brian Neve, Norma Barzman, and Thomas W. Devine, to name just a few. Wherever possible, I asked these authors to help me dig into Sapphire and its special place within discussions of the Cold War and the blacklist. It's not easy to position a hugely capitalistic venture within the context of persecution, but they helped me do it.

Hannah Weinstein's story and that of Sapphire Films necessarily involve the story of the Hollywood Ten and the blacklist. Those two terms do not include the thousands of people who were not on any official list of the major studios, or even "graylisted"—those who were able to find work at smaller studios but not the majors. These Cold War nadirs are important backdrops in a story about a woman who saw a world that was changing—a Western empire that had won a terrifying war in the name of freedom and democracy, only to emerge from the carnage with new enemies it could not directly engage with. And although women and minorities and first-generation immigrants had been an integral part of America's winning the war, they still did not have the same rights and pay as white, native-born male citizens.

Most importantly, this book is about a woman who knew that her native country—to show its public that the loss of 420,000 Americans was not in vain and that it would not succumb to fascism—was suppressing freedom of expression and organization and was persecuting its own citizens. She articulated this time and again, but I think the best summary came in 1970, long after her decade of exile in Europe, when Weinstein helped her great friend Lillian Hellman form the Committee for Public Justice, Inc. (CPJ), which aimed to counter the "repressive tendencies" of J. Edgar Hoover's FBI.[6]

Weinstein's concerns about the American government and world affairs in the middle decades of the twentieth century are no different than the concerns I had as I started writing this book in late 2019. It was easy to see some politicians from the last few years as Joseph McCarthy-type figures: powerful people of questionable mental health bent on repressing individuals who don't agree with their views, weaponizing government agencies, and using misinformation tactics against political rivals. It was also easy to see some of these politicians and their advisors playing the role of Hoover. As with some of our lawmakers today, few in the 1940s and 1950s had the courage to speak out against, let alone subvert, McCarthy until the Warren Court trimmed his wings and the Senate finally grew brave. Even the Kennedys were friendly with McCarthy—they were fellow Catholics who feared godless Communism.

The attack on the US Capitol on January 6, 2021, has led to an ongoing series of existential questions about what Americans are willing to tolerate and fight for to preserve the freedoms we do have—imperfect freedoms, but ones that are perhaps better than anywhere else on the planet. The point is, Weinstein understood—as many do today—that consolidation of power under the guise of patriotism can quickly lead to fascism.

Weinstein's story resonates with me. I admire her belief (and practice) that change starts with our own actions. The 2010 Supreme Court case won by the conservative nonprofit Citizens United opened the floodgates for corporations to have undue influence in American elections. Because of this and the increasing disparity between rich and poor in America,

I've come to believe a certain amount of activism must be woven into our daily lives to preserve basic freedoms and opportunity for everyone.

Sometimes, benefits or results from this grassroots effort seem elusive. There are too few of us asking questions, writing letters, making phone calls . . . resisting. Leah Finnegan, one of my favorite bloggers, expressed this well when discussing French poet Charles Baudelaire's quote that the evil of modernity was simply this: apathy.

> *Anyway, ennui—commonly defined as boredom, but better defined as the refusal to interrogate your rapidly changing surroundings—was a simpler concept in Baudelaire's time. Back then there was ample access to opium and zero access to the internet. Everyone had syphilis and died at 40. Is that better than living until 110, and having to work as an Instacart shopper until you're 108 because the labor infrastructure of America has dissolved? I can't say.*[7]

We can see the proverbial writing on the wall: the rise of anti-intellectualism, anti-Semitism, white supremacist hate groups, and gun violence. Even one of these entities in this nation makes it a dangerous place for many people to be, and this is certain to worsen if some commonsense reform does not prevail.

Hannah Dorner Weinstein was far from perfect. She could be impatient, indomitable, and opportunistic—even allowing for the sexist lens of the times in which she lived. But she was also passionate, compassionate, and an incredibly loyal friend, mother, and advocate. She recognized that if she could not bring equality to people on a global level, she could start by doing so within a smaller group of persecuted people. "What few people knew at the time," said producer Louis Marks, "was that at considerable professional risk to herself Hannah Weinstein had insisted on engaging leading Hollywood screenwriters who at the time were banned from work in their own country by the McCarthy blacklist."[8] Moreover, Weinstein did it all on her own terms.

Not one single person in this book ever tried to overthrow the government of the United States; to my knowledge, no television episode mentioned in this book has spurred anyone to try.

Chapter i

Beginnings

THE FIRST EPISODE OF *THE ADVENTURES OF ROBIN HOOD* DEBUTED IN Canada on September 12, 1955. It then appeared for the first time in Britain three days later, and finally, in the United States on Monday, September 26, 1955, at 7:30 p.m. Eastern Time. It was the first filmed British series to appear on an American television network. It was also the first television series to be seen simultaneously in three countries, and the first costume-based drama series to air on broadcast television.[1] Its creator and executive producer was forty-four-year-old Hannah Dorner Weinstein.

That night, executives at CBS Television, its advertising agency partners, its distributor Official Films, and its producer Sapphire Films held their collective breaths. Board members from Wildroot Hair Tonic Company and Johnson & Johnson prayed that their investment had paid off. They hoped that the early, youth-oriented timeslot would garner enough attention that mothers and wives would purchase the goods that supported the show.

They needn't have worried. *The Adventures of Robin Hood* was a huge hit. Ben Gross from the *New York Daily News* called it "the answer to those who have been crying for entertaining quality shows for young-sters," and that its swordplay and historical authenticity would appeal to old and young alike.[2] In 1955, when only thirty-one million American households—64 percent—had a television set, some thirty-two million people tuned in for its debut. It took top spots in Canada and Britain, too. Subsequent airings pulled millions more people into its regular viewership—and they stayed until the very last of its 143 original episodes aired in 1960, then tuned into repeats for decades.

Robin Hood fulfilled the very definition of "broadcasting"—the idea that a program should appeal to as many people as possible in what was considered the traditional American family. And though the drama aired at what was considered a "right before bedtime" timeslot for younger viewers, it attracted just as many parents and other adults in the household, earning its label as "family friendly."[3] *TV Guide* and *Variety* praised the show's success in breaking America's Davy Crockett and Superman spell, and said it could "very well be the answer to a mother's prayer about Westerns," and "a welcome relief from 'they-went-thataway' school of children's hour programming."[4] That first season, it led into the top-rated George Burns and Gracie Allen Show, then starting its sixth season.

Sapphire Films—the show's producer in Surrey, England, had cleverly formulated a program that would appeal to children on its surface, but also one that would appeal to adults, too. "For younger viewers," media historian James Chapman posits, "such episodes have a transgressive appeal in the idea of an outlaw lifestyle free from parental authority, while parents in turn could identify with Robin's predicament in finding himself in the role of a surrogate father who has to control unruly children." Other commentators saw the main character, played by actor Richard Greene, as sort of "everyone's favorite uncle."[5]

What most viewers did not realize was that they were watching a thinly veiled commentary on the plight of the blacklisted writers and McCarthy hysteria in general. According to one historian, even the very first episode, "The Coming of Robin Hood," must be considered as the setup for all the ones that followed. In the opening scenes, Robin—the protagonist—has been locked out of his ancestral home. A Norman lord produces false documents proclaiming the death of his predecessor and his own inheritance of the manor. This action forces Robin, who is returning home from the Crusades, to enter his home via a secret route. These opening scenes resemble the narrative of the American writers who reached their native audiences by using the alternative path of a new medium produced in a foreign country.[6]

The genius of *Robin Hood*, too, was that it appealed to viewers on all points on the political spectrum. The basic myth of Robin Hood was—is—probably the most "ideologically flexible" of all popular heroes—a fact that did not escape Weinstein or her writers. For the Right, Chapman explains, Robin (both in myth and in TV series) was a warrior-patriot and a staunch defender of the Crown; his allegiance is to King Richard and, according to the legend, he fights to protect the absent king's throne from the ambition of his treacherous brother Prince John. For the Left, Robin was a proto-socialist engaged in the redistribution of wealth; according to the legend, he robs from the rich to give to the poor.

Weinstein was careful to avoid this overt trope, but many episodes feature Robin forcibly reclaiming monies or onerous taxes taken from villagers and returning them. There's even an environmentalist reading: Robin as a forest-dwelling back-to-nature eco-warrior, harvesting the natural resources of the greenwood and leading an alternative lifestyle outside the capitalist system.[7]

The Robin Hood character as embodied in the filmed series *The Adventures of Robin Hood* reflected Left ideology, whether viewers realized it or not. In "The Miser," for example, Sir William (Laurence Naismith) raises the taxes on his tenant farmers, then threatens to throw them off their land if they don't come up with the money. Robin comes up with a plan to get the villagers their money back, but it involves Friar Tuck keeping them in church while he does so. In "A Jongleur," Bartholomew (Peter Hammond) upsets the Sheriff of Nottingham and ends up as Robin's guest for dinner. He is soon recruited to help Robin and Little John in a plan to relieve the sheriff of the unfair tax money.

More specifically, in some cases, the episodes frequently pushed back on Red Scare culture with their choice of plots. In several of them, conflict centers on the lower-class members of Nottingham being denied political rights as well as some economic rights. In episode twenty-nine, "Children of the Greenwood," for example, a boy and a girl are made into serfs after their father is framed for murder. In other words, the family loses its autonomy because of Norman tyranny. In "The Vandals," the sheriff interrogates a village ironsmith to make the man confess that he has made arrow tips for Robin Hood. "I know you are a decent citizen now," the sheriff goads him, evoking the language of the House Un-American Activities Committee inquisitors that sought to guilt former radicals into naming names of Communists and fellow travelers. In another episode, "Blackmail," a man stumbles upon Maid Marian and Robin talking in the forest and threatens to inform the Sheriff of Nottingham of Marian's fellow-traveler-like association with the outlaw. And in "The Ordeal," the sheriff hatches a plot to turn villagers against Robin's band of merry men by framing one of them for murder. Nottingham sows rumors among the villagers, precipitating a mob mentality that quickly grows out of control. The zealous villagers plant evidence to affirm their suspicions that the outlaw Edgar has committed the crime and force Edgar to face a trial in which he will have to grasp an iron rod that has been heated in a fire. In true "witch hunt" form, he will be deemed guilty if his hand blisters.[8] And so on.

Unknown at the time to everyone except Weinstein's close circle, the program was written by American writers who had been blacklisted by the McCarthy Communist witch hunt. They had to write the *Robin Hood* scripts behind pseudonyms, and use a very labyrinthic, anxiety-producing system not only to write and deliver the scripts but to get paid. Principle writers Ring Lardner Jr. and Ian McLellan Hunter foresaw the pitfalls in this process when they first agreed to take the job:

> *There is just one other problem to all this from our point of view and that is money; when we get it, and how. We had assumed the fact that you were working through a lawyer's office would make it practical for the loot to be delivered directly to us, or at least to a relative or close friend, and that there would be no particular problem about a formal contract.[9]*

Of course, there were many problems. Fees had to go through lawyers, advertising agency administrators, and network accountants—and this was just on the US side of the Atlantic. The notes and accounting coming from the United Kingdom side could be intercepted at any time. For every script, at every stop, there was the potential for a writer's real name to be discovered. Ironically, good work was their Achilles heel. "We each had a steady name for checks, but if you had the same name on more than a couple of scripts, then the executives at CBS or wherever might want to see that writer."[10] Then, like now, network management and talent agencies constantly tried to poach writers who were connected to a hit show.

The woman at the helm of this entire endeavor was Hannah Dorner Weinstein. By her mid-forties, Weinstein had already lived a lifetime before ever setting foot in Europe.

***

Before the Cossacks, before the Nazis, before the Soviets and Putin, there was the thriving Jewish community of Krystynopol, Austria.

Today, the city is better known as Chervonograd, in the L'viv region of far western Ukraine. Situated roughly halfway between the Baltic and North Seas, it was one of the most beautiful and vibrant centers in eastern Europe. By 1900, Jews had lived here and nearby for nearly five hundred years. They had coexisted mostly peacefully with Greek and Roman Catholics, Turks, Armenians, and any number of other religious and ethnic populations, in spite of the constant strictures placed upon them by kings. By the turn of the last century, Jews comprised nearly three-quarters of Krystynopol's population.

But in 1903, the massacres against them started. Russian imperial authorities needed a distraction. They were faced with growing unrest stemming from the empire's losses in the Russo-Japanese War. It granted reactionary newspapers and ultraconservative loyalist groups a free hand to agitate against "Jewish machinations" as the cause of the social upheavals of the time. Nationalism contributed to anti-Jewish feeling, too. In nearby cities such as Lemberg and Brodi, Ukranian peasants waited until the men were at synagogue on the Sabbath. Then they raided their homes, smashing windows and furniture and stealing belongings. Women who refused to leave their houses were beaten, raped, and sometimes thrown from second- or third-story windows. Reports from Vienna told of Jews, including children, being clubbed to death or set on fire.

Against this backdrop of violence, and most certainly the threat of being conscripted into the Russian army, twenty-year-old Israel Dorner left his mother, father, and siblings in Krystynopol. The young fur merchant boarded a train in Lemberg—now called L'viv—and some days later arrived at the ferry to Southampton, England. From here, he sailed on to America. Dorner arrived in New York City on Christmas Day of 1904.

He found work as a furrier with a firm in the city and a few years later married Celia Kaufman, also from Krystynopol and the daughter of a rabbi. The pair moved from her parents' apartment to their own in the city, and on June 23, 1911, daughter Chana—Hannah—was born. Two years later, brother Albert was born, and in 1917, brother Seymour. The Dorner children grew up in various rented homes, all close to the future Yankee Stadium. The South Bronx was rapidly becoming "the place to be" for working-class immigrants with upwardly mobile prospects. By the middle of 1925, it was populated by grocery stores, restaurants, vegetable and fruit markets, tailors, and hardware stores. There were new public schools, and inhabitants throughout the borough shopped in department stores and boutiques at 149th Street and Third Avenue, an area known as the Hub, which also had movie palaces and vaudeville theaters—all of which was a fifteen-minute walk for the Dorners. By 1930, the family lived on the 1400 block of trendy Grand Concourse, a wide street modeled after Park Avenue and the Champs Elysees in Paris.[11]

It's not clear if Weinstein's parents had anything to do with any formal political party, but in the 1920s and especially the 1930s, the Communist Party dominated the garment and needle-trade unions, especially those in the fur industry, so its presence would be hard to avoid.[12] They were almost certainly enmeshed in the travails of her aunt Sarah Dorner, a dressmaker. Sarah came to the United States in 1910 and quickly rose to the highest ranks of the powerful New York City branch of the International Ladies' Garment Workers (ILGW). In 1923, its general executive board expelled her, along with eighteen others, for their work with labor agitator and leader William Z. Foster. Broadly speaking, Foster led efforts to unite factions within different unions, so that they might gain even more leverage in negotiating rights for workers within different sectors. The ILGW found the eighteen guilty of holding separate caucuses outside union headquarters and sharing internal information with outsiders, including Foster's Communist representative for New York.

Ms. Dorner spent the remaining decades of her life working on behalf of the ILGW in Los Angeles, resisting demands by factions inside and outside the union that wished to force its members to sign affidavits that they were not Communists.[13]

In fact, like Hannah, Sarah was a registered Democrat, not a member of the Communist Party. One daughter recalled that Hannah was "a Marxist and socialist but not a Communist."[14] But even if she was, it would have meant something totally different then than it did after the lens of Stalin's purges. As radical feminist and essayist Vivian Gornick summarized, there was good reason that some Marxist tenets found eager listeners in the United States:

> *The Communist Party USA (CPUSA) was formed in 1919, two years after the Russian Revolution. Over the next forty years, it grew steadily from a membership roll of two or three thousand to, at the height of its influence in the 1930s and 1940s, seventy-five thousand. All in all, nearly a million Americans were Communists at one time or another. While it is true that the majority joined the Communist Party in those years because they were members of the hard-pressed working class (garment district Jews, West Virginia miners, California fruit-pickers), it was even truer that many more in the educated middle class (teachers, scientists, writers) joined because for them, too, the party was possessed of a moral authority that lent concrete shape to a sense of social injustice made urgent by the Great Depression and World War II.*[15]

Between 1927 and 1939, ordinary citizens watched as the very rich got even richer by consolidating their holdings and gobbling up undervalued assets like oil and real estate, and paying labor a fraction of what it was worth. At the same time, there were few social safety nets to help the most impoverished and struggling.

After World War II ended in 1945, the US government made beneficial programs available to those who had managed to keep their lives—the G.I. Bill and the implementation of some New Deal reforms, for example. But some Americans were alarmed—rightfully so, as it turned out—that capitalists were driving the country's post-war agenda and dictating overseas policy. They criticized Truman's $3.75 billion loan to Britain as helping the latter claw back its pre–World War I empire. This, plus the larger Marshall Plan, they thought, was the start of America's own imperial designs—designs that would enrich a few, impoverish millions, and require more bloodshed to protect.

Though actual numbers of CPUSA members were low in the context of America's population (and many of those members never even set foot in a meeting), there were millions more who considered themselves sympathizers and fellow travelers. The party had an in-your-face daily newspaper that liberals as well as radicals regularly read. "As one old Red put it," Gornick wrote, "'Whenever some new world catastrophe announced itself throughout the Depression and World War II, *The Daily Worker* sold out in minutes.'" At that time, in that place, the Marxist vision of world solidarity as translated by the Communist Party offered a feeling of structure, safety, and shared humanity.[16]

Weinstein entered New York University in the fall of 1927, at sixteen, to pursue a degree in journalism. She attended for four years but left just shy of obtaining a degree. In a memorial to her, friend and colleague Louis Marks recalled that she went to work on the foreign desk of the *New York Herald Tribune* at the age of seventeen.[17] She appeared to be working full time for the paper by 1930. For the most part, she was assigned coverage of women's sports figures. Instead of just reciting their stats and athletic prowess, though, she highlighted the women through a feminist lens, asking questions about obstacles to having both a marriage and a career; how more young women could become involved with sports; how universities and communities should provide equal training facilities for both men and women; and how advanced degrees help women stay independent after their athletic careers are over.[18] She occasionally grabbed a more substantive piece, like the one she wrote on the state of affairs in the nation of Liberia, which was created in the 1820s by free and formerly enslaved people of color from the United States.[19]

The Great Depression landed as Weinstein reached adulthood, and though her family was relatively comfortable, the effects of it no doubt affected her worldview and interest in progressivism. By 1930, thirty million Americans were out of work, and that number doubled the following year. As most educated people knew, the economic boom of the 1920s and rampant speculation had led to this crash. Workers in the mass production industries—steel, auto, rubber, textiles, oil, chemicals, and so on—were unorganized and at the mercy of employers, who derived huge profits at the expense of the sweat and fatigue of their workers. They had no rights, and anyone who stood up for the workers' rights ran the risk of being accused of being a "Communist," "a Red," or a "Bolshevik." With no safety nets in place for workers when the world markets crashed, millions of Americans lost their entire life savings, their homes, and their livelihoods. Many suffered permanent effects of malnutrition and inability to pay for health care. The Depression affected people of color more harshly and permanently than whites.

In 1933, Weinstein got a job on the campaign staff of Fiorello La Guardia, who ran for mayor of New York City. Though his mother was Jewish and he had been raised in an orthodox home in Trieste, La Guardia chose not to wear his Jewish heritage on his sleeve. All the same, he was an ardent advocate for Jewish rights. Later, this would crystallize into a virulent and vocal crusade against Hitler and his regime, but when Weinstein joined his mayoral campaign, anti-corruption and anti-Tammany Hall was his focus. Though a Republican, La Guardia worked closely with Franklin D. Roosevelt, and insisted he would spend his public service days raising the quality of urban life. During the depths of the Depression, with the city's treasury on the verge of insolvency, he managed to reform the welfare system and make it one of the nation's most progressive. Weinstein met her future husband, Isadore ("Pete"), as they toiled on speeches for La Guardia in the basement of Gracie Mansion.

After La Guardia's successful campaign, Weinstein worked to elect East Harlem's Vito Marcantonio to Congress, and was possibly on staff when he switched parties from Republican to the American Labor Party and won in 1938. That same year, on May 26 at 2:40 p.m., Hannah and Pete married at the New York City clerk's office.

CHAPTER 2

"Girls Like That"

AFTER THEY WERE MARRIED, PETE AND HANNAH SETTLED INTO AN apartment on West 103rd Street, where a lot of other young advertising, marketing, and publishing professionals lived. Their first daughter was born in March of 1941, at which point the couple moved to a more spacious apartment on West 92nd. Another daughter arrived almost exactly two years later. Pete worked in public relations for the dairy industry. Since the end of the La Guardia campaign and between giving birth, Hannah had been working for Bernard Lichtenberg's Institute for Public Relations as a copywriter and associate strategist. The institute focused primarily on business issues on American soil, such as wage conditions in certain industries, and re-branding the view of alcoholic beverages as something to be served at home as opposed to the saloon—the image of which was permanently tarnished by Prohibition.

The firm kept promoting Weinstein. By 1940, she'd risen to top management. In 1941, she took charge of a new account: the National Council of American-Soviet Friendship (NCASF).[1] The council, composed largely of professionals who were sympathetic to socialism, believed that the USSR and the United States should join in their common fight against autocracy. There was plenty of branding work to be done with the NCASF given the non-aggression treaty signed by Joseph Stalin and Adolf Hitler in August of 1939. Though Hitler would break this pact a little less than two years later, many members fled, never to return.

Leading up to World War II, the NCASF's mission was more about cultural exchange and education between east and west. But on June 22,

1941, Adolf Hitler's army invaded the Soviet Union, thus ending the alliance of two totalitarian empires. Now, NCASF had a more sharply defined goal: for America and the Soviet Union to form an anti-fascist alliance. Continued cooperation between the nations, the group trilled, could become an "inclusive system of collective security" for a post-war world. A secondary benefit to come from such an alliance, it said, was the sharing of scientific and educational research that could increase the world's food production, keep its water clean—maybe even cure cancer at some point.

Hollywood also got its chance to yoke itself to this idea of American-Soviet friendship when Japan attacked Pearl Harbor on December 7, 1941. While thousands of performers and artists considered themselves proponents of left-wing causes, or even Communist sympathizers, there were those who were proud members of the Communist Party of the United States. For party members in America—those who saw Marxism and Leninism as a means to utopia—this awful event of Pearl Harbor provided some relief. They were no longer socially reviled in some circles because they could, very crudely speaking, be on the "right side." Fascists had attacked the Motherland, and overnight, party members were fighting alongside Roosevelt, Churchill, and Stalin for their "world of the future." They might not have been ideal dinner guests at mainstream Hollywood parties, but internally, they could feel more closely aligned with fellow Americans of all political stripes and the Western world at large.

When Japan attacked Pearl Harbor, Communist Party members joined with the rest of Hollywood in fighting a common enemy. Because of its proximity to Hawaii, the West Coast was immediately affected by the war. Los Angeles and environs had blackouts, its harbor was ringed with barbed wire, and Hollywood stars heard the same air raid sirens that other citizens did. Naturally, the film capital of the world turned itself into a hub of resources for the war effort. The Motion Picture Academy set up a research council composed of talent from all the top studios to produce training, historical, and public relations films for the US Army.[2]

About 12 percent of those employed in the film industry joined the armed forces, including those who were members of the CPUSA.

Michael Blankfort, a screenwriter who would later become a front for the blacklisted Albert Maltz for the latter's screenplay of *Broken Arrow* (1950), joined the marines. So did Michael Wilson, who would go on to write *The Bridge on the River Kwai* alongside Carl Foreman, neither of whom received credit for it until 1984, after they were both dead. Wilson would eventually write some scripts for Weinstein in Europe, as would Paul Jarrico, who enlisted in the merchant marine. Ring Lardner Jr. and Maurice Rapf, who would work for Weinstein and be so integral to the success of her television shows, tried to enlist in any service that would take them, but even at this early stage, their political views made them a security threat and they were denied.[3]

The arts and entertainment community in Los Angeles were among the first to respond to America's entry into the war, setting a course for their colleagues in New York, Chicago, and the rest of the country. Communists who remained in Hollywood had plenty of opportunities to support the war effort. Three days after Pearl Harbor, film colony veterans formed the Hollywood Victory Committee, a clearinghouse for volunteer war efforts by the film community. Just one week after Pearl Harbor, party stalwarts created the Hollywood Writers Mobilization (HWM), which comprised members of every guild imaginable: Screen Writers, Radio Writers, Screen Cartoonists, Independent Publicists, and so on. Its goal was to satisfy the urgent demand for speeches, shorts, advertisements, entertainment, documentaries, and so on in support of the war effort. Notable members of its first editorial board were playwright and screenwriter John Howard Lawson and writer-director Abraham Polonsky, who—years later—would become intrinsic components of Weinstein's empire.[4]

Again, crudely speaking, America's entry into World War II demanded that true Communist Party members and Hollywood liberals unite in combat against Hitler's fascist ambitions—in reality, something many had done since the dictator had risen to power in 1933, and since Franco had come to power in Spain a few years later. For many artists (and, of course, Americans at large), the Hitler-Stalin pact two years earlier spurred many to leave the Communist Party and Communist-associated groups like NCASF. Those who remained could now unite against a single fascist enemy. After Pearl Harbor, the party even declared its support for interning Japanese Americans on the West Coast, and the prosecution of Trotskyists for conspiring to teach and advocate the overthrow of the US government. The party essentially remade itself into the left wing of FDR's New Deal coalition. This was the world from which Hannah Weinstein drew her friendship and talent.

The war also ushered in a new era of public relations opportunities and missives for both the government and the private sector. If there was one common denominator that organizations and agencies of all political stripes had, it was that they all had a vested interest in not just reporting numbers and facts, but also in creating a public image that lent credibility to politicians, government bureaus, and private enterprise. More narrowly, the profession evolved very quickly as a way for America and other industrialized countries to sell a war.

For Weinstein, public relations offered a good and respectable way for a smart, engaging young mother to work outside the home. The Institute for Public Relations handled accounts for everything from whiskey makers in Kentucky to meat packers in Chicago. Now it was becoming a quasi-lobbying body, often working on behalf of trade unions and running interference between industries and political candidates. In the months leading up to America's formal declaration of war, for example, it sent speakers to Albany and Buffalo, to counsel manufacturing firms about looming war debt and how to smoothly shift from consumer goods to national defense production.

To get more attention for NCASF, Weinstein helped spearhead the creation of an event—a "congress"—that would draw attention and legitimacy to the council. Such an event would be held in the fall of 1942, the twenty-five-year commemoration of the October Revolution and the creation of the USSR. She decided that the best way to get newspaper and radio coverage was to recruit celebrity sponsors and speakers for an inaugural event—a rally—to be held at Madison Square Garden.

By all accounts, the two-day rally was a huge success. Every seat was sold out—an estimated twenty-three thousand people jammed MSG on November 7 and 8 to attend panels and workshops about Russian engineering and education. There was speech after speech praising the

Red Army; about the possibilities of joint Arctic, oceanic, and space exploration; and about mobilizing women for more jobs in technology and manufacturing. Weinstein got every major newspaper in the country to cover the entire forty-eight hours.

For the most part, the rally highlighted the ideals of world security and prosperity possible if these two gigantic allies could share information. Thousands cheered when Mayor La Guardia shouted that every Nazi who entered Moscow would do so as a captured and crushed prisoner of war. Governor of New York Herbert H. Lehman compared the Mother Country to New York City, both melting pots of different religions and nationalities that worked peacefully alongside each other. From Washington, D.C., President Dwight D. Eisenhower wired a message saluting the Soviet army, which was read at the rally.[5]

According to her FBI files and other sources, Weinstein became a "concealed Communist" at this point. In later analysis, the CIA vacillated on her status, then concluded she was not.[6] But whether she was or not is irrelevant. She was surrounded by avowed party members and her work for the council inextricably tied her to subversive activity, so as far as the government was concerned, she was. In her memoirs, ex-Communist (and close friend of Mayor La Guardia) Bella V. Dodd didn't name Weinstein specifically, but she was clearly describing her and the rest of NCASF and similar colleagues when she penned this:

> *The Communist Party made the most of this. Now there emerged the Russian Institute with its imposing headquarters on Park Avenue. This was a sophisticated propaganda agency; it brought American educators, public officials, artists, young people of families of wealth into this left-wing world. Famous names, Vanderbilt, Lamont, Whitney, Morgan, mingled with those of communist leaders. The Russian Institute was so respectable that it was allowed to give in-service courses to New York City schoolteachers for credit.*
>
> *In Albany and in Washington, a new crop of young, native American Communists swarmed into the legislative halls as legislative representatives and public-relations and research aides to legislators. With inside information on what was happening, they were*

able to guide legislators in the direction of Soviet-American unity. They helped produce dozens of important public figures at Madison Square Garden rallies, organized under various labels but filled by the rank and file of devoted party members. It was a glittering society that was emerging, made up of Russian diplomats and Russian business agents, of Americans in evening clothes, and artistic Bohemians in careless dungarees, all of them cheering the repeated avowals of friendship with the Soviet Motherland. . . . The Independent Committee of Artists, Scientists and Professionals, under the chairmanship of Jo Davidson, the sculptor, was under strong Party direction.[7]

***

Dodd wrote about Alexander Trachtenberg, the unapologetic leader of the CPUSA and publisher of translated works by Lenin, Stalin, and other Marxist theorists. It was Trachtenberg, she said, who was most gifted at pulling the strings of all these leftists. He told her, she said, that when Communism came to America it would come under the label of "progressive democracy." It would come, he added, "in labels acceptable to the American people." In other words, Dodd claimed, Trachtenberg planned to manipulate someone like Hannah Weinstein to create an organization that Communists could use to indoctrinate unsuspecting citizens.[8]

Trachtenberg and Weinstein were in constant contact in the early to mid-1940s and held meetings at the Weinstein's newest apartment on Riverside Drive. According to FBI informants, Trachtenberg and Harlow Shapley freely spoke of their association with Weinstein as a fellow Communist, though these admittances were never verified. Again, whether Weinstein adhered to the party line was immaterial—her competencies at getting publicity or raising money or both for any left-wing cause that had true believers among its leadership made her useful to the party. Her work for the Joint Anti-Fascist Refugee Committee, for example, helped raise $75,000 for humanitarian aid to those who had fled Spain's civil war and were stranded in other nations. But, like its chairman, actress Dorothy Parker, she was placed under the same scrutiny as other members, like declared Communists Dalton Trumbo, Paul Robeson, and Martha Dodd Stern.[9]

All the same, Weinstein and other major drivers of the rally and its goal of creating a permanent organization had already been criticized for being naïve or willfully ignorant or even supportive of the horrors of Stalin's purges and authoritarian goals. Joseph E. Davies, FDR's recent ambassador to the Soviet Union and a co-founder of the rally, embarrassingly lauded Stalin and Soviet diplomats for their "intelligence, ability, judgment and fearlessness."[10] Suffice it to say that, in this time and place, Weinstein had a job to do, and she did it extraordinarily well.

Weinstein's organizational skills with the convention caught the attention of its new chairman. In 1943, he appointed her member of a committee to reorganize the foundation that sponsored the event and turn it into a permanent, national institution. Still using her maiden name professionally, she helped coordinate the opening of at least thirty local affiliates across the country. In turn, these affiliates, particularly those in New York, Chicago, and Los Angeles, sponsored various conferences, concerts, and exhibits. Dozens of mayors across the United States proclaimed November 9 as "American-Soviet Friendship Day" and sponsored scores of cultural events held in city forums and in public schools.[11]

Keeping the momentum going, Weinstein planned a second rally at Madison Square Garden for November of 1943, this time for three days. British scientist and Marxist J. B. S. Haldane showed films from Russian biologists resurrecting dead animals by way of a special organ regenerator apparatus. Panels featured women who presented best practices in childcare in times of war and peace. Explorer Sir Hubert Wilkins discussed ways that east and west could collaborate on Arctic research. Secretary of the Interior Harold Ickes lashed out at newspaper conglomerates, arguing that they were part of a machinery working against a Soviet-American alliance for peace. The media rivaled Hitler, he said, in their "lack of scruples about deliberately saying what is not true."[12]

Director Orson Welles joined the core group of politicians and celebrities pitching for the Soviets, and by now, Ambassador Davies's film, *Mission to Moscow*, had been released to widespread controversy, drawing more attention to the rally. Commissioned by FDR when the

United States and Soviet Union were allies, *Mission* whitewashed Stalinist repression. Even though the film fervently stressed Davies's belief in capitalism and democracy, it surprised few that the now four-year-old House Committee on Un-American Activities (HUAC) chose to scrutinize the film and everyone associated with it, including studio mogul Jack Warner, writer Howard Koch, and actor Walter Huston.

Weinstein then organized another celebration, this time on February 21, 1944. It was a celebration of Red Army Day, complete with a dinner and speeches by military personnel and words of praise from Generals George C. Marshall, Dwight D. Eisenhower, and John J. Pershing, to name a few.[13]

As the months of 1944 crept along and the Soviet army took Ukraine and Allied forces prepared for D-Day, the Democratic Party worried about Franklin Delano Roosevelt and whether he could win or even run as a fourth-term president. His health was already on the decline due to his hardening of the arteries that had been worsened by the stress of serving during the war. He also suffered from hypertension, acute bronchitis, and congestive heart failure, some of which didn't become public knowledge until decades later. Roosevelt followed his doctor's regimen of reduced working hours and a very strict diet and recovered enough energy to push for a final term, motivated by his desire to see the war to its end.

FDR also wanted to avoid the fate of his predecessor Woodrow Wilson, who saw America through World War I only to have his idealistic plans for lasting peace fall apart in the years that followed. And so, his running mate this term became of paramount importance; FDR knew that there was a very real likelihood he would not make it through all four years. Before he accepted the nomination, Roosevelt decided to drop his running mate, whom he saw as too left wing and eccentric, in favor of Missouri senator Harry S. Truman. The jilted candidate was fifty-six-year-old Henry Wallace, who had served as FDR's vice president in his recent third term.

FDR selected Truman in order to gain more votes from moderate Democrats, but opponent Thomas Dewey, the moderate Republican governor of New York, ran a strong campaign to get these voters, too. He wouldn't undermine social and economic New Deal reforms, Dewey said, but rather make them more efficient. The Republican also made subtle and not-so-subtle attacks on FDR's age and health. While FDR's third-term candidacy had been tougher in many ways, winning in 1944 was not a foregone conclusion, and many far-leftists in the entertainment and artistic communities panicked at the thought of the Republican Party designing a post-war roadmap for peace and prosperity. This was exactly the fear of sculptor Jo Davidson, soon to be Weinstein's top political partner.

In today's world of television and social media stars and influencers, it's hard to understand just how famous a clay-and-stone artist could be. During the first half of the twentieth century, though, there were few craftsmen who routinely made the front page of national newspapers for their work. "Biographer in bronze" Davidson was one of them, and his personal and political work was hugely influential.

Davidson, who had grown up in a poor Jewish family in Manhattan's lower east side, had met and modeled almost all the significant figures of modern times. Among those who'd sat for him were General John J. Pershing, John D. Rockefeller the elder, Andrew Mellon, Sinclair Lewis, George Bernard Shaw, Benito Mussolini, Mahatma Gandhi, several prime ministers from Britain and France, and intellectuals from the Soviet Union, to name just a handful. In 1934, President Franklin Roosevelt sat for the sculptor, and by the end of their collaboration, Davidson was convinced he was one of the greatest statesmen of all time.

For about ten years leading up to World War II, Davidson had been telling the media and his friends and politicians that he felt the world was inching closer to a showdown between fascism and socialism. He wanted to do something about it. These feelings became more acute when he was in New York in June of 1940. While he was meeting with patrons and friends like Gertrude Vanderbilt Whitney and Helen Keller, the Nazis formally took over Paris. The stocky, bearded, fifty-seven-year-old and his wife assumed that their home there and all the artworks in it would probably be destroyed or stolen.[14] For the time being, they resettled at their Dutch farmhouse, built in 1780, which rested on a hundred acres in Bucks County, Pennsylvania, and their studio loft in New York.

In August of 1944, Davidson and Weinstein met at his studio, along with Davidson's wife and a few others. They decided the best way to boost Roosevelt's chances for a fourth term was to convince scientists, film and stage stars, and writers to get out of their "ivory towers" and join the cause. Hannah crafted a letter to send out to about five hundred people well known in the artistic or scientific disciplines. They didn't expect so many swift and positive replies. Some of the luminaries who signed on to play an integral role included Keller, literary critic Van Wyck Brooks, painter Tom Benton, actresses Tallulah Bankhead and Ethel Barrymore, and many others.[15] Encouraged, the pair sent out even more invitations, and more acceptances poured in. They decided to call their group the "Independent Voters Committee of the Arts and Sciences for Roosevelt" (IVCASR). Davidson recalled that Weinstein was the most "amazing," tireless, and active founder. She was designated as the group's executive secretary, and "if it had not been for her extraordinary sense of organization," he said, "we would not have gone very far."[16]

By now, Weinstein was an old pro at packing a venue. She booked Madison Square Garden and, on September 21, 1944, it was once again sold out. To the horror of the head of the Democratic National Committee, she and Davidson had Henry Wallace as one of the headliners.[17] Reporters and government figures were increasingly calling Wallace out for being oblivious to the actual situation of the Soviet people. It didn't help that on a recent trip to the USSR, Wallace didn't realize he was given an entirely staged tour of Kolyma, complete with a faked luxury apartment and surrounded by healthy, good-looking bureaucrats acting as farmers and repentant prisoners.

Still, the jettisoned candidate pledged his support for both Roosevelt and Truman, as did stars like Bette Davis, Orson Welles, and Frederic March. He received a standing ovation at the Garden rally. A month later, Weinstein produced a fundraising dinner at the Hotel Astor for 1,700 people. It raised $40,000 for FDR, using the draw of celebrities Frank Sinatra and Ethel Merman, journalist Quentin Reynolds, Pulitzer Prize–winning playwright Robert Sherwood, and more.[18] On October 5, Weinstein traveled to Washington, D.C., with Davidson, Brooks, singer Jan Kiepura, Harvard astronomer Harlow Shapley, and actors Dorothy

Gish and Joseph Cotten. The White House received the delegation, which pledged its support for his candidacy, resulting in a very helpful photo opportunity and widely disseminated image of the group and the president.

The fact is, Roosevelt needed independent voters, whatever pundits might have thought of Wallace at this time. His opponent, Dewey, was a successful prosecutor of organized crime in New York City, and went after high-profile, white-collar criminals, too. Since 1942, he'd been governor of New York, raising his own profile even more. As late as October 24, 1944, polls showed that chances of either winning the presidency were fifty-fifty. Most voters thought that either candidate could create a post-war foreign-policy roadmap. Dewey had a Republican Congress. Roosevelt was a beloved and proven entity, but some undecided voters thought he came with the baggage of the strident, pro-labor force with openly Communist members. The president told Davidson that he knew it was necessary to accept Weinstein and Davidson's help, along with the rest of the committee. He would "hate to win or lose by a small margin."[19]

He also knew he needed female voters: A national survey came out that October that showed women were expected to cast more than 60 percent of the total vote. Women were also shown to be largely responsible for registering all eligible voters in general, through their work with various action committees, including Weinstein's IVCASR.[20] As member Bette Davis noted, 1944 was the first year that more women than men were eligible to vote. "This year," she said, "our men are overseas, arguing a mortal dispute that could not wait. The women here at home will be the conscience of those silenced soldiers and sailors."[21]

Some press made fun of IVCASR's effort. Not surprisingly, most of these outlets were in heavily Republican counties, in Dewey's "home turf" of upstate New York, and mocked Frank Sinatra, Orson Welles, and particularly Gypsy Rose Lee. "The 'Independent Voters Committee,'" one said, "certainly enrolled some dandies!"[22] Nevertheless, Roosevelt won reelection for a fourth term, though with fewer electoral and popular votes than he had for his third, thanks in large part to the efforts of Weinstein, Davidson, and the rest of IVCASR. Watching the returns and then celebrating in the ballroom at the top of the Astor on election night and into the early hours of the next day, Weinstein and the rest of IVCASR's board decided that their committee should be continued as a permanent engine for change, and not just for getting people elected, but also for getting legislation passed. They also decided that they could accomplish these goals on a local level, too. They called their new iteration the Independent Citizens Committee for the Arts, Sciences and Professions (ICCASP).

In fact, though, this may have just been lip service paid to work that the board of IVCASR was already doing. In the spring of 1944, the US Treasury Department asked for ICCASP's expertise in presenting the Bretton Woods narrative to "the people."[23] Bretton Woods was, simply speaking, a high-level meeting of economic minds from forty-four nations that sought a new international system after World War II. This new system would draw on the lessons of the previous gold standards and help with post-war reconstruction, and also help avoid the worst effects of another Great Depression. In July of 1944, about 730 delegates met in the namesake city in New Hampshire. Ultimately, the Bretton Woods Agreement created two important organizations—the International Monetary Fund (IMF) and the World Bank. The "founding fathers" of the Bretton Woods institutions were economist John Maynard Keynes, from Great Britain, and Harry Dexter White, Assistant Secretary of the Treasury of the United States.

White approached Weinstein by way of a radio writer named Allan Everett Sloane. As he told the HUAC and the FBI some ten years later, Sloane briefly flirted with the Communist Party during the war. Fellow writer Millard Lampell persuaded him to join, and it appealed to his "fuzzy-minded attitude" as a liberal, though "liberal in the best sense of the word." Four days before the opening of the conference, Sloane testified, Weinstein called him. "Allan," she said, "something has come up and we thought you'd like to be in on this." A very important government official, she said, was passing through New York and had graciously offered to meet with a small group of people to discuss this important subject. Would he come to the Astor Hotel?[24] White passed away a few years later under a cloud of suspicion of being a Soviet agent, an idea disputed by more recent scholarship.[25] All the same, at the time of Sloane's

1953 testimony about this era, Joseph McCarthy and HUAC labeled him as such, and therefore Weinstein's interaction with him was suspect, too.

Sloane recalled that it was Weinstein who often summoned him for other projects to be hashed out in the group's offices on the eighth floor of the Astor. "I do not mean to imply this person was known to me to be subversive, but she was the one who always called me. Sometimes she would call and say, 'Allan, something has come up and would you like to do a piece for the Teachers' Union?' He returned to her importance a few lines later:

> I believe she was the person who, in that particular organization, as in many organizations, knew various people. She knew that (I) Allan Sloane was a radio writer who could be had and she knew that So-and-So was an actor who would cooperate, and So-and-So a director. She knew people all over. You find girls like that in many organizations who always seem to know who to call and where they can be found and things like that.[26]

This "girl" in the form of thirty-four-year-old Weinstein had Sloane and Lampell continue to write important missives. The association with Sloane bolstered the FBI's position that she was a concealed Communist when he turned "friendly witness" for HUAC just a few short years later.

After Roosevelt's triumph, Hannah and her family took a brief trip to Florida to rest, though she still found time to meet with reporters. Getting some sun outside while knitting a sweater for one of her girls, she explained that this new, enlarged organization would welcome all kinds of people. To be sure, there would be actors, playwrights, journalists, artists, and the like, but also scientists, doctors, dentists—any kind of "white collar workers." All these people had gone to bat for Roosevelt, she said, and they'd done it in an interesting way—showing him how to connect with Americans and explain his peace policies through radio talks, countless luncheons and banquet speeches, and, of course, rally coverage. She also emphasized that women had been an integral part of getting him elected.[27]

This may have been the last time Weinstein got any rest for years while she led the growth and prominence of ICCASP. On December 20, 1944, the *Daily Worker*—the primary newspaper for the CPUSA—announced, "[L]eading Americans yesterday united for organized political activity as the Independent Citizens Committee for the Arts, Sciences and Professions." Its national board read like a Who's Who of the entertainment and science and artistic world at that time. Frederic March, who'd won an Academy Award twelve years earlier for playing Dr. Jekyll/Mr. Hyde, was made treasurer, while Broadway director and producer Herman Shumlin was appointed chairman of the finance committee.

Others included scientists Albert Einstein and Linus Pauling, radio writer Norman Corwin, actresses Olivia de Havilland and Florence Eldridge (married to Frederic March), playwright Lillian Hellman, screenwriter Howard Koch, and talent agent William Morris, to name a few. Davidson was national chairman. Weinstein became executive director, tasked with keeping all these often-disparate personalities tied together to further the goals of ICCASP. Broadly speaking, their goals were to extend democracy in the United States and abroad; to promote worldwide peace through the United Nations; to end discrimination against women and people of color; and to provide support for policies that would lead to full employment and a "decent standard of living for all."[28]

Predictably, the entertainment world was enthralled by the group. *Daily Variety*, for example, praised ICCASP for not letting politicians be the only faction to shape world policy.[29] The committee's first dinner was held at the Waldorf-Astoria on February 18, 1945, and highlights from it were broadcast on CBS radio.[30] Screen idol Edward G. Robinson spoke for many when he responded to a reporter's question about why he joined. "I belong to ICCASP because the atom bomb, when it exploded over Hiroshima, blew up every ivory tower in the world. America is in crisis. I am part of the world. I am a citizen of America and caught in this crisis." Humphrey Bogart responded, "I belong to ICCASP because I believe in the principles promulgated by Franklin Delano Roosevelt."[31]

The formation of ICCASP generated a lot of hurried discussion between several "alphabet groups." The most prominent of these was the

Hollywood Democratic Committee (HDC), which had also corralled talent to get out the vote for Roosevelt but was pretty much limited to Los Angeles-based stars.[32] What if, Weinstein argued to Davidson and the other board members, they could more fully plumb celebrity name recognition and talent from Hollywood, in return for lending ICCASP's more East Coast, intellectual patina? There was already a lot of overlapping membership. Weinstein wanted to create a unified organization that would combine the glitter of West Coast celebrities with East Coast writers and academics. Their work was a "nation-wide job," she wrote to Davidson, and she was "particularly anxious to have a Hollywood-affiliated or cooperating body."[33]

Just three weeks after the launch of ICCASP, Weinstein reached out to George Pepper, film producer and executive director of HDC. Pepper was understandably protective of his image-conscious membership, especially since the HDC was bipartisan, despite its name. It supported policies that generally aligned with liberal-leaning legislation but could just as easily promote a Republican or Independent candidate if their platform included those reforms. The two agreed, though, that voter registration and widening access to the polls were the most crucial priorities for their membership. Then, she raised the stakes, sharing a more direct concern with Pepper:

> *We are planning to start a campaign on a "hard peace" for Germany. As you may know, a directive according to these lines was agreed upon at Yalta, by Roosevelt, Churchill, and Stalin. The directive went into the work upon Roosevelt's return so that it could be sent to Government agencies and chiefs-of-staffs. Since Roosevelt's death this directive has been sitting on Truman's desk and he has done nothing.*

Weinstein referred to the Kilgore Plan, the informal name for a congressional committee led by Harley Kilgore, a West Virginia Democrat. Kilgore and many others in the US government pointed to overwhelming evidence that instead of destroying the German/Nazi monopolies and corporate trusts—all geared toward war—certain Allied capitalists along with those from neutral countries like Switzerland were deliberately protecting them.[34] This ran counter to agreements made at the recent Yalta Conference. Could the HDC, Weinstein asked, help ICCASP with a public relations campaign to get Truman and reticent members of Congress to commit to holding all parties to the letter of the agreement?

It could and did. Moreover, in June of 1945, HDC's membership—with some prodding by Weinstein and Davidson and others—voted to become the Hollywood Independent Citizens Committee for the Arts, Sciences and Professions (HICCASP). After an unsuccessful film career but a very distinguished one in the recent war, James Roosevelt, FDR's son, joined ICCASP as Director of Political Organization. Harold Ickes, recently Secretary of the Interior, joined as executive chairman. Approximately 3,300 artistic professionals joined one or both groups, including future president Ronald Reagan.

The senior Roosevelt had passed away on April 12, 1945. When Harry Truman took office, he for the most part embraced ICCASP—at least initially. Over the next year or so, though, it became clear that most of the organization (or, at least, its leadership) would not be deterred from a more conciliatory relationship with the Soviet Union, whereas Truman was moving toward containment.

The most heated arguments were about the atomic bomb. Many Americans (and members of ICCASP) believed that Truman dropped the atomic bomb on Hiroshima and Nagasaki when he had other means to end the war. Many members—led by information provided by scientists—felt that control of atomic energy should be turned over to the UN and include the Soviet Union in overseeing security in these processes. This, coupled with the fact that many, if not most, members were party members earned suspicion from the FBI and HUAC. It didn't help that CPUSA took credit for ICCASP at its secret summer 1945 convention. Its cultural section head read, "We built the Independent Citizens Committee of the Arts, Sciences and Professions and it is a great political weapon. The radio and film propaganda organizations can help our activities as communists. We can bring in the middle strata."[35]

***

On June 6, 1945, when the HDC decided to formally change its name to the Hollywood Independent Citizens Committee for the Arts, Sciences and Professions, it had already been using the name informally for a couple of months. Despite its name change to closely resemble Weinstein's organization, it emphasized to the public that it would stay independent, even welcoming Republicans and Independents. Now, however, there were even fewer distinctions between the two than there had been earlier in the year when Weinstein opened discussions with James Cromwell, the actor and director that served as its head.

Their combined efforts brought more recognition and resources to both, but ICCASP really benefited by its ability to cross-pollinate legislative action with faces recognizable to the general public. *Mademoiselle* described Weinstein as ICCASP's "spark plug," and the idea generator behind marrying celebrities with certain legislative goals. For example, she got ballet dancer and *Beauty and the Beast* star Sono Osato to travel to Washington the day after she had fractured her rib, to put pressure on Congress to pass the Fair Employment Practices Act. She got glamorous actresses Virginia Gilmore and Judy Halliday to stand in Times Square and Radio City and gather women's signatures on a petition urging senators to approve the United Nations Charter.[36] And so on.

By October of 1945, Weinstein was trying to persuade ICCASP to turn against the new president. She elevated the concerns she had previously shared with Pepper and the HDC. Truman showed "no will" to fight with "reactionary" members of Congress, she told her board, arguing that they had to oppose the "incipient native fascism" coming from the new administration. She urged the board to adopt measures to show the public that there was no longer any "democratic purpose" to American foreign policy.[X] Members who were not as anti-Truman as Weinstein, Shapley, Davidson, and others still had to concede that the president had dismissed surviving members of FDR's progressive political family, casting doubt on any further New Deal–type legislation. Frances Perkins, Harold Ickes, Henry Morganthau—all stalwart and motivated progressives in the previous administration—were all gone. They knew their influence at the highest levels of government was dwindling, and they'd soon have to do something about it.

On May 20, 1946, the intensely misogynistic and anti-FDR journalist John O'Donnell wrote his usual political column for the *New York Daily News*. In it, he took aim at Weinstein and her "pinko outfit," ICCASP, along with America's first political action committee, the Congress of Industrial Organizations (CIO-PAC). Days before, these groups announced they were teaming up with smaller New Deal offspring to create a serious workshop for young people. It would be based at the Willard Hotel in Washington, D.C., and it would teach political strategy. It was aptly called the School for Political Action Techniques, or "SPAT." Along with other sarcastic barbs, O'Donnell wrote that Weinstein, Sidney Hillman of CIO-PAC, and other political and public relations specialists would instruct the "boys and girls in (S)PAT" on "how to put the squeeze" on voters and Congress:

> *Everything from doorbell-ringing and rabble-rousing to the crude but essential chore of dough-raising will be covered in 39 separate courses. They range all the way from the effective use of radio, leaflets and posters by minority groups to harass Congress into denial of majority opinion, down to such ancient and time-tattered Tammany tactics as "How to Build a Ward and Precinct Organization."*

O'Donnell went on to list the other civil rights groups and PACs involved in educating the next generation of activists. In a parting shot, he wrote that the names were the very same as those that had "popped up, over and over again" in the printed testimony of HUAC as being identified as fellow travelers and/or members of the Communist-front organizations in the United States.

O'Donnell was smearing a large group of well-intentioned individuals and groups who wanted to show young people how to flex their democratic rights and get out the vote in a non-presidential election. But his sarcasm did express the suspicion that large numbers of Communists were quietly infiltrating all levels of government. The HUAC—now a permanent, standing committee—started labeling groups like ICCASP and the CIO-PAC and American Youth for Democracy as "communist fronts."

At its peak, ICCASP had eighteen thousand members. But by mid-1946, as the press and right-wing foes and government officials increasingly called it "infiltrated," people dropped off its rosters and donor lists. Some of this was because of natural attrition during an off-year election cycle, but most of it was because some members no longer believed they were truly independent progressives. On October 7, 1946, Ickes sparred with Weinstein about ICCASP's strong criticism of the US atomic control proposal and threatened to resign. By October even Eleanor Roosevelt was saying privately that the organization was "Communist-dominated," and Jules Stein was warning his client Bette Davis, "You had better get out." Weinstein, who persuaded Wallace to throw his support behind a fellow traveler, radio commentator Johannes Steele, against a Democrat in a special New York congressional election, earned the group more scorn from the mainstream Democratic Party.[38] James Roosevelt dropped out after denouncing ICCASP as a "communist outfit." Future president Ronald Reagan, still a registered Democrat, began supplying information presented in HICCASP meetings to the FBI, but soon left the local and national organizations.

In September of 1946, *Time* magazine printed that "like almost any liberal political organization," ICCASP had picked up some Communists. Both its critics and members, it said, felt that the organization was being turned into a Communist front. To underscore this notion, it quoted an unnamed Chicago member of ICCASP, who supposedly said, "The Commies are boring in like weevils in a biscuit."[39] Both Davidson and Weinstein balked, saying Communists had no more to do with ICCASP than "fleas to a dog." To the question of Communist influence, Davidson replied, "Have you stopped beating your wife?" Weinstein was even more dismissive: "Says who and so what? If the ICCASP program is like the Communist line, that is purely coincidental."[40]

As if to underscore this point, President Truman fired ICCASP's faithful friend in the White House, Secretary of Commerce Henry A.

Wallace. Weinstein played a minor role in his sacking, but a gigantic one in his subsequent bid for the first progressive president of the United States.

CHAPTER 3

Moving Spirits

IN JUNE OF 1946, RUMORS IN CONSERVATIVE CIRCLES SWIRLED THAT Weinstein and the rest of the board at ICCASP were formulating a plan to run a Communist in the 1948 presidential election.[1] A young Arthur M. Schlesinger Jr. explained in popular *Life* magazine that, in fact, most members of ICCASP and the like were simply naïve—that they were "organized for some benevolent purpose, and because of the innocence, laziness, and stupidity of most of the membership, perfectly designed for control by an alert minority." Its celebrities maintained their membership, but not their vigilance for democratic causes, he charged.

ICCASP's national board of directors rebutted Schlesinger's various charges against it in a subsequent issue. It may well have been Weinstein who wrote the tongue-in-cheek preamble: "Sidestepping the implication of the word 'celebrities,' may we point out that this letter is at least evidence of our vigilance."[2]

Weinstein planned an ICCASP rally for Madison Square Garden to be held on September 12, 1946. Its goal was to get out the vote for New York Democrats ahead of the midterm elections, but also to be a showcase for post-war American-Soviet relations. Henry Wallace would be the primary speaker, and the whole event was titled, "The Path to Peace." It turned out to be a public relations disaster for President Truman, and Weinstein played a part in Wallace's downfall in the administration.

Newsweek offered a play-by-play of the debacle in its next issue, including Weinstein in a photo "lineup" of people who took part in it, and a forensic explanation of how it happened.[3]

37

Though he had not expressly said it yet, Truman had, since March of this year, signaled to the press, his cabinet, and the world that he would pursue a policy of containment when it came to the Soviet Union. The lone dissenter in his Cabinet was Henry Wallace. This thorny point aside, Truman wasn't unhappy to see Wallace the morning of September 10—after all, Wallace was his secretary of commerce.

In line with Cabinet custom, Wallace showed the president a speech he planned to make two nights later, at a New York campaign rally sponsored by ICCASP and the National Citizens Political Action Committee (NC-PAC). Truman had made it tacitly clear to Wallace that he was not to discuss foreign policy—among many other blunders, the latter had recently cost America a military presence in Iceland by railing against it, leaving the Icelandic government no choice but to pick a side. They picked the Soviet Union. Still, Truman was happy to have him speak to Weinstein's MSG crowd—he hoped Wallace could hold New York's radical left in line for Democratic candidates for governor and senator.

Each man had a copy and read through the high points of each paragraph together. Truman approved the speech. Then, on the morning of the 12th, Weinstein provided Capitol Hill reporters with advance publicity materials. The reporters could not believe what they were reading and sped to Truman's usual press briefing. Almost immediately, hands shot up. Had he approved Wallace's speech in its entirety? Yes, he replied. All of it? Again, the answer was yes. Incredulous, the Washington press corps raced back to their desks and began making phone calls. What they did not know at the time was that Truman either zoned out while flipping through pages six and seven, or somehow, new text was inserted after the fact.

That night, Wallace delivered his speech to a full house at MSG, proposing that peace with the Soviet Union could be had if the United States would stop supporting imperialistic British interests and stop chasing oil in the Near East using the lives of American soldiers. "On our part," he said, "we should recognize that we have no more business in the political affairs of eastern Europe than Russia has in the political affairs of Latin America, western Europe, and the United States."[4] Truman's Secretary of State, James Byrnes, was furious, threatening to resign after not sleeping for seventy-two hours, forced to take calls from panicked heads-of-state and reporters.

Ironically, the CPUSA condemned Wallace's speech because it contained some mild criticism of the Soviet Union. Wallace himself later recalled that Weinstein had persuaded him to delete several sentences that criticized that nation. And since the crowd booed loudly when he did offer criticism, he opted to skip over some of it on his own accord. Within a few days, though, the CPUSA changed their tune, acknowledging that Wallace "did say a lot of good things in his speech at Madison Square Garden."[5]

None of these nuances mattered to the White House. Wallace had expressly undermined Truman and Secretary Byrnes's foreign policy, and this was the last straw for the president. He fired Wallace on September 23 and replaced him with W. Averell Harriman.

Almost immediately, the influential leftist magazine the *New Republic* hired Wallace to be its new editor. This move was cheered by most labor movements and the most left of the Democratic and Independent parties, and certainly by members of ICCASP. By way of the magazine, Wallace and others blasted the White House for turning its back on Democratic ideals, and for what they perceived as an attempt to push the country into another world war using the nuclear bomb.

Weinstein aligned with Wallace on the fraught issue of nuclear power and information-gathering between nations. Some argued that it was the other way around—that Wallace deferred to Weinstein. Regardless, the major fractures both within ICCASP and between the organization and external factions of all political stripes had to do with atomic energy and weaponry.

The first prominent defector from ICCASP was atomic physicist Harold Urey; he and several colleagues pulled out in July of 1946, convinced it was a Communist front. A few months later, Weinstein sparred with atomic physicist J. Robert Oppenheimer, who was serving as an ICCASP vice president at the time. The scientist was infuriated by a position statement of the group disseminated at a Chicago conference the day after Wallace was sacked. It was a joint declaration with representatives of NC-PAC and CIO-PAC, making it a very powerful one.

Loosely speaking, it endorsed the Baruch Plan, which would give America the right to inspect, control, and license the world's nuclear power capabilities, given that it was the first to obtain this capability. In return, America would reduce its atomic stockpile in steps, as each phase of international cooperation was implemented. The Soviets balked at this, arguing that negotiations could never proceed as long as the United States could use its atomic monopoly to coerce other nations into accepting its plan.

Weinstein and Wallace balked at this, too. Their postwar vision was similar to that of some other atomic scientists, who believed that basic scientific knowledge could not be contained because science had no national boundaries.

Oppenheimer disagreed with Weinstein and her more polarized colleagues. He called Wallace's recommendations "illusory," among other things, and resigned. After receiving his letter of resignation, Weinstein quickly wrote back. Among other points, she assured him that ICCASP had not made a final decision on its atomic recommendation. "I realize that it is difficult for someone with as many demands upon his time as you to attend meetings of the ICCASP. . . . I often hear how often you are in New York. If you would only let me know about these visits you could, I am certain, find a few hours to attend some of these meetings."[6] Her subtext was clear: Decisions were made by those who showed up.

A bigger problem for Weinstein was Harold Ickes's defection, spurred in part by the same issue. Ickes told the *New York Times* that he hadn't been present when the Chicago statement was approved by ICCASP's executive committee, but that when he heard about it, he was "pretty damn sore." He added that he followed up with Ben Baruch and assured him that he was on board with his American atomic plan. The joint declaration, he said, directly contradicted his own thoughts and, moreover, "tying the conference to the kite of Henry Wallace" represented "some fast work on the part of Harold Young," Wallace's principal advisor. He called the Soviet atomic proposals "childish," and, without expressly naming her in this article, he made it clear later that Weinstein never asked for his input. He told the *Times* that he sent his letter of protest to Weinstein at ICCASP headquarters but had received no reply.[7]

In truth, Ickes had offered his resignation months earlier, in June of 1946. He did not get along with Weinstein and the rest of the staff, who felt that his high salary entitled the ICCASP to more than token services and the use of his name. Also, the organization was, by midyear, more than $100,000 in debt. In July, Weinstein had to ask Ickes to forego two months of his salary. "I am sure that his Scotch blood froze cold at the thought of it, but he gave in," she wrote Jo Davidson. He agreed to withhold his resignation until after the midterm elections, but in September, he was enraged by the letter of protest the group made to Truman protesting the firing of Wallace.[8] By the time the Chicago conference and protest of the Baruch Plan arrived, Ickes needed little prompting to jump ship.

Ickes's departure was a blow, but not unexpected. Weinstein and Davidson had already been looking for ways to shore up membership and find like-minded people to help promote the late FDR's platform for peace and prosperity. Weinstein reached out to Calvin Benham "Beanie" Baldwin, to talk about merging his NC-PAC with ICCASP. She, Baldwin, and CIO attorney John Abt met and strategized about ways they might join forces.

Of particular concern to all these left-wing groups was the upcoming midterm elections. At an ICCASP rally, Democratic senator Claude Pepper from Florida warned of what was at stake. Republicans planned to attack labor unions harder than ever and depress living conditions of Americans:

"Republican Old Guarders" have no platform, and no promises to offer the people. So, they had to find a political profanity to hurl. And they hit on an ugly word—Communism. And according to that crowd, everybody who doesn't believe Hoover was the greatest President this country ever had is a communist.

Pepper went on to say that "about 10 powerful Republican families have tossed in about a million dollars" to the campaign fund. But when a faction like the CIO-PAC, he continued, takes up a collection in which its members voluntarily contribute, "they want to make you Public Enemy No. 1 in America."[9]

The Republican party swept the 1946 midterm elections. Because of this, and Wallace's firing, NC-PAC and ICCASP decided to pull the trigger. On December 29, 1946, along with eight smaller liberal groups, they held a merger conference at the Hotel Commodore in New York. That day, they announced their new, combined juggernaut. It was called the Progressive Citizens of America (PCA). La Guardia gave a keynote speech, as did Wallace, soon to become a third-party candidate for the president of the United States, with his campaign run by Hannah Weinstein.

***

"What Are U.S. Communists Up To?" *Newsweek* laid it all out for readers in June of 1947. Progressive Citizens of America was the prime example of how Communists could infiltrate liberal organizations and "make them soapboxes for Communist propaganda." Jo Davidson was co-chair of the newly formed PCA, along with radio commentator Dr. Frank Kingdon. But, the magazine said, "the real boss is Hannah Dorner [Weinstein], executive vice chairman. Miss Dorner denies that she is pro-Communist but she has traveled for years in pro-Communist circles," along with friends and board members Lillian Hellman, Van Wyck Brooks, and Paul Robeson, and others.[10] According to the hyperbolic piece, Baldwin and Weinstein were manipulated by the Communists to merge, given that they were each "the moving spirits" of their previous organizations. But Weinstein was the most influential, it said. "A Wallace friend explained this very simply: 'Henry,' he said, 'just can't resist when Hannah calls him up.'"[11]

Within the first six months of operations, the PCA gained some twenty-five thousand members in addition to the roughly fifteen thousand that already adhered to at least one of the former groups that combined to make up the new body. In a lengthy program adopted at their first convention, PCA outlined plans to strengthen several pro-labor acts, economic and diplomatic sanctions against Spain and Argentina, and a ban on the manufacture of atomic bombs and the destruction of existing stockpiles; support a dissolution of monopolies, trusts, and cartels; promote civil rights and voting rights; and more. It took aim at the Democratic and Republican Parties, claiming the former "woos privilege" and the latter could no longer call itself "liberal" in any sense of the word.[12]

From the moment of its inception, PCA was hammered by the press as a Communist-run organization. Baldwin was simply a Wallace subordinate, said one syndicated article, which advocated loudest for the CIO's "suicidal strategy" of trying to unite with Communists. Weinstein, it said, was the "female bird of the same feather, only rather more so."[13] Weinstein and Davidson flew to the West Coast in January 1947 to drum up support from labor unions and mainstream and progressive Democratic groups. They were relentlessly peppered with questions about their communist affiliations. In Seattle, for example, they were asked if Communists would be "cleaned out" of the PCA. "Did you ever hear of the Bill of Rights, or Thomas Jefferson?" Davidson thundered. "Tom Jefferson was called names. So what? He stood for a principle and he worked for that principle. That is what our organization is doing."[14]

The PCA never lost sight of its original goals, but it had to react quickly to three high-profile actions taken by Truman and Congress. These were what became known as the Truman Doctrine, Executive Order 9835, and HUAC's citations of contempt for the men who became known as the Hollywood Ten.

On March 12, 1947, Truman appeared before a joint session of both houses of Congress to request an immediate appropriation of $40 million of military and economic aid to Turkey and Greece, and to be able to send American civilian and military personnel to those countries. This was necessary, he said, to provide a bulwark against internal Communism and external threats, presumably from the Soviet Union.[15] The PCA board was having a lunch meeting when Truman's address came out on the radio. Chairman Dr. Kingdon pounded the table so hard with a water glass that it broke. "That man has just set us on the road to war!" Weinstein was a bit calmer. "Don't you think," she asked him, "you could run a Garden meeting around this?"[16]

Kingdon agreed, so they reached out to Wallace to see if he would headline a "Crisis Meeting" at the Garden later that month. In the meantime, Weinstein and her assistants put out a release denouncing Truman's proposal as heading the country toward war, announcing "the end of an American policy based on one world" and substituting one "which divided the world into two camps." These two camps, the PCA said, would eventually and necessarily move to an atomic arms race and total world destruction.[17]

That Wallace agreed to headline a rally was notable because he'd taken a self-imposed silence on politics after taking the editorship of the *New Republic* two and a half months earlier. Davidson, Weinstein, Baldwin, and other PCA honchos asked the magazine's owner, Michael Straight, to meet for a discussion about freeing Wallace from his editorial desk a bit so he could go back to in-person political work again. Straight chafed, having gambled hundreds of thousands of his family's dollars to make the magazine compete with *Time*. He didn't want to give up a popular editor and writer. He also didn't want to get embroiled in Wallace's political spats with other factions of the Left. Jo Davidson pressed him, and finally Straight agreed to come to dinner to discuss the matter. "Ouch," he said to himself, as Hannah's handshake belied her diminutive figure. Davidson, Kingdon, and Weinstein pressured him hard—but he didn't relent until a few days later, with the announcement of the Truman Doctrine—a step too far for Straight's own politics.[18]

Wallace didn't wait until the MSG meeting to speak, though. Just a day later, on March 13, he gave a radio address. In it, he excoriated what he perceived as Truman's coming to the aid of Greece and Turkey when other nations more friendly to the United States needed it just as much. The money, he shouted, would effectively be used to police Russia's borders.

The PCA had to add another item to its crisis meeting scheduled for the end of the month. On March 21, 1947, Truman signed Executive Order 9835, which essentially established the first loyalty program in the United States. The goal of the order was to eliminate Communists from all areas of the US government. It also empowered the FBI to investigate federal employees and created presidentially appointed Loyalty Review Boards to act on reports from the FBI. Some in the press called it the "Domestic Truman Doctrine."

On October 18, 1947, HUAC convened a hearing in Washington, D.C. Its goal was to investigate subversive activities in the entertainment industry. The targets of this investigation were forty-one screenwriters, directors, and producers, who were subpoenaed. Most of these witnesses were "friendly." They were willing to respond to the committee's central question, which was: "Are you now or have you ever been a member of the Communist Party?" Those who answered "yes" were given the opportunity to name "fellow travelers," thereby regaining their good standing with the committee and, by extension, the American film industry.

Ten witnesses banded together in protest, refusing to cooperate on First Amendment grounds. These ten included Ring Lardner Jr. and Adrian Scott, both later so integral to Weinstein's television series. All of them were or had been party members but did not think it was any of the government's business. HUAC disagreed: It found the so-called Hollywood Ten in contempt of Congress, fined them each $1,000, and sentenced them to up to a year in federal prison.

Weinstein formed committees to deal with the issues of loyalty oaths and the Hollywood Ten on the one hand, and Wallace's looming campaign as a third-party candidate on the other. There was an understanding that Baldwin would have all financial control of the PCA, and that on May 15, 1947, he would take over as the sole executive vice chairman for the PCA. This was supposedly a mutual decision, with the understanding that there could not be "two bosses." Whether this was a "face-saving" measure, as one historian called it, because the two butted heads, or there was some other reason isn't clear. When the day arrived, Weinstein did not want to quit, but she did. She continued as a member of the board of directors. The rallies she planned were pulling in some $300,000 per event, to be used however this new "people's party" saw fit.

Even as late as September 1947, Wallace still hoped to run under the auspices of the Democratic Party, as an alternative to Truman's more conservative platform. For her part, Weinstein found herself managing several Wallace advisors who all had different visions of themselves as parts of the Wallace machine. There were the aggressive strategizers, John Abt and Lee Pressman, former Communist Party members and sympathizers, and overlapping general counsels for the CIO. There was

Harold Young, Wallace's longtime "affable and rotund" assistant, who had few ideological connections to a progressive party but wanted to be a "kingmaker." Of course, there was Baldwin, who was the public face of the emerging third party. There was the "bearded and leonine" Davidson, the de facto leader of the creative world that wanted a third party—more a social contact than a political one for Wallace.[19] And then there was top PCA leader Robert W. Kenny, a progressive strategist from California. Kenny hoped to build up Wallace's strength within the West Coast Democratic Party and dangle the threat of splitting the party—he could then force moderates to compromise on some other candidate to unseat President Truman.

Among all of these "background advisors," argued *Harper's Magazine*, Weinstein was a "top mover and shaker," and "one of the "best high-pressure political saleswomen" around. She moved quietly and efficiently, it said, and was instrumental in rallying names, talent, influence, and money for third-party causes. She was working at nefarious purposes, though, the article intimated. "Those whom she rounded up discovered too late—if they looked around at all—that many with whom they had been brigaded were Communists."[20]

By late November 1947, most of those "movers and shakers" who had plans for Henry Wallace realized that he really had no platform except—simply speaking—"peace." He had few ideas about the American economy, except for some generalized attacks on "Wall Street." Kingdon had come to recognize the lack of support for a third party and resigned his position from the PCA. Notably, the CIO declined to have Wallace speak at its annual November convention. Even Harold Young was against it, realizing too late that Democrats were not going to absorb Wallace as a candidate. Kenny realized this too and begged him not to announce as a third-party candidate, but that even if he did, to consider letting his name be entered into the California and Oregon primaries for the Democratic ticket. Kenny later recalled that he celebrated a strange New Year's Eve at Weinstein's apartment in New York, during the worst blizzard in years. Paul Robeson, Beanie Baldwin, and a few others from PCA were there, as well as Wallace and Young. "There was a tremendous effort," he said, "to persuade Young and me to go along with the third-party idea but we declined."[21] Kenny, though, changed his mind shortly thereafter.

On January 18, 1948, the PCA board met in Chicago. It voted to authorize its merger into a third party planned by Henry W. Wallace in his bid for the presidency.

CHAPTER 4

Wallace and Waldorf

AFTER ANNOUNCING WALLACE AS A THIRD-PARTY CANDIDATE, THE PCA issued a twelve-page, seventy-two-point platform that articulated its primary objectives and Wallace's platform, including rejection of the Marshall Plan, immediate withdrawal of American military personnel and aid from Turkey and Greece, a repeal of the Taft-Hartley Act, and more, including a substantial housing bill that would alleviate overcrowding in slums.[1] Its "number one plank," though, was its commitment to uphold the rights of labor and to create full employment in America.[2] The group elected two hundred officers, and Robert W. Kenny was named national chairman. The FBI's eponymous name for this third-party candidacy was "Operation Wallace." Weinstein's involvement with his campaign was enough to have informers provide coverage of her activities.

Wallace running for president ostensibly as a tool for the Communists was of paramount concern for the agency at this point, as was Weinstein's involvement in it. But of equal or greater concern for the agency in these early days of that campaign was her simultaneous leadership of the Committee of One Thousand. It would work closely with the Committee for the First Amendment, an existing, Hollywood-based version with virtually the same ideals. The committee's statement-of-purpose termed HUAC's members as "betrayers of American ideals, those who use terror, innuendo, hearsay and smears, ignoring the common rules of evidence and all precepts of fair play."

Their plan was seemingly simple: to gather at least one thousand influential people from around the country and enlist them to go back to their communities and networks to communicate just how intrusive and anti-democratic HUAC was. While persecution of the Hollywood Ten took up most news coverage because it was innately glamorous, Weinstein's committee correctly assessed that the same persecutions were happening to scientists, academics, playwrights, and others. Harvard's Shapley noted that among many other "little un-American activities committees" that HUAC had been spawning all over the country was one looking into physicist Edward U. Condon, at that time an extremely important atomic leader for the government and a one-time member of the scientific division of the National Council of American-Soviet Friendship (NCASF).[3] Sponsors included Albert Einstein, Helen Keller, Rabbi Stephen S. Wise, and radio star and writer Norman Corwin.

Meanwhile, the new Progressive Party planned to hold Wallace's nomination at their convention in Philadelphia the third week of July 1948. The candidate drafted an acceptance speech to deliver at Shibe Park, but Weinstein thought it was terrible—she didn't like Wallace's ethereal depictions of himself as the biblical Gideon leading a new army. She asked Allan Sloane and Millard Lampell, her colleagues from ICCASP, to write a new one. And though neither Sloane nor Lampell were Communists at this time, their sympathies shone through, and later, the FBI served up this Weinstein chore as an example of their subversive behavior.[4]

One scholar called the Progressive Party convention "an astonishing affair by all accounts." Most of the delegates were "plain people with little practical political experience." Howard Smith, writing in *The Nation* that summer, reported that there were hundreds of people who hitchhiked to get there, with many of them staying in tents in the convention hall parking lot. Those who worked for the party got rooms at the Hotel Bellevue-Stratford and spent a month before the convention preparing for it.

Also at the Hotel Bellevue-Stratford were agents . . . of a sort. They were men working for a group of four former FBI agents, all of whom left the bureau between 1945 and 1946. These men worked for an association calling themselves "American Business Consultants" (ABC), in New York. The real FBI described ABC as a group of former special agents who had "formed what might be looked upon as a sort of private F.B.I. for the purpose of detecting and exposing Communists and their activities and recommending to the American people what can be done about them."⁵ ABC founders felt their former employer didn't go far enough to expose Communists, Socialists of any kind, Soviets, Progressives, or really, any remotely leftist activities within the ranks of business. More narrowly, it was vehemently anti-union and felt that the way to beat Communist infiltration in America was for corporations to take matters into their own hands. Its newsletter, *Counter Attack*, exhorted its readers to write protest letters to the corporate sponsors of programs featuring actors with purported links to the Left. The Wallace campaign was an obvious target.

A few weeks before the convention, men from ABC rented rooms at the Bellevue-Stratford, on the third floor, where the Progressive Party planned to do most of its administrative business for the convention. They got at least two rooms in strategic locations: one between Lee Pressman, for years general counsel for the CIO and now serving as advisor to Wallace, and public relations men Ralph Shikes and Steve Fischer, both of whom had worked for progressive causes and various newspapers. They got another room situated between Hannah Weinstein's and one used for committee meeting purposes. The ABC men placed small, flat microphones under Hannah's door and those of the PR men and any strategy meetings that happened to interest them. When people left their rooms, the interlopers took all the paper they could from wastebaskets. They'd bring it up to the sixteenth floor, where they had commandeered a linen room. There, they would examine the paper for any "evidence" of subversive plans.

ABC didn't cover its tracks very well, though they may not have cared to. Wallace (and by extension, his campaign workers) had always charged that they were subjected to intimidation efforts and spying, and not just by the ABC or the FBI. In addition to several more-rogue groups, there was the British Security Coordination (BSC), covertly run by MI6 to report on Wallace's anti-imperialist rhetoric. Notably, fledgling writer Roald Dahl was an agent, and passed along information he learned while socializing with the erstwhile politician, even serving as his tennis partner. Anyone attending Wallace's speeches and rallies could expect that men in suits would not hide the fact that they were copying down license plates or speaking to their employers. Reporter George Mills of the *Des Moines Register* noted that almost everyone working the convention knew the rooms were wired.[6]

If their mikes were hot, the ABC must have had to drink as much coffee as Weinstein and the rest of the board trying to write Wallace's party's platform. The first half of that week was spent just trying to decide whether to include "Communist" in Wallace's preamble or not.

Over the next few months, Wallace suffered from ill-defined, or mixed, or even absent messaging, depending on any one person's point of view. In his book *Henry Wallace's 1948 Presidential Campaign and the Future of Postwar Liberalism*, Tom Devine describes the problem Wallace had with a liberal-Communist alliance and non-Communist Progressives:

> *These primarily middle-class men and women—lacking political experience but closely following current events and genuinely concerned about the outbreak of another war—had gravitated to Wallace hoping that his deep commitment to peace would allow him to win the Soviets' trust, as Franklin Roosevelt had done. Idealistic, perhaps to a fault, they also admired Wallace's refusal to participate in the seamier side of politics, convinced he would never compromise the ideals of the New Deal for political gain (as, some acknowledged, even FDR had done).*

But as these men and women waited for Wallace to denounce the behavior of some Communists at the convention and within various state organizations, their confidence began to erode. "As they waited in vain for Wallace to condemn such behavior and distance the Progressive Party from the Communists, they gradually came to see their hero both as less idealistic and less independent."[7] The Wallace-Taylor ticket finished in fourth place in the election, winning 1,157,328 votes (2.4 percent), behind the States' Rights Party.

***

With Wallace's campaign over, Hannah turned her attention back to abolishing HUAC. "ICCASP" was now reconstituted as "NCASP," the first letters standing for "National Council," though sometimes the names were used interchangeably. John Howard Lawson wrote the cover letter sent out to thousands of past and present members. With enough pressure, he wrote, they had a chance to force Congress to abolish the committee in its eighty-first session.

Weinstein's coup de grace before leaving the United States was undoubtedly the Cultural and Scientific Conference for World Peace. Planned for March of 1949, the three-day event brought together artists, intellectuals, and scientists to "meet, to discuss and to seek a basis for common action on the central question of peace as it affects our work and our aspirations in the various fields of culture." As the title of the event suggests, panels included natural sciences, physical and mental health, economic and social sciences, fine arts, and more. General themes included the role of the United Nations, the dangerous nature of NATO (which excluded the USSR), criticism of US foreign policy, intellectual freedom, and the general climate of fear.[8]

As one Cold War historian said, "The ostensible, if naïve intention of the Waldorf conference was the promotion of cultural exchange across international boundaries, peaceful coexistence, and the diminution of growing tensions between the Soviet Union and the United States."[9] Writer Howard Fast later took credit for coming up with the idea, which only served to bolster its reputation as a Comintern-planned event. In fact, though, it had no direct or obvious connection to the Soviet Union in terms of planning, organizing, or sponsorship. It was borne out of discussions between Harlow Shapley, Weinstein, Fast, and other recent Wallaceites with a burning desire to keep the candidate's plans going, if not the candidate. Shapley made assurances to Secretary of State Dean Acheson: "Our conference is not related in any way whatever to conferences that have been held elsewhere or that are being planned."[10]

All the same, the American press ignored this distinction or was unaware of it or both—it treated the event as though it was just another one of the many peace conferences around Europe that were, in fact, Communist Front organizations. It would be hard not to, given that many invitees were prominent Soviet Party members, whether of their own free will or not.

Fanning the media's anti-Communist fury against the conference was Professor Sidney Hook, a leftist scholar, critic, and then head of NYU's philosophy department. Hook had published several magazine and newspaper articles in which he called for the immediate dismissal of university professors and instructors who belonged to the Communist Party, and to at least suspend and investigate those who had been in the past. If Communist ideals were only thoughts, he said, it would be no problem. But by mere association, he claimed, these professors would be unable to avoid indoctrinating students—you could not be a Communist without blindly following a party line, whatever that may be. Academic freedom should not extend to university instructors, he thought, because party members simply could not help but be indoctrinators. Hook's critics noted that his views had nothing to do with the truth or falsity of the views taught, or even the classroom behavior of the teacher. A non-Communist professor, for example, could teach the same material and be protected by principles of academic freedom.

Hook was invited to talk about his position, but he was angry that he wasn't getting more attention. He was only given a spot at a panel meeting. "Anybody can do that," he told the press. "There is no guarantee that I would be recognized." He wanted his name on the program and be given a dedicated time to speak without jockeying for position with others. More specifically, Hook claimed, Shapley was prone to the machinations of Hannah Weinstein, and Communists, and they would not allow him a spotlight.

A CIA officer keeping tabs on Weinstein and the others during the conference relayed his experience, which mostly amounted to complaints that Hook shared with him and others from his own rooms that he'd set up for the event. Soon after the Waldorf conference was announced in January, Hook wrote a long letter to Albert Einstein and other intellectuals who had been announced as headline speakers. "I believe," the CIA agent wrote, "he sent the letter as one distinguished scholar to others, asking their opinions and asking what they thought could be done to see that these views were clearly defined at the conference so that this viewpoint would receive proper expression."[11] According to Hook, he got no reply, so he wrote Shapley, and had others do so on his behalf, too.

Shapley, though, never received these letters, or at least denied that he did. He did not communicate with Hook, who grew angrier by the day as the Waldorf event drew near. Hook rented a bridal suite at the hotel and, through his own action group, sponsored protests of the event. Meanwhile, he decided to call Weinstein directly. According to Hook, it took two days to get her on the phone, and when he did, she told him that he would have no more opportunity to speak than any other session attendee, and that the possibility was up to recognition by the chairman. Weinstein rebuffed his continued attempts:

> He then asked her to read him the agenda, but she said she did not have it at hand. He asked, if he called later, would she be able to tell it to him. She said, no she would not. He then said he would be glad to talk at one of the other sessions. She regretted that those too were all filled up, and again replied she could not give him details on them. He then asked when he could get details, and she finally got nettled and told him she could not give him the agenda and furthermore his views would not receive expression at the conference.[12]

Hook burst into a conference room at the event and cornered Shapley as to why he had ignored all of his communications. Shapley denied ever receiving anything. Hook and the CIA agent concluded that it was not Shapley's fault—he was not a liar by nature. Therefore, the entire non-exchange was "conclusive proof" that Communists were keeping Shapley in the dark, as well as intercepting mail and other communication at NCASP. More to the point, they felt Weinstein was doing it on behalf of the party. "Hannah Dorner is supposed to be behind the scenes running this conference," the latter wrote. "She is well known in Communist circles—and is almost certainly a party member. She runs all sorts of affairs that they put on like this one." This Hook situation, the agent's report continued, was reminiscent of the ones Wallace was often in—another not-so-subtle attachment to blame Weinstein. "Shapley thinks he is running the show," the missive summarized, "but he is not."[13]

The State Department warily relaxed its policy of not admitting known party members into the country, but just for the week of the conference. These Soviet visitors were eighteen renowned writers and editors, ballet dancers, musicians, and economists. Acheson did, in fact, revoke several visas for French, Italian, and British delegates, using the lackluster explanation that American officials in the embassies of those countries halted them. At the end of what NCASP and thousands of intellectuals considered a resounding success (the event was plentifully covered by press worldwide, with varying opinions of its usefulness in bringing attention to the opening of the Cold War), Weinstein and the rest of NCASP tried to get its Soviet visitors to embark on a countrywide "tour." The State Department unilaterally denied this and sent the visitors home.

On March 23, 1949, two days before the start of the conference, the California Senate Factfinding Subcommittee on Un-American Activities, headed by virulent anti-Semite politician Jack B. Tenney, placed ICCASP, NCASP, PCA, and hundreds of other groups and people including Weinstein on its own list of Communist fronts. Operating in much the same way as HUAC, the California version tried to institute loyalty oaths in labor and universities, promoted book and film banning, and tried to dismantle labor organizations.

On February 24, 1950, the flamboyant theatrical impresario Billy Rose used his newspaper column to attack Weinstein and her Independent Citizens Committee of the Arts, Sciences and Professions. He wrote that a few years earlier, he had been invited to a small gathering of theatrical people at a private residence, where Eleanor Roosevelt made some remarks—which he recalled in astounding detail:

> *Confession is good for the soul, and tonight I have something to confess to all of you. After thinking it over for a long time, I've come to the conclusion that I've been taken in, duped and used by various organizations to which I've lent my name and support. And since most of you are connected with the Independent Citizens Committee, I want you to know that I consider this particular organization the most*

*insidious and dishonest of them all. I have resigned from it, and I've
come here tonight to plead with all of you to do the same.*[14]

As the attacks by the press, Republicans, and some mainstream Democrats mounted, NCASP continued to lose funds and membership. Weinstein and some members of the Hollywood Ten and other blacklisted and
sympathetic writers and performers tried to help each other out, using
their shared connections to refer work that could earn under-the-table
cash. They even created a "vaudeville night," called the "A. S. Prevue," that
performed every Friday night at the openly FBI-monitored Yugoslav
Hall on 41st Street. A portion of the ticket sales would go to NCASP,
and some to the writers. Lester Cole, recently released from prison for
his contempt charge, proposed to Hannah that they take the revue to the
"Borscht Belt," the colloquial term for the chain of summer camps in the
Catskills.[15] Unfortunately, this opportunity never materialized.

***

On June 20, 1950, former Communist Party member Louis Frances
Budenz identified Weinstein as a Soviet sympathizer and party member.
The FBI created a new folder for her, and copies of the photo she submitted with her month-old passport application were slipped into it for
reference. In the image, Hannah stares resolutely into the camera, her
dark blonde hair bobbed smartly with a flip at the bottom and deeply
colored lipstick accentuating her resemblance to Olivia de Havilland.

Budenz, fifty-nine years old, sat for hours in the FBI's New York
City offices while a stenographer took notes about his recollections of
Weinstein's pro-Soviet activities. The FBI had developed a questionnaire
for Budenz to use for each individual whose information he deemed
important to hand over to the agency. Some of the questions were:

- Was the individual active in front organizations?
- Was individual ever involved in secret work? What work? Who
  knew it?

- Can you recall any trips abroad particularly to Russia and the approximate date of the trips?

- Did this subject appear to have entrée to the Russian Consulate or did he receive special consideration and attention from known Russian Agents or Communist Officials in the U.S.?

- Do you know of any other members of his (her) family who are Communists?

- Do you know of any other activity on the part of the individual, which would indicate that the individual is a concealed Communist?[16]

Budenz described Weinstein as a "concealed Communist"—one who did not hold herself out as one and who would deny membership in the party.[17] These interviews marked the beginning of the FBI's twelve-year surveillance of Hannah and her friends, associates, and family.

Budenz was a study in contrasts. He had been an avowed party member for more than a decade. But in 1945 he returned to the Roman Catholic Church of his upbringing and became an informant for the FBI. The former activist—who resembled a cross between actors William Holden and Ian McDiarmid, known for his Emperor Palpatine role in the *Star Wars* trilogies—spent an estimated three thousand hours with FBI agents in interviews. He began testifying at various House and Senate hearings about Communism in December 1945 and was called on thirty-three different occasions over the next nine years.

Budenz later estimated that he was paid $70,000 for his information during the various trials and hearings. It was he who spearheaded the FBI's case file against Hannah Dorner Weinstein and helped her earn a Security Matter–C designation—"C" meaning "Communist."

In fact, the FBI had been following Budenz's career and activities since he graduated from law school in 1912 when he was only twenty-one. He was baptized Catholic but paid little attention to the faith growing up. The Indiana native was aggressively reform minded. He had organized strikes for labor unions and had been arrested twenty-one times during such efforts in Wisconsin, New Jersey, and Ohio. He had served as secretary of the Saint Louis Civic League and as publicity director for the ACLU. The FBI knew that he had worked with agitator Abraham Johannes Muste, a pacifistic yet powerful labor leader, and that he had flirted with Trotskyism.

Before he turned into an informant for them, the FBI's biggest concern with Budenz was his work for the Communist Party, which he'd joined in October of 1935. He had served as labor editor of the *Daily Worker*, the official mouthpiece of the CPUSA. He briefly served as editor of a Communist paper in Chicago and then returned to the *Daily Worker* as managing editor and American correspondent for its London edition.[18] Even when colleagues left the paper and the party when Hitler and Stalin formed a pact in 1939, Budenz and others remained staunch supporters of Stalin and all Soviet policies. They targeted individuals and organizations including the Catholic Church. Hoover had copies of all his dispatches to London, and reading them agitated the bureaucrat to no end. He pushed hard to get Budenz indicted for failing to register as a foreign agent. As it turned out, Hoover only had to wait for the opportunity to bring him in.

Opportunity came in the form of Fulton J. Sheen. Monsignor Sheen was a high-ranking professor at Catholic University of America in Washington, D.C. He was also host of the popular show *The Catholic Hour* on NBC Radio. Millions of people tuned in every week, including a curious Hoover. How could the church, Budenz thought, be against those who were trying to help the poor and downtrodden? In fact, he criticized Sheen and other Catholic leaders in the *Worker*: "How strange it is to see in a world so set up, where Catholic spokesmen in so many instances belabor communism." Budenz and Sheen began communicating both through the press and privately.

Perhaps incensed, perhaps intrigued, or both, Budenz agreed to meet with Sheen to discuss the matter. The exact time and date has never been discovered, but they met sometime in 1939 and stayed in touch. Budenz tried to convince Sheen that Catholicism could be aligned with Communism; Sheen slowly convinced Budenz it could not. Sheen eventually prevailed. In 1945, Budenz wrote the monsignor a letter: "I'm returning to the Catholic Church," he said, "and bringing my family with me."

The activist confessed his sins, and Sheen baptized him—and notified Hoover that they had a man who would be willing to name names.[19]

In fact, Sheen and Hoover had been regularly corresponding since 1944, when the religious leader wrote Hoover to thank him for a copy of a speech he had sent him. The monsignor routinely publicly denounced Communism on his radio shows (and later his television shows), earning a closer look by Hoover, an invitation to dinner, and ultimately a plea to help the FBI "root out" this evil. Because of Sheen's reach with American audiences and because of the volume of hate letters the priest received and turned over to the agency, the FBI kept a detailed file on Sheen. Hoover hoped that the radio host might bring some of the most hardened Soviet and Nazi sympathizers to Hoover's attention when he had occasion to interact with them.[20]

Sheen delivered Louis Budenz. The result would be catastrophic for the livelihoods of hundreds of people.[21]

Sheen had tipped Hoover off to Budenz's planned defection. The bureau closed its active criminal investigation of Budenz under the Foreign Agents Registration Act and instead arranged extensive interviews with him. The interview process, which began at a hotel in South Bend, Indiana, was lengthy and exhaustive. The bureau prepared typed lists of roughly seven hundred questions covering every phase of the party's operations and Budenz's career to guide the interviews. (At Budenz's insistence, both interviewing agents were "practical Catholics.")[22]

Budenz testified that it was Alexander Trachtenberg who had officially informed him that Weinstein was a concealed Communist "of some years' standing" back in 1944. Trachtenberg and several others, Budenz said, met in his office at the *Daily Worker* and discussed how they could form the Independent Committee of the Arts, Sciences and Professions. The group included (Jo) Davidson and the others, like Ickes, Brooks, and so on. They decided, said Budenz, to put Weinstein in "the really key position as executive" because of her Communist associations.[23]

The FBI's power to investigate Weinstein and many of her colleagues derived from Executive Order 9835. President Harry Truman signed this directive—sometimes called the "Loyalty Order"—on March 21, 1947, prescribing "procedures for the administration of an employee loyalty program in the executive branch of government."[24] The order was designed to root out Communist influence in the US government.

Weinstein, of course, was not a federal employee, nor did she aspire to be. But after the order was implemented, Truman's attorney general, Tom C. Clark, quickly followed with his own directive, which was to provide resources for one particular criterion in the executive order: whether "reasonable grounds exist for belief that the person involved is disloyal," which would be a finding of "membership in, affiliation with or sympathetic association" with any organization determined by the attorney general to be "totalitarian, Fascist, Communist or subversive," advocating or approving the forceful denial of constitutional rights to other persons, or seeking "to alter the form of Government of the United States by unconstitutional means."[25] In other words, it didn't matter if someone was a federal employee; if she was a member of a group deemed subversive, she could be investigated. As Clark's list of subversive groups grew, so did Hoover's purview to investigate the people within them. As an active board member of at least three of these groups, Weinstein was a natural candidate for continued investigation.

***

FBI Special Agent John P. DiMarchi was put in charge of cultivating and collecting special informants to report to him about Weinstein's past and present activities. These would have to be new sources—not just the erstwhile special investigator in the NYPD who provided "padding" for Weinstein's file regarding her involvement with ICCASP and her husband's work for the Yugoslav Relief Committee.

Earnest, methodical, and needing little sleep, DiMarchi drove from his home in Stuyvesant Town in Manhattan to FBI headquarters every morning when he wasn't out in the field. Many of the informants he and his colleagues found were of little consequence—they were simply clerks or agents in state and county vital records offices or the Board of Elections office or the New York Customs and Immigration office. Sometimes an "informant" was not even a human, but rather just a body of information extracted by an agent pretending to be a pollster or advertiser and using the pretext to call Weinstein at home, as DiMarchi himself did once or twice.

The informants in Weinstein's file fell into general categories of informers developed by Hoover in the late 1940s. Many were "confidential sources": individuals who furnished the FBI with information available to them through their employment or position in the community. Under no circumstances would the FBI disclose such an informant's identity; he or she might be a high-ranking Communist Party member. Usually—and ideally—this person would be employed in government service so as to inform on others who had Communist sympathies or had infiltrated government service or turned Communist while doing so.

There was the "established source": any source with whom the FBI developed a relationship over time and who was trusted to keep that relationship confidential—perhaps somebody who was a secretary for an organization suspected of Communist activity. There was also the "office contact": usually a businessperson who could be relied upon to provide information—Walt Disney is thought to have been one of the most famous examples of such an informer. Last, but not least, there were other government agencies or businesses that relied on government regulation that merely supplied general information: passport and customs offices, rail companies, telephone companies, airlines, and so on.

These categories seem interchangeable, and they were. There were even hierarchies within each category. Some informants were paid, and some weren't. For someone not employed by the government, Hoover preferred "a professional man, a banker, a lawyer, a doctor," or someone else the agency deemed reliable. "When that type of man gives us information in confidence," Hoover said, "we of course are going to treat it in confidence." For a mere "next-door neighbor or fellow employee" who insisted on anonymity, Hoover demanded that the agency investigate whether this person was "activated by malice" and, if so, the reason for that hostility. If the person was not willing to make a signed statement or testify, the situation had to be evaluated by the Loyalty Review Board.[26]

The Loyalty Review Board was a body of people set up in an informant's place of employment. Each federal agency had its own board, composed of individuals it deemed worthy of the task of hearing evidence of an employee's incorruptibility.

Budenz himself was labeled Special Informant T-36. The assessment of Weinstein he provided that late spring day in 1950 was broken up into chunks throughout her file; statements provided by other informants embroidered these chunks. Virtually none of this information was any secret. She played pivotal roles in organizations such as the Joint Anti-Fascist Refugee Committee, Progressive Citizens of America (PCA), and the National Council of the Arts, Sciences and Professions (NCASP). She raised thousands of dollars for the relief of Spanish Republicans and in support of various labor organizations around the country. And some informants were clearly plucked from investigations of other prominent left-wing activists and actors.

DiMarchi, though, seems to have cultivated some informants that Weinstein may not have noticed. One, for example, worked closely with Weinstein and Dr. Harlow Shapley. It was this informant who advised DiMarchi and his colleagues that on April 16, 1948, Alice Prentice Barrows and Dr. Shapley had agreed that Weinstein was to be named one of the executive directors of the NCASP. Barrows was a teacher and had been a secretary in the Office of Education during the early days of the New Deal. She was an unabashed Communist and worked for many labor organizations in addition to NCASP. In addition, she told the FBI that Weinstein had close relationships with President Truman, Interior Secretary Oscar Chapman, former secretary of war Robert Patterson, and other government officials. The inference was clear: Hannah, the journalistic housewife, was thought to have the ability to manipulate figures at the highest levels of government and sway them to Communist endeavors!

The FBI's greatest concern with Weinstein appears to have been her agitation against the Internal Security Act of 1950. Sponsored by Nevada senator Pat McCarran, it called for the registration of organizations and persons deemed dangerous to American national security. It would force citizens to disclose any membership in organizations that might be considered somehow seditious, and it would allow companies to fire employees it deemed directly or indirectly sympathetic toward

Communist, Socialist, or Fascist ideals. It would also implement a more stringent screening of people trying to immigrate to America and Communists (concealed or just sympathetic). Also, members of other organizations considered dangerous to public safety could be deported from the United States.

Whatever power this informant thought Weinstein had brought to bear against the president, he or she was clearly overreaching, or perhaps the FBI was, or both. Truman always proclaimed that he would veto the bill in its original form, and he did so on September 22, 1950. This was just one day after this tipster provided the information to the agency.[27]

Still, the intelligence agency pulled together a case against Weinstein that was damning in quantity, if not quality. Confidential Informant T-34, for example, "of known reliability," recounted how on March 16, 1949, the activist badgered Sergei R. Striganov—the cultural attaché and first secretary at the Soviet Embassy in Washington, D.C.—to get renowned Russian pianist Dmitri Shostakovich to play for the World Peace Conference held in New York City in 1949. It was common knowledge that Joseph Stalin pushed hard to get such invitations, owing to his goal of burnishing the Soviets' reputation for producing cultural and artistic icons, though such artists faced persecution at home. Moreover, said the informant, Weinstein planned to make movies about any Soviet delegation to the conference—insinuating that she planned to distribute pro-Soviet propaganda films. Weinstein's machinations could only be perceived as enabling Stalin.[28]

Other informants gave information that could only be interpreted as Weinstein's working as an agent for the Soviet Union. T-3, for example, was Margaret Harwood, the brilliant director of the Maria Mitchell Observatory in Nantucket, Massachusetts. Harwood was both a close friend and colleague of Harlow Shapley. She allegedly told the FBI that Weinstein made contact with some Soviets via mail drop—letters were left for her at the Royalton Hotel in New York City under the name "Sidney Rowen." Another informant—whose name remains redacted—advised the agency that Weinstein had told Shapley she possessed some "inside data" on relations between Washington, Berlin, and Moscow, which she would furnish Shapley the next time they were together. Whatever the "inside data" was is not described.[29]

Also of great concern to the FBI was Weinstein's involvement with the Committee of One Thousand. Shapley and Weinstein formed this organization in 1948 with the goal of abolishing the House of Representatives Committee on Un-American Activities (HUAC). The committee's statement of purpose termed the members of HUAC as "betrayers of American ideals, those who use terror, innuendo, hearsay and smears, ignoring the common rules of evidence and all precepts of fair play."[30] The FBI was also troubled by Weinstein's leadership of the NCASF—an organization that fell under the purview of Executive Order 9835.

Other informants noted Weinstein's association with John Howard Lawson, known as the "Great White Father" of the Communist Party movement in Hollywood. Weinstein, it seems, helped him prepare a full-page ad in the form of an open letter to President Truman, calling for the dismissal of Attorney General Clark and the appointment of a citizens committee to investigate the FBI. With these statements, Weinstein was yoked together with members of the Hollywood Ten and, in a broader sense, the California Committee on Un-American Activities.

As was true with so many targets of Hoover's Communist witch hunts, there were huge problems with the veracity of the confidential informants in Weinstein's case. To be sure, some were willing to spy in return for cash on a weekly or piecework basis or may also have had ideological motives. Some were individuals who suffered some sort of legal or practical vulnerability out of which his or her handlers exacted quid pro quo informant work. And yet another group of informants included those who furnished private information to the authorities out of a desire to "keep the door open" or develop a special relationship that could stand in good stead if things got difficult or serious troubles developed—such as arrest, or a violent uprising of some kind.[31]

There was a fourth category of informants in Weinstein's case and that of many others. This was that of the "unwitting informant"—one who provided privileged information to the bureau without fully realizing how they were being used, and how their role was being portrayed in FBI paperwork. All that was required for this was for an agent to telephone or visit and somehow contact this person and ask for updates on the organization at large—updates that might even already have been published in the newspapers. This was the case with "informants" like Weinstein family friend, Hugh Houlihan, who worked for press relations at the American Committee for Yugoslav Relief.

This was also the case with Hannah's friend, columnist and activist Ileene Heiman, who was sourced several times in the Weinstein file. Heiman's daughter recalls that her mother worked on behalf of Jewish charities, and that their Chicago home was a place of refuge for aging sharecroppers, some of whom were driven from their homes in the middle of the night by white hate mobs. In addition to working with Weinstein in Progressive Citizens of America (PCA), Ileene was handpicked by W. E. B. Du Bois to be the Chicago spokesperson for the NAACP. "It would have been totally out of character for my mom to have taken an action that may have jeopardized someone else's well-being," her daughter said. "She hated J. Edgar Hoover."[32]

***

On June 22, 1950, just days before the start of the Korean War, a pamphlet called *Red Channels: The Report of Communist Influence in Radio and Television* started making the rounds at advertising companies, TV networks, and movie studios. It was eventually distributed to four thousand executives. *Red Channels* took full advantage of the earlier indices of names as well as the panic that accompanied the conflict in Asia. Published by American Business Consultants (ABC) from a small office on 42nd Street, *Red Channels* listed the supposedly Communist associations of 151 performing artists. These publishers encouraged the use of their list whenever making hiring decisions, they said, as a bulwark against the efforts of the Communist Party to infiltrate every phase of American life. The party, they claimed, used television programming as "sounding boards, particularly with reference to current issues in which the Party is critically interested: 'academic freedom,' 'civil rights,' 'peace,' the H-bomb, etc."[33]

Most of the producers, writers, and actors who were accused of having had left-wing leanings found themselves blacklisted, unable to get work. Actor Jean Muir was the first actor to lose her job because of her appearance in *Red Channels*; NBC fired her after receiving about thirty phone calls protesting her role in the television program, *The Aldrich Family*; the advertiser, General Foods, requested her dismissal. The apparent cause of Muir's appearance in *Red Channels* was her six-month membership in the Congress of American Women, deemed subversive by the HUAC. Soon after, other artists began losing their jobs in droves, including Weinstein's close friends Dorothy Parker, Lillian Hellman, and Philip Loeb. "The $500 million-per-year broadcasting industry now accepts '*Red Channels*' almost as a bible," one columnist wrote, noting that the advertising companies that supported programming allowed themselves to be intimidated by nothing more than a tiny pamphlet written by people with no special standing or any authority within the community.[34]

CBS Television—*Robin Hood*'s future home—most strongly reacted to the *Red Channels* list and general anti-Communist measures. In December 1950, reacting to Truman's declaration of national emergency, the network asked its 2,500 employees to sign loyalty oaths like those required of applicants for federal jobs. It also placed armed guards at transmitter sites and in master control rooms to prevent sabotage of equipment or service.[35]

Weinstein was not listed in *Red Channels*. She wasn't working in any visual medium yet. Still, she was lumped in with her friends in Hollywood and New York working in radio and television. As historian Carol Stabile recounts:

> *Although their names appeared on no official lists, people like Gertrude Berg, Joan LaCour Scott, and producer Hannah Weinstein were rendered unemployable through rumors of their association with blacklisted people. Because the blacklist occurred at such a transitional moment in the broadcast industry, in which writers were migrating to television from theater, radio, print, and film, many of those named by Red Channels were singled out not because of their work in broadcasting, but because conservatives were concerned about the work they might do.*[36]

The FBI began corresponding with the CIA regarding Hannah's activities. Both agencies followed her for the next twelve years. In sometimes humorous, ham-fisted attempts, they cultivated sources as inane as the teenaged doormen at various apartment buildings in which she stayed when she flew back and forth to the United States. Other times, these were subtly chilling, like when they followed her father and her brothers. They would call her apartment under some pretext and if one of her daughters happened to answer, they would dig for information from them.

In particular, the agencies were concerned with her brother Seymour, who had allegedly set up a corporation in the United States to finance Sapphire Films and its Communist enterprises. And of course, the bureau cultivated an informant to monitor communication between her and Walter Bernstein, the blacklisted writer and producer, and Gene Frankel, the actor and theater owner. Both were considered leaders in the Communist Party USA and thought to be the nuclei to sprawling spy rings within the entertainment world.

As for Louis Budenz: There is an admission in his perfunctory cover memo at the beginning of Weinstein's voluminous file. It says that although he conversed with her on the phone, he'd never actually met her.

**

In mid-1950 the board of directors for the Institute for Public Relations demanded that she give up her political activities or lose her job. She promptly resigned. Moreover, she and husband Isadore—"Pete"—decided to separate. There were other reasons for the split, too, but as Weinstein told her close friend Peggy Phillips, "I can't really blame him. He's worried the liberal paint could smear off him and might affect his livelihood."[37] By now, Pete ran his own boutique advertising agency, after resigning as director for the American Committee for Yugoslav Relief, deemed "subversive" in 1949. He was intimidated by his wife's far greater ambitions and success. He also hadn't wanted children, or at least not so many of them, according to one source. Paternalistic friend Harlow Shapley helped tell the girls their father was not going to live with them anymore, and Weinstein decided not to ask for alimony and child support. As one daughter recalled, it wasn't so much that she was looking to be a Herculean character. "It's just that if she was seen as fragile, I think that she was probably terrified that she would be, so she just didn't do it."[38]

Around this time, Weinstein learned through friends that HUAC planned to subpoena her to appear before its committee about her own work on ICCASP and her other organizations deemed "communist fronts." She was just as likely to have been subpoenaed by McCarthy's office, too, given Budenz's testimony and her close association with three of the senator's primary targets: Harlow Shapley, John Abt, and Lee Pressman. Of particular interest to the FBI was her continued contact and friendship with Alfred and Martha Stern, the Soviet romanticists who were later charged with espionage. Her files indicate the agency hoped to turn her into an informant against the couple.[39]

Weinstein taught her girls never to open the door, for fear of a subpoena being pushed into their little hands. By April of 1950, Weinstein knew the FBI was following her. Friends already in Europe encouraged her to come over before the government confiscated her passport. And so, a few days after the end of Chanukah, she and her girls sailed for Europe and an unknown future.

CHAPTER 5

France and Scotland Yard

On December 15, 1950, President Harry Truman proclaimed a national emergency. In previous months, the United Nations had successfully tamped down Soviet forces in Korea. But in November, China had joined those forces on the peninsula, and it was clear that Communist leaders intended to take more territory. Truman announced that he was setting up a new government department with unprecedented power to mobilize the United States against "world conquest by Communist imperialism." The Office of Defense Mobilization, Truman continued, would retain full authority over civilian agencies already at work building US war strength. In newspapers and speeches and radio addresses, the president called upon every citizen to put the country's defense "ahead of everything else."[1]

The next day, with winds whipping up around Pier 88 on New York's North River, Soviet foreign minister Andrei Y. Vyshinsky boarded the French liner SS *Liberté* to go back home to Russia. He lamented his departure to the many reporters and cameramen clustered at the steamship to watch him board and read a statement that said, in part:

> *Those who have followed the work of the fifth session of the United Nations General Assembly could not have failed to observe its distinctive feature which was that, not only the basic principles of the United Nations Charter, but also the General Assembly's rules of procedure were systematically violated whenever they happened to be*

inconvenient for the United States delegation, whose lead is followed
by the delegations of the other members of the North Atlantic pact.[2]

More specifically, Mr. Vyshinsky continued, the United States refused to curb its aggression in Korea and put controls on its nuclear arms production. Would Mr. Vyshinsky care to comment on Truman's "national emergency" speech? a reporter asked. Coyly, the diplomat declined, saying that he was asleep at the time of the president's announcement. Another reporter asked the foreign minister about his thoughts on Truman's recent statement that war was not inevitable. Vyshinsky assured him that the Soviet Union had always maintained that all "honest and reasonable" people would rather avoid war, that the only people who felt otherwise were interested in profit and world domination—an unsubtle criticism of the United States. After delivering some Christmas platitudes, the sixty-seven-year-old Ukrainian-born diplomat retired to a luxury suite on the ship and prepared to sail back to Russia and the opposite side of the Cold War, by way of Paris.

Away from the reporters and cameras focused on Vyshinsky, a petite woman ushered her three small girls, ages nine, seven, and five, onto the *Liberté,* too. Their cabin was significantly smaller than the diplomat's first-class one, but all the accommodations on the newly refurbished ship were considered luxurious by the day's standards. On the ship, Vyshinsky greeted the woman who looked at least ten years younger than her thirty-nine years. She was his friend, Hannah Dorner Weinstein.

Weinstein and Vyshinsky became acquainted in 1942, when the National Council of American-Soviet Friendship (NCASF) put her in charge of its publicity. She wrote or helped write many speeches for him to deliver at events sponsored by NCASF. Perhaps her best was the one Vyshinsky delivered to fifteen thousand people at Madison Square Garden, on December 2, 1946. In it, he warned of the "clever and artful prophets of evil" that were attempting to "undermine the friendly and cordial relations" between the United States and the Soviet Union.[3]

The Weinsteins and their nanny arrived in Paris five days later and were greeted by her friend Johnny Weber. Until recently, Weber had been head of the William Morris Agency's literary department in Los Angeles and was, in fact, a member of the Communist Party. In Hollywood, he'd worked closely on creative and party pursuits with John Howard Lawson, Weinstein's HICCASP counterpart. An open Marxist, Weber trained in national-level Communist leadership through the Depression years, organizing marches to bring awareness about hunger and unemployment. A gifted writer and reader with a knack for finding narratives that sold well, Weber eventually rose to his position at William Morris and advised and promoted the careers of many progressive writers and actors. Along the way, he founded the organization that became the Screenwriters Guild of America, the powerful union that advocated for wages and credits for writers.

Boss William Morris and the rest of the agency's management had no qualms with Weber's activism, knowing that progressive writers tended to be the "cream of the talented crop." Morris even sent affidavits of his support of Weber to the HUAC in 1947, when it first subpoenaed him. But then there was a change in management at the agency. Weber was quietly terminated and blacklisted. In 1950, he moved to France with his wife and two small daughters.

For the first month after they arrived, the Weinsteins stayed at the Hotel Bellegarde in Paris, and then Weber installed the family at the Hotel Derby where he and writer/director Bernard Vorhaus were staying. He then connected Weinstein with Russian-born novelist Vladimir Pozner, with whom she and her daughters lived for a time in Chatou, a suburb of Paris.[4]

Here in France, Weinstein joined a group of eclectic artists and personalities who were warmly welcomed by their adopted country. Rebecca Prime, author of *Hollywood Exiles in Europe: The Blacklist and Cold War Film Culture* and a forthcoming work on blacklisted writer/producer/director Jules Dassin, summarizes the host country's attitude toward these newcomers:

> *Arriving in France at a time when the influence of the French Communist Party was at its peak, the Hollywood exiles found that their political orientation provided them with a sense of belonging to a broader community. "Although no longer party members, we*

continued to feel like Communists," Norma Barzman recalls. "And
since we were in a country where the Communist Party was a mass
party, winning a large bloc of votes, we felt part of the mainstream."
For John Berry, his political beliefs helped him feel integrated into
French society. "You'd go to a manifestation for the [Ethel and Julius]
Rosenbergs with a great sense of being together. There was kind of that
solidarity in every area."[5]

According to her CIA file, Weinstein initially thought about a career
importing dolls made in Italy to America. Accurate or not, the plan could
not have lasted long, given the pull of the enormous writing and producing talent surrounding her. Hannah's social scene in France included
Boris Karloff, the actor famous for playing Frankenstein's monster, and a
cluster of exiled screenwriters and producers including Norma and Ben
Barzman, Vorhaus, writing team Lee and Tammy Gold, director John
Berry, Dassin, and writer Abraham Polonsky, to name a few, all of whom
had gone to France in the late 1940s and early 1950s. "Blond, small and
slim," recalled Norma Barzman, "she looked determined, had a business-
like manner, was a powerhouse of enthusiastic energy."

Weinstein knew nothing about filmed entertainment, Barzman
recalled, but she had a lot of ideas—they just weren't crystallized. Before
leaving the United States, Weinstein had formed a company with Sam
Wanamaker with the idea of making a film about Judah Maccabee, the
Jewish priest who—with his brothers—rebelled against the Hellenistic
empire that ruled ancient Judah. The Maccabees eventually restored wor-
ship at the temple in Jerusalem in 164 BCE. The film would be a fiction-
alized version based on the novel *My Glorious Brothers* by Howard Fast.

Her goal was to learn how to produce films—at first, maybe just
some shorts that were so popular in theaters at that time.[6] She was
intelligent, and a quick study, Barzman also recalled. "Jack [Berry]," she
remembered, "took her to a TV show I wrote, filming by the Seine. They
taught her [basic camera and production work] in a few days."[7]

After producing a film with Berry about the French resistance, Weinstein—with Polonsky and Karloff, began planning a TV program. It was
called *Colonel March Investigates*, and it would star Karloff as an urbane,

eye-patched sleuth who solved unusual mysteries and locked-room murders.

***

Colonel March was the catalyst for Sapphire Films. It brought together half a dozen entities that created the blueprint for Weinstein's success over the next ten years. More broadly speaking, *March* signaled the transition for the "lower reaches" of the British film industry. It shifted from the production of "program fillers" and supporting features to making filmed TV series. As film historian Dave Mann writes, Hannah saw the potential in this shift earlier than her British counterparts. She also recognized that the American market might be ready for something that differed from the heretofore popular variety shows fronted by former Hollywood stars—like the domestically produced *Douglas Fairbanks Presents*.

American novelist John Dickson Carr, writing as "Carter Dickson," created the Colonel March character. Then, like now, Carr was considered the master of "locked-room" mysteries—the "impossible crimes." Though originally published in a variety of magazines, the stories featuring this private eye were mostly located in a collection published in 1940.

In the books, Colonel March (first name "Perceval," but never used) headed "D3," a little-known department of Scotland Yard. Within the Yard, the department was fondly referred to as "The Department of Queer Complaints." Colonel March fielded any case that seemed outlandish and impossible. Most such cases turned out to be the products of overactive imaginations, but some turned out to be very serious, involving thieves, spies, and menaces of unknown origins. These were not cases for any ordinary policeman or even an experienced detective. Colonel March, however, was able to take the inexplicable and the bizarre and find a rational explanation. The character's prowess was more a function of him being well and widely read as opposed to having special, Sherlockian deductive powers. The books were extremely popular.

Weinstein was interested in Colonel March for several reasons. As Mann explains, the crime genre had long been a staple of the British film industry. It could be made cheaply because contemporary locations, props, and costumes were readily available. The early television industry followed suit, typically exploiting the internationally marketable mythologies of Scotland Yard and/or the English eccentric sleuth. Between 1929 and 1952 there were at least twenty films or television shows that had shown in theaters or over the airwaves with "Scotland Yard" in the title—and scores more without it but set against the Yard backdrop. Many of these titles had been sold into other countries, too. The true "explosion" of Scotland Yard television fare would follow right on the heels of *Colonel March* (as evidenced by the proliferation of shows in the mid-1950s, like *Calling Scotland Yard* and *Stryker of the Yard* and *Fabian of the Yard*). Clearly, *Colonel March* was a harbinger of what was to follow.[8]

For his part, Karloff was interested in a vehicle that would showcase his versatility as both a film and television actor. It would also allow him and his wife to visit his beloved home country, which he had not visited for nearly thirteen years. As a founding member of the Screen Actors Guild who was committed to safe working conditions for performers, Karloff was pro-union when the situation required it, and was certainly against the McCarthy hysteria. Thus, the actor probably appreciated the irony of making a filmed version of one of John Dickson Carr's characters.

Carr was so disgusted with the New Deal politics of the pre-war era that he often pontificated about an idealized perception of English conservatism. He even moved to England in 1933 and stuck by his adopted country through the war years, but he left in 1948, finding the Welfare State agenda of the Labour government intolerable. He returned in 1953 when the Tories had reestablished themselves. Most of his stories were about pre-war England—one uncontaminated by social strife or class enmity. "One of Carr's purposes in writing mystery and historical dramas for the BBC," said one historian, "was to relive the horrors of war by presenting cosier and, with the solutions at the end of each play, more manageable horrors."[9] For Weinstein, *Colonel March* had to be an interesting experiment. As Mann points out, the production was unique in that it articulated a proxy confrontation between two ideologically opposed American writers: Colonel March's creator, the right-wing American anglophile Carr, and the series' left-wing, progressive writers in the form of her blacklisted friends.

In early 1952, Weinstein began negotiating with Carr's British lawyers for the film rights. Hannah asked her friend Walter Bernstein if he would write the show. She had originally approached Arnold Manoff, but he was busy writing for producer Charles ("Charlie") W. Russell on the CBS drama *Danger*. All the same, Manoff, Bernstein, and Polonsky had formed a sort of "mutual aid" trio. If one got a job and another really needed the money, they'd pass the job along.

A member of the Communist Party USA, Bernstein appeared in *Red Channels* in 1950, effectively putting him on the "do not hire" list almost immediately. Polonsky was called to testify in front of HUAC in 1951, at which he refused to do so, earning him the designation of "a very dangerous citizen" by Illinois Republican congressman Harold Velde. Manoff was "outed" by both a director and another screenwriter. All of them—and their families—were being relentlessly harassed by the FBI. Since working with Hannah in ICAASP in the late 1940s, Bernstein had been busy adapting a thriller and was writing for the *Philco Television Playhouse*, a program sponsored by a giant electronics manufacturing company. For *Philco*, Bernstein's friend, Eliot Asinof, acted as his "front."[10]

Despite their blacklisted status, Bernstein, Polonsky, and Manoff were busy. They were all writing for the CBS program *You Are There*. It was a serious news-entertainment program, in which Walter Cronkite sat behind his anchor desk and an actor portraying a historical figure sat behind another. Every week featured a new reenactment of some pivotal moment in the past, like on April 26, 1953, when the show featured a dramatization of Ben Franklin and others finessing and signing the Declaration of Independence. Producer Russell had no apparent interest in any political content in *You Are There*, but allowed his secret writers to pick and choose what topics they wished to write about and how they wanted to portray them, if they were factually correct. "In that shameful time of McCarthyite terror, of know-nothing attempts to deform and defile history, to kill any kind of dissent," Bernstein recalled, "we were able to do shows about civil liberties, civil rights, artistic freedom, [and] the Bill of Rights." Polonsky concurred. "You don't have to lie or change the facts of history," he said, "but you have to be able to select them properly." Thus, the three men forged a distinctly anti-McCarthyism foundation for each of the programs, choosing to narrate the stories of individuals who, for one reason or another, had become political or cultural pariahs because of their assumedly virtuous beliefs or principles. They chose subjects such as Joan of Arc, Galileo, Socrates, and John Milton, to name just a few.[11] In some episodes, they simply featured women and African Americans in non-normative roles, to challenge the usual stereotypes of females and people of color.[12] In other words, the trio had become extremely adept at using sociological subtext to build wonderfully entertaining teleplays.

When Weinstein floated *Colonel March* to Bernstein, he and Polonsky asked her if they could team up. It would be better if they worked on it together, they explained, because it would be easier to create and solve the puzzles required for a detective show. She agreed, happy that two blacklisted screenwriters would have work instead of just one—although they would have to split the fee between them.

Weinstein still had a passport, so she was able to fly or sail to the United States when she needed to. According to the FBI's Confidential Informant T-4, Hannah was in New York City in April 1952, met with Bernstein on the 22nd, and had arranged to obtain pictures of some kind from him "in the afternoon." Most certainly, the two were not planning espionage so much as discussing projects for which they could work together, and probably discussing *Colonel March*. Weinstein had already engaged Karloff, so Bernstein and Polonsky would need to write a role for the actor who, at sixty-seven years old, would play a Colonel March who was thin and wore an eye patch—whereas the book character was obese and had no eye problem.

They would also need to create a name for themselves, since both were blacklisted. When Bernstein was first banned from scriptwriting, he thought he could just put a different name on his scripts. He simply typed "Paul Baumann" on some. For one reason or another, advertisers and television executives got suspicious. When people asked Russell where his writer "Paul Baumann" had gone, he simply said that he had "moved to Denver." Executives got even more wary and started insisting on in-person story conferences. If this happened, Russell said that Baumann was living a secluded life atop a mountain in Colorado and had no access to a telephone. In one instance, a desperate but stalwart Russell told CBS that "Baumann" had gone to Switzerland for treatment of a rare tropical disease. As pressure increased to produce evidence of Baumann's existence, Russell finally spread the sad news that Baumann's disease had proved fatal and he passed away in a Swiss hospital. Eventually, though, Bernstein had to drop "Mr. Baumann."[13]

For Bernstein and Polonsky, like many other blacklisted writers and creators were also realizing, using a pseudonym would not work any longer. They would have to use a "front." Bernstein enlisted real people who offered their names to put on his scripts in return for a percentage of the earnings. The pair started using the bucolic "Leo Davis." Leo was, in fact, a real person who agreed to act as a front for the pair. They got to work reading the books and working out different plotlines.

Over the next several months, Hannah flew back and forth between New York, Paris, and London. When in New York, she stayed at the apartment Pete had rented for her in his name at 41 West 96th Street. The FBI occasionally dropped by to speak to the doorman and his supervisor, but they could provide no information about her activities except to say she seemed to be unemployed and occasionally stayed at the apartment with three small children. The agents did take note of her presence at an ICAASP board meeting at the Hotel Brevoort on June 21–22.[14]

A week later, Carr's lawyers in England signed off on an agreement with Weinstein's then-named company, Panda Films, for the film rights to *Colonel March*. According to Carr's biographer, Weinstein secured a highly advantageous deal, paying only £2,000 total for the rights, a surprisingly small sum that greatly disturbed his American agent, who apparently was not consulted, and neither was Carr himself.[15]

While in the states, Weinstein stayed in close contact with a consortium made up of three brothers, whose Eros Films would fund part of the production of the series. In return, their US branch, American-British TV Movies, would get the television distribution rights for the United States. At least, that was the original idea. The consortium signed Donald Ginsberg, a Brit fresh off the mystery feature *The Armchair Detective*, to produce the first three episodes. They figured that if they could package the three episodes as a feature, and if it showed well in the UK, perhaps they could use it as a "calling card" for a potential series.

Hannah flew back to France in May to work with Karloff and Polonsky, who, though blacklisted in 1951, was also somehow able to keep his passport. They agreed that the Carr stories were more cerebral than cinematic, but Weinstein didn't much care, Bernstein recalled—they could easily be rewritten, or new stories could be created. And so they batted ideas back and forth across the Atlantic over the phone, but eventually Weinstein and Bernstein decided it was time for Bernstein to meet with Karloff and get him on board with the character they'd fleshed out.

In December, Karloff and his wife returned from Europe to their apartment at the iconic Dakota building in New York City. The Karloffs invited Bernstein for tea. The writer took an elevator and then climbed a winding set of iron stairs to get to the home. "It seemed appropriate," Bernstein recalled, "like climbing to the bell tower where he held Gloria Stuart captive," referring to the 1932 horror film, *The Old Dark House*. The actor made him feel right at home, giving constructive criticism and advice on the ideas he and Polonsky had come up with thus far. They discussed the pitfalls of making a detective story into a film, particularly how the movie frequently became static at the end because the detective had to stop the action to explain the case. They talked about ways to make those endings active, at which point the dry-humored Karloff suggested that they not make them too active because he was not as young as he used to be.

Karloff and his wife sailed to Britain in July of 1952, with a newly grown moustache for his detective role. Reporters clamored for a quote as they stopped off the ocean liner. No horror films this time, he joked. Instead, he was looking forward to a more "light-hearted" and "benign" role.[16] The indefatigable actor had appeared in three television shows this year already, and one film—*The Black Castle*—in which he starred alongside another British-born actor: Richard Greene.

In London, leftist play director Mark Marvin introduced Weinstein to Cyril Endfield. At thirty-nine years old, Endfield was a fairly prominent Hollywood director. He'd grown up in Scranton, Pennsylvania, in an affluent Jewish household. The Great Depression severely affected the family's finances, but Endfield was able to secure a scholarship to Yale in 1932. Here, he managed to keep his studies up while making money on the side teaching card tricks to other students. By 1935 Endfield was involved with theater and radical politics. Endfield's biographer Brian Neve recounts that he joined the John Reed Club (a Communist Party organization) in New Haven and became a member of the Young Communist League—though he never joined the Communist Party. When he left Yale he went to New York, where he did odd jobs and took part in activities with the New Theatre League, another left-wing group.

Endfield decided to move to Hollywood in 1940, and he was eventually offered a job as a director with the MGM shorts department. This brought him into contact with Dalton Trumbo and playwrights Hugo Butler and John Wexley, names that would appear alongside so many others on the list of HUAC's subversives. He worked on a few shorts, wrote some scripts for radio, and attended occasional Communist Party meetings. Endfield's Communist associations would turn up to haunt him a few years later, according to Neve, but he always maintained that, by 1948 or so, he had become suspicious, if not totally disillusioned, about the party's motives.[17]

By the end of 1951, Endfield had three large budget films under his belt, including *The Sound of Fury*, which did not do very well in the American box office but garnered decent attendance in Britain. Before his next film, *Tarzan's Savage Fury*, could make its debut in theaters, Endfield had to leave the United States. In March of 1951, he was called to testify before HUAC. He refused, but in September 1951, "serial testifier" Martin Berkeley, a screenwriter, named Endfield and 159 others. It was obvious that Endfield himself would soon be called to appear before HUAC, and rather than wait for the subpoena, and then have to face the dilemma of how to respond, he decided to leave the United States. Luckily, he had a passport or would otherwise have been denied one, and on December 23, 1951, Endfield sailed the *Queen Mary* to England.

Endfield took up residence in Chelsea and got permission from the director's section of the Association of the Cine Technicians (ACT) to be able to work in Britain without being a full union member. Some key members of ACT's legislative committee were at that time also members of the Communist Party, including producer/director Sid Cole. Union leadership was sympathetic to political exiles, but fiercely protective of its native-born members. Brothers Phil and Syd Hyams, who owned distributor Eros Films, were also sympathetic, having watched HUAC persecute friends like musician Larry Adler, who also fled to the UK in 1951. The brothers wrote the Home Office, testifying that Endfield was essential to the production. Ultimately, the Home Office let him work, but only if he had a British director on set as a stand-by. However, he could work under his own name, which he did when Hannah tapped him to direct *Colonel March*.

Physical production was planned for Southall Studios, in what is now West London. This facility was then the home of "Group 3," a company that set up low-budget films and was also sympathetic to Weinstein's politics. It's not clear where all the funding came from for those first three *March* half hours, but it's likely that at least some of it came from left-wing actors and producers, some American, some British. The FBI tried to figure this out by keeping tabs on Panda Productions's office on Madison Avenue, but to no avail.

Polonsky and Bernstein—"Leo Davis"—wrote three initial scripts with input from Hannah and Sid Cole. The first one, "Hot Money," set up the format of the show. *Colonel March Investigates* had the same format as the mystery program *Danger*, for which Bernstein and Polonsky had also written; it would be a half hour with an act break in the middle. They had a great time writing the shows, according to Bernstein. "We discovered we were adept at creating the puzzle and our first acts usually ended on a high, expectant note of suspense." Unfortunately, it proved harder to write the second acts. "Our puzzles were so good they were unsolvable. The question was not how to make the endings more active but how to end them at all." Bernstein noted that no one else seemed to worry about this, least of all Weinstein. "So long as she got something to shoot, she was happy. If the endings made no sense, that did not bother her."[18]

Weinstein produced three episodes of *Colonel March* in conjunction with Criterion Films, a London-based outfit formed by Douglas Fairbanks Jr. Her goal was to have three pilot episodes that could be stand-alone programs or could be strung together into a feature film that would be shown in the UK in the hopes that it became popular enough to garner more investment from Eros Films, which took distribution in

Britain. In this deal, Karloff was entitled to a cut of any profit earned by sales of the program—how much isn't clear.[19]

Though she was involved in every facet of production, with Cole's assistance, she did not take a production credit. This probably wasn't so much to avoid attention paid to her writer "Leo Davis" as much as it was forward thinking. If shown as a feature film, a distributor would have had to declare the salary costs for *Colonel March Investigates* to the Board of Trade to fall within a British film quota. The combined salaries of Hannah as producer and Cy Endfield as director would have pushed *Colonel March Investigates* outside the threshold of eligibility. However, if Hannah didn't take a producer's credit, her salary would not be counted in the production costs.[20]

***

The writers stayed faithful to Carr's stories in the sense that they indulged the novelist's preference for "locked-room mysteries," for which he was famous, as well as misdirection and sleight-of-hand. Similarly, they kept most of Carr's supernatural elements (for example, in "The New Invisible Man," a man insists he saw a pair of disembodied, white-gloved hands shoot a man dead). However, Weinstein let Bernstein and Polonsky have free reign to inject whatever satire or veiled commentary they felt like injecting. And the duo deviated from Carr's celebration of the omniscient super sleuth. Instead, they promoted the "experts found wanting" paradigm. Their disdain for real-life, self-appointed fanatics and organizations that had ruined the lives of so many of their friends was fairly evident in their narratives. Mann summarizes:

> *Plainly we see the shadows of these "abominable" zealots threatening the likes of paranoid and perfidious members of Himalayan Mountaineering Club; or tracking down "ghosts" armed with the era's most innovative technology, like so many Madame Richters; or infiltrating the naïve though sincere idealists of the Society of Interplanetary Communication whilst secretly bent on their own venal agenda.*

There were plenty of analogies, Mann continues, to HUAC, SISS (the Senate Internal Security Subcommittee responsible for investigating the supposed Communist infiltration of the radio and television industries), the FBI, and so on.

Another important recurring motif of *Colonel March*—in contrast to Carr's original depictions—was the celebration of professional and resourceful women. The series boasted three murderesses during its run and at least three intrepid female investigators of various sorts. Mann posits that at least one of these might have been an homage to Weinstein—shown when March meets up with a character who is the director of a documentary film on the abominable snowman. The colonel concedes that male chauvinism has kept female investigators out of the rarified pool of special investigators. At the end of the episode, the woman is ceremoniously admitted to the "club."[21]

In April 1953, *Colonel March Investigates* premiered as a movie to lukewarm acclaim. One trade magazine said that it was an "acceptable novelty for public halls," and another wrote that some of its characters were "wildly extravagant." Theater owners would not commit to more episodes to combine for feature release. They were already largely suspicious of the same efforts by Douglas Fairbanks Jr. An anthology that his company released around the same time was the subject of an exposé in *Picturegoer*, which warned readers that "a new type of British film" was heading their way, and that the British cinema screen was in danger of becoming a "second-hand window" for American commercial television interests. But most other trade magazines praised the talents of Karloff and his co-lead, Ewan Roberts. Whatever their regional criticisms or praise of the film, movie halls kept it as a staple for the better part of a year.[22] It was a solid draw for adults looking for an escape on a Sunday afternoon.

Spurred by *Colonel March*'s relative success, Weinstein used the movie as a calling card to get more funding for a full series. Eros Films decided it could probably sell the series in the UK and invested about a third of the costs up front. So did Emmet Dalton, a former officer for the Irish Republican Army and head of its intelligence unit who was now a prominent movie producer. Again, whatever costs that weren't covered by these entities would remain a secret among Hannah and a few close associates.

Endfield's relationship with the series came to an end once the first three episodes were done and the resulting feature was released. He was irritated because he'd had to do some unpaid writing tasks for the first three episodes, and experienced "some rough spots" with Weinstein "off the set."[23] In any case, he moved on to other projects, so the direction of *Colonel March* was absorbed mostly by two extremely capable men: Bernard Knowles and Arthur Crabtree (a few were helmed by Phil Brown, Terence Fisher, Donald Ginsberg, and Paul Dickson).

Bernstein and Polonsky continued writing the bulk of the *March* episodes, except for a few that were written by Waldo Salt and two others. The only problem was they had to drop Leo Davis as a front. The real Davis eventually became a successful producer, but in those early years of the 1950s he was fairly poor. He sent what money he could home to his elderly parents. Then he started getting hired to write more scripts—both as a front and as himself—which made his life impossible, recalled Bernstein. "Friends kept telling him, 'You're living in a shithouse [while] making [all of] this money.'" His parents also wanted more money, thinking he was earning the full payment for something he didn't write. Davis had to drop the charade.[24]

Bernstein and Polonsky found a front who would end up becoming the name on the bulk of their *Colonel March* scripts. Leslie Slote had been friends with Bernstein since they were kids. He later recalled that when Walter told him about the blacklist, "I didn't have a television set, so I didn't know what the hell he was talking about." He didn't hesitate when Bernstein asked to use his name. "He explained that every once in a while I would get money from CBS. I would deposit it in my checking account and then write a check for that amount to him." Slote had no aspirations to be a television writer. He was working for a civil-service newspaper called *The Chief*. He liked the playacting, and would not take any money.[25]

It wasn't always easy, though. As more and more Bernstein and Polonsky–written episodes of *Colonel March* hit the airwaves, Slote's name became a known commodity. He was also fronting for the pair on

Danger and had already been called into the studios of the production so everyone could meet this "wonderful writer," Slote recalled. "I just sat in a booth and watched this thing, and that was all. I wasn't nervous." Another time Walter called him and said, "The agency people want to meet you." Again, Slote embraced the playacting. He put on a tweed jacket and got a pipe, thinking this would make him look like a typical writer. He showed up at the agency and met with Charlie Russell (who must have been praying this deceit worked) and a roomful of advertising men. Afterward, Russell assured Bernstein that Slote was a "big hit."[26]

Slote wasn't even aware that he was tethered to the series called *Colonel March*. After his name appeared on about twenty episodes, Bernstein called him and said, "You've got to go up to CBS's spook department," to see a former FBI agent. "I went to the CBS building," Slote recalled. "I got off the elevator on the eighth floor, and there was no name on the door of his office. Inside was a secretary and not a paper to be seen anywhere. It was the cleanest office I have ever seen. He asked me a few very cursory questions, and thank you and good bye."[27]

Colonel March was a triumph for Weinstein in two ways. As Mann deftly points out, she built on the precedent set by Douglas Fairbanks Jr. and successfully introduced American-style production strategies into the fledgling British TV/film sector. In fact, she was the first to base her production strategy around the work of writers experienced in this format—writers who also had a shrewd appreciation of American market requirements. To be sure, she read and gave notes on every single draft of the *March* scripts, but she trusted Bernstein and Polonsky to establish the series' format and redefine characters taken from the work of an internationally successful author. With "an astute pragmatism," she exploited the mythology and iconography associated with Scotland Yard and the eccentric English detective to differentiate a British series from its American rivals. In short, she developed a serial program that would resonate with both British and American sensibilities.

Weinstein accomplished something less obvious, too—at least, less obvious to all but a few in her inner circle. In engineering the adaptation of Carr's work, she and her writers were able to conduct an "amusing and gently subversive campaign" that challenged the American Right. In the process, Mann adds, the British cultural landscape, particularly the domestic generic tradition, became the site of ideological struggle. With this in mind, Weinstein decided to try to sell an even bigger series.

CHAPTER 6

Sherman Drive and Sherwood Forest

BACK IN THE UNITED STATES, A HOUSEWIFE IN INDIANAPOLIS WAS making headlines all over the nation. Ada White, a vocal member of the Republican Party, was increasingly alarmed by what she perceived as subversive, Communist indoctrination. In 1952, letters to the editor of the *Indianapolis Star* signed by "Mrs. Thomas J. White, 3501 N. Sherman Drive" made regular appearances in the paper. "Back in 1930," she wrote in one, "our Commie educators said that it was useless to indoctrinate our school children in socialist ways and not at the same time re-educate the parents." Of concern to Mrs. White was a book lauded by the National Congress of Parents and Teachers, which advocated "five socialistic measures: Federal aid to education, socialized medicine, public housing, economic security for all, and UNESCO." Just four years earlier, she warned, was when the Parent Teacher Association lobbied Congress for federal aid to education. "It is still repeatedly admitted by Communist educators that Federal control of our schools is a must for thorough indoctrination!"[1]

Mrs. White grew increasingly disturbed about text disseminated in schools, convinced (like many other Americans) that juvenile delinquency, Communism, and a general anti-American attitude were being instilled in the country's population by way of textbooks like *Adventures in Reading* and *Adventures in Appreciation*. These two alone, she said, each had thirty-eight authors and references listed in the un-American index. Twenty-one of them, she said, were affiliated with Communist fronts. "The literature books stress the breaking and contempt of law, indifference to parental authority, the sneer at religion, and the futility for one's rights, whether property or country. If our children are not Communists at the end of their schooling we can well thank the home and church."[2] In May of 1953, Mrs. White managed to get herself onto the Textbook Adoption Commission for the Indiana State Board of Education. She wasted no time in extolling textbooks that promoted capitalism and character as being intertwined.

In mid-November of 1953, she took aim at Robin Hood. "There is a Communist directive in education now," she said. "They want to stress it because he robbed the rich and gave it to the poor. That's the Communist line."[3] White was specifically alarmed about one version found in a seventh-grade textbook. It was called *Excursions in Fact and Fancy*, published by Laidlaw Bros. in Chicago. The story, the newspaper report said, was written by Mary MacLeod, and asserted that MacLeod was labeled a "party-liner" in a report of the Investigating Committee of Education in California.[4] The main points in the Robin Hood story that Mrs. White objected to were these, in bold to indicate how she made her notes:

> *Unhappily, the luckless boy slew a knight of Lancashire and to pay the heavy penalty exacted from him to save his rights* **(a slam at lawyers)**, *I was forced to sell my goods.*
>
> *Besides this, Robin, my lands are pledged until a certain day* **(a slam at mortgage holders)** *to a rich abbot* **(a slam at the church)** *living close by here at St. Mary's Abbey.*[5]

The Indianapolis school superintendent announced that he would re-read the story and decide whether he should take any action, but could not immediately infer anything subversive about Robin, Will Scarlet, Maid Marian, and the rest.

But within a couple of days, the wire services had helped make the story an international one. William J. Vox, the real High Sheriff of Nottingham in 1953, got several phone calls about it from America. "I have told all inquirers that the Communists will never be able to steal Robin Hood. . . . The Communists may claim a lot of things but they can't claim Robin Hood. We're really proud of him." Another British politician said that Robin Hood "would have been horrified at communism," and furthermore thought Robin would have shot Karl Marx. The Soviets got in on the action, announcing that author N. Gribachev had published "A New Ballad of Robin Hood" in the Communist newspaper *Pravda*. L'Humanite, an organization of the French Communist Party, went so far as to make a tongue-in-cheek claim that White objected to Little Red Riding Hood based on the color of her hood.[6]

In fairness to Mrs. White, she told the *Indianapolis News* that reporters had blown her recommendations out of proportion. "You can't be anti-communist these days," she complained to a reporter. "They'll smear you." She said she never stated that Robin Hood should be banned from Hoosier schools. "I did state that the Communists were promoting the Robin Hood theme of 'rob the rich to give to the poor' wherever and whenever possible." It wasn't the sort of thing that seventh graders should be reading, she added.

The zeitgeist created by the Ada Whites of America, coupled with the universal theme of Robin Hood as a fighter of an unfair ruling class and the story's origins in her immediate surroundings, gave Hannah Weinstein an idea.

***

In January 1953, Harold "Hal" Hackett was burned out. Tall, graying, handsome, the New York native had spent almost twenty years as an executive with RCA, helping build first its radio departments and then its fledgling television ones. But at nearly fifty, Hackett recalled, he just got sick of it all and left. Money wasn't really a problem—he'd done very well at RCA and at NBC before that. But he was bored and decided to take a vacation to think about his next venture. He sailed to the Bahamas, where he just happened to run smack into Isaac "Ike" Levy.[7]

Levy was a veteran Philadelphia radio and television entrepreneur. He was also a longtime stockholder and board member of the CBS networks. In late 1949, Levy was among a group of prominent broadcasters and entertainers who bought a controlling interest in Official Films. This group included correspondent Edward R. Murrow and Columbia Records president Ted Wallerstein. To them, buying into Official seemed like a good way to buy into a company that was leading the way in providing content for the relatively new medium of television.

Founded in 1945, the distributor was originally a home movie company, selling 8- and 16-mm shorts and features. The catalog offered hundreds of titles for sale, and quickly added two thousand musical shorts. By 1949, it was grossing over $1 million annually and was considered number two in the home-movie field. Its original owners focused on selling to "home—school—church." Levy and the others decided they would shift their efforts and sell to "home—television—bar."[8]

During its first year under new management, Official went into debt by nearly $200,000. Hurting for more television films, the consortium ran an experiment. In 1951, it purchased the Jerry Fairbanks studio and most of its already-produced entertainment, like *Front Page Detective* and the *Bigelow Theatre* series. By doing this, Official believed it could pick up a stockpile of films to syndicate and be able to produce its own fare on the Fairbanks lot in Hollywood. Unfortunately, this arrangement didn't work out. Fairbanks built his own sales division and managed to buy back most of the product he'd sold to Official. By the third year of management under Levy, the company was running nearly $1 million in debt. The succeeding year, 1952–1953, was a critical one.

The executives decided to go for broke, spending credit and cash to get two titles that would play on the NBC and CBS networks, and one that was sold into syndication. It worked, grossing Official a whopping $5 million and earning them a profit of about $75,000. They paid down their debt, and tentatively hired five salesmen to increase their presence in the marketplace. While this was all positive, Levy knew that if they lost even one sponsor of the three programs, it could spell disaster for the company. He needed someone to steer it in the right direction.

Enter Hackett. While their families played in the ocean at Paradise Beach, Levy convinced Hackett to come over to Official Films as president, which he did in April of 1953. The first thing Hackett did was dispel any notion of the company going into the production business. The only way to continue to make money, he declared, was to become solely a distributor. Sure enough, Dunhill cigarettes canceled its sponsorship of *My Hero* on NBC, and Canada Dry canceled its sponsorship of *Terry and the Pirates* in syndication. This freed up both properties for Official to resell to independent stations all over the country, which it did very successfully, becoming known as one of the leading distributors in America.

Official's ascendancy was in large part because its board could see which way the wind was blowing in terms of technology and government, both of which made it possible for these kinds of distributors to emerge. In the early 1950s, most television programming was broadcast live from New York City, and a lot of its dramas were based on theatrical productions. Hollywood studios started to get into the TV business by supplying films. The Walt Disney Company began supplying programming to ABC in 1954, and Warner Bros. followed the next year. Independent Los Angeles production companies such as Desilu, which began producing *I Love Lucy* in 1951, had started supplying programs on film even earlier. All the same, 80 percent of network television was still broadcast live in 1953.

This all changed when AT&T finished laying a system of coaxial cables from coast to coast. These precursors to the now familiar cables that run from cable TV wall outlets to today's tuners had enough bandwidth, or electrical carrying capacity, to transmit hundreds or even thousands of telephone calls as well as television signals. Now, ABC, CBS, and NBC could become "true" networks, although they only owned about five or six stations apiece at this time. The rest were either independently owned and operated or chose to affiliate with one of the three networks and carry its programming.[9]

By late 1953, the networks had to concede that live television would soon be a thing of the past. They'd been able to control their stations because the latter had to receive live feeds from the networks according to a specific schedule, whereas stations could air taped or filmed programs whenever they chose to run them. The networks and the television critics also insisted that live television programming was creatively superior to filmed fare. Nevertheless, the lower cost and reliability of recorded programs finally prevailed. As TV historian Michele Hilmes explained, "[B]y breaking down their own restrictions against the use of recorded programs, the major networks paved the way for the gradual disappearance of unwieldy and unpredictable live programming and the rapid rise in the use of film, as Hollywood wedged a toe in the door by means of syndicated film series."[10] In turn, this paved the way for Official Films and other syndication companies like it to feed the growing demand for wholesome drama and comedy series for the whole family. Now, Hackett and his colleagues just had to find that pipeline.

***

During one of her many trips home in 1953, Weinstein met with Hackett. What if he could sell *Colonel March* into the American market? She'd lost Endfield, but Bernard Knowles and Arthur Crabtree were equally talented and perhaps even a bit more economical—and didn't have the McCarthy albatross around their necks. Additionally, she thought she could secure the musical work of Edwin "Ted" Astley, who had just started hiring himself out for television and whom the budget-conscious Danziger brothers had recently used on some of their programs.

Could Weinstein film at least twenty-three more episodes, for a total of twenty-six, Hackett asked? He would need that many to sell into markets, which would not want to repeat them too quickly. Moreover, another firm was planning to sell another Scotland Yard–based program in the United States—also produced in England, by the daughter and son-in-law of Prime Minister Winston Churchill. That outfit only had thirteen episodes planned for their show; if she could assure Official of twice that amount, Hackett would have more leverage to sell into the late-night markets. She did.

At the same time, rapid developments in television were taking place back in the United Kingdom. On June 2, 1953, millions of viewers in Britain gathered around newly purchased television sets to watch the coronation of Queen Elizabeth II. Homes, pubs, and community centers were packed with people, all eyes fixed on the grainy, black-and-white images from the television set. It seemed like the entire nation lay hushed as the broadcast got underway, and over twenty million people in England watched the popular young Queen Elizabeth II swear the coronation oath; another seven million tuned in from other parts of the United Kingdom. This number reflected an average of seventeen people watching each set and almost twice the radio audience. Canadians and

Americans got to see the eight-hour affair with just a few hours delay, thanks to an elaborate relay system using RAF fighter jets and local police escorts to get BBC films to stations in North America. Australia was able to see the event about fifty-five hours later. Eventually, tens of millions of people around the world were able to watch highlights of it. In the two months preceding the Queen's formal ascension, British viewers bought more television sets than in any previous comparable period, bringing the country's grand total to about 2.5 million by the time the event aired.

Set sales aside, this broadcasted pageantry ushered in a new era of television in Britain and made *The Adventures of Robin Hood* possible just two years later. It was the first coronation to be filmed in full, and the first major world event to be broadcast internationally on television. But it also signaled some cultural shifts. One of these was the question of whether such a rarified and solemn occasion should be shared with millions of commoners. Most members of royalty and Parliament thought, "No." One member even asked, "Might there, even, be something unseemly in the chance that a viewer could watch this solemn and significant Service with a cup of tea at his elbow?" The Queen herself ended this debate by insisting that it be televised, paving the way for royal pomp and circumstance and even personal events like weddings to be filmed and broadcast.[11] Over the next decade, this became a practice not only accepted but expected.

The other cultural shift was Britain's reluctant acceptance of commercial television. This discussion had already been the subject of hot debate in Parliament and in the public sphere, and certainly among advertisers. But it was stoked even hotter by reports of how the coronation was shown in the United States. The British government had some strong words for NBC and CBS, which interspersed the proceedings with some sponsor plugs. NBC committed the most heinous offense, which was a five-minute "interview" about the coronation with J. Fred Muggs, the *Today Show*'s resident chimpanzee.

In 1953, there was still very strong resistance to going commercial—resistance led primarily by the National Television Council.[12] This powerful group was mainly composed of two political groups within

Parliament, leaders of the Church, and opinion-formers within the media who favored centralized social and cultural messaging, and who were afraid that commercially funded television programming would erode traditional values and morals. Simply put, they believed that the BBC (British Broadcasting Corporation) should be the entity to "inform, educate, and entertain," and that introduction of commercial values in broadcasting would "mark an apparent trend toward the 'Americanization' of British cultural life."[13]

All the same, the coronation's broadcast signified the last gasp of anti-commercial protest. Britain's post-war economy was improving, and manufacturers of television receivers needed more reasons to increase the sales and rentals of their equipment. The expansion of the economy also led advertisers to look for new and bigger markets for a range of consumer goods, which could be done by advertising those goods on television. A lobby called the Popular Television Association (PTA) led those in favor of commercial television as a new way to distribute new programs and services.

What ultimately pushed through legislation for commercial television was a small handful of members of Parliament. The Conservative government, elected to office in 1951 under the leadership of Winston Churchill, only had a majority of sixteen seats in the House of Commons. Some of these sixteen were opposed to any kind of monopoly—not just the one the BBC had in broadcasting—and believed the world of business was best served by free enterprise and competition. The chairman of the party agreed that the government would legislate for commercial television as long as it did not threaten the BBC's monopoly on radio. This was not very controversial: Radio was still considered the more prestigious and established medium, while television was considered new and somewhat experimental, and had a minority audience.[14]

With this governmental obstruction out of the way, seasoned film producers and entrepreneurs alike clamored for office space and set space to film new product for both television shows and the commercials that were now allowed to be shown (albeit with some strict limitations—at first). But almost a decade after the end of World War II, the domestic British film industry was still in decline. Studios started renting out space to non-British entities like Columbia Pictures and the omnipresent Douglas Fairbanks Jr. Between the gap in production of the first three episodes of *Colonel March* and the series, Weinstein and her crew lost their space at Southall Studios. She saw this as an opportunity. Why not take an ownership position in a studio, instead of just renting?

In mid-1954, Weinstein started discussions with the Hyams brothers. Philip, Syd, Nathan, and Michael "Mick" Hyams were the sons of a Russian immigrant baker in the East End of London, who had helped finance a popular film theater in Stepney in 1912. As teens, Phil and Syd worked there at night to learn the business. In the mid-1920s, the pair struck out on their own, buying rundown buildings and refurbishing them into movie theaters. The brothers, eventually joined by Mick, went into several businesses together with Gaumont Films, creating theater and broadcast centers that were not only immensely profitable but also architecturally stunning. Queen Mary and other members of the royal family often came to live and filmed events shown at The Trocadero, a magnificent theater built in the French Renaissance style, in central London. Fearing the threat of looming war, the Hyams brothers sold off some of their inner-London properties in 1939 but kept The Trocadero—which unfortunately lost money because people were understandably scared to enter taller buildings after the Blitz. The brothers sold it to Gaumont, just before the post-war boom in attendance made gold mines out of their theaters.

Not to be deterred, the impresarios started yet again in 1947, when they launched a distribution company called Eros Films. Initially, they reissued old Hollywood favorites like *Beau Geste* and *The Road to Singapore*. Soon they added new, British films for which they supplied some or all of the financing, like *The Runaway Bus* (1953) and the war drama *The Sea Shall Not Have Them* (1954). By 1954, they owned four of the biggest cinemas in London. But the Hyams brothers also wanted to be in the television business.

So did Lew Grade.

This cigar-chomping impresario would turn out to be the lynchpin between Weinstein and her success in creating Sapphire Films. Born as Lev Winogradsky in central Ukraine, Grade immigrated to Britain in

1912 at five years old, to escape the Jewish pogroms there. His parents were entertainers, and to keep the family afloat they performed vaudeville in the East End of London. Lew flourished in school, possessing a photographic memory and an exceptional command of math. Although he received scholarship offers for university, Grade decided to follow the advice of a family friend and get some practical work experience. He apprenticed at a clothing manufacturer and showed such a natural flair for business that within a year he had his own thriving business with more than a dozen employees.

Despite his long hours at work, Grade found time to dance. The Charleston was becoming all the rage in England like it was in America, and Grade was incredibly good at it because his parents had taught him the acrobatic, Cossack-like moves they'd brought with them from Europe. He picked up prize after prize, and even became the "Charleston Champion of London." A few years later, this arduous dancing wore his knees out, and he was bored with the clothing business and looking for something new. Lew had become friendly with a booking agent named Joe Collins, the father of actress Joan and future authoress Jackie. Grade recommended several acts to Joe that he had seen while traveling through Europe. Every act that Lew recommended, Joe hired. By the early 1930s, Grade figured he could book acts, too, and decided to formally go into business with Collins. Together, they built a very busy talent agency, only to lose some of it when the country went to war in September 1939.[15]

In spite of this setback, Grade had built enough of a reputation that the War Office hired him to handle entertainment programs for British troops. Meanwhile, Grade's younger brother Leslie had started his own agency, and at the war's end, because relations between Collins and the older Grade had become strained for various reasons, Lew accepted Leslie's offer to run his agency when he was called up for service. One of the people with whom Leslie did business was Val Parnell, managing director of a large theater group and one of the most powerful men in entertainment at this time.

When Leslie returned from service, the brothers merged all their contracts, which included bookings for stars like Abbott and Costello,

Lena Horne, Jack Benny, Dorothy Lamour, and Judy Garland. By 1951 Lew and Leslie Grade Ltd. had offices in London, New York, and California. Lew Grade was by now a major player in the world of entertainment. He was held in high regard as a man who would honor his word, look after his clients, and get the best deals. In 1953, when the British government started to grant licenses for commercial television, the assiduous Grade decided he must get one.

To be a candidate for getting a license, entities had to show proof of initial capital of £3 million. Grade thought he could scrape together £1 million between him and his brother, but there was no way he could raise three. He dismissed the notion of pursuing a license, but then a friend in the business called with an idea. This gentleman was in business with an American named Suzanne Warner, an ambitious and exceptionally connected publicist working in Britain at the time. He thought Warner might have some information that could help.

Grade called Warner; indeed, she did have information, but she was being cagey about her client, perhaps to avoid contenders who weren't serious. He asked, "Suzanne, who is going to put up the £2 million?" According to Grade, Warner replied, "I can't tell you that." The impatient Grade hung up on her. She called back almost immediately and gave him the name of the wealthy family willing to put up two-thirds of the money. Grade then called every theater chain owner who owed him a favor and his own banker and managed to come up with the rest. He then completed the application, suggesting he and theater impresarios Prince Littler and Val Parnell would lead the board.

They were denied. The Independent Broadcasting Authority told them that together, they controlled too many theaters and managed too many actors in Britain. In other words, the IBA accused them of having a monopoly on entertainment in the country. Why not, the IBA suggested, simply supply television programming to companies that would eventually be given licenses? The entrepreneurial Grade was extremely disappointed. But, between him and his brother and a few others, he had raised £500,000 in immediately available cash, so he figured he might as well take the IBA's suggestion to heart. All that remained was one question: How did one go about producing commercial television programming, and making a profit from it? They took a good look at *Colonel March Investigates*, and its producer, Hannah Weinstein.

In the United States, Wilen Wines sponsored the detective show, and by the end of 1954, the series—renamed *Colonel March of Scotland Yard*—could be seen in virtually every television market in the nation, usually in a 9:00 or 9:30 p.m. timeslot. *March* was not a ratings bonanza—it usually landed in the middle of a long list of winners for any given week—winners decided by a ratings system in its infancy, and one that did not necessarily rank late-night programs. But even in the beginning of 1954, it was getting good press in America. Wilen claimed that the program offered viewers something "entirely new and out of the ordinary," a "refreshing format with a decided twist."[16] The Karloff topper kept its regular audience from week to week and offered stations solid advertising dollars. When the show originally broadcast, *TV Guide* pointed out that the series had a "tightly budgeted" look; the sets were "inexpensive and showed little variety," and the supporting actors were usually young and virtually unknown. But it did concede that Karloff did a "smooth and entertaining job," the younger actors were convincing, and that Ginsberg and Endfield had good eyes for talent.[17]

***

In mid-1954, Weinstein talked to her friend Sid Cole about making a series. Cole was an associate producer at Ealing Studios when he met Weinstein through a mutual film world contact. He was a committed Socialist and Union activist. The forty-seven-year-old Londoner was the accomplished producer of several left-wing documentaries about the Spanish Civil War. When Cole came to work with Hannah, he came with more recent credentials but had received much acclaim for producing *The Man in the White Suit* (1951), starring Sir Alec Guinness as a humble inventor who develops a fabric that never gets dirty or wears out. The fabric turns out to be a boon for mankind, but, of course, garment manufacturers take issue with it and try to suppress it.

Weinstein told him she was considering a program based on either King Arthur or Robin Hood. Which one, she asked, did he think was best? He immediately said the latter. The Robin Hood myth, he told her, was well known around the world—a show about bandits and underdogs fighting powerful, corrupt rulers could eventually be sold into more nations than just the United Kingdom and America. It would allow viewers to root for outlaws. "You could be against the law and still with it as it were," he said. He signed on for *Robin Hood* as associate producer.[18]

As historian Andrew Paul writes, "Weinstein could have done worse than to select the legend of Robin Hood as a means to challenge the cultural climate of the cold war and allegorize the contemporary geopolitical conflicts of the period."[19] By mid-1954, Hannah had her "core group" ready to develop a series based on the mythological story.

CHAPTER 7

Brylcreem Boy

IN JANUARY 1953, ACTOR RICHARD GREENE TOOK AN INTERVIEW WITH
Marjory Adams of the *Boston Globe*. He was starring in *Dial M for Murder* at the city's famous Wilbur Theater. He couldn't help but prevaricate
when Adams asked him about his film career: "I admit I wouldn't refuse
a really good role if someone offered it to me," he said, "but I'm not going
to make any more 'Black Castles' and films of that type, unless I need
money a lot more than I think I shall."[1]

Greene was referring to a horror film he'd co-starred in the year
before, with Lon Chaney Jr., Rita Corday, and Boris Karloff.

At thirty-four, Greene was still a tiny bit boyish looking, even at six
feet tall, with blue-gray eyes and dark, glossy hair, and a slim nose but
strong chin. In the 1930s, the British-born actor had fairly walked into
several leading man roles because of his good looks. But in Hollywood,
being too good-looking could get one typecast into shallower roles
praised for their athleticism more than their speaking lines, which is
exactly what happened to Greene, much like his friendly rival, Tyrone
Power. And while he wasn't making the amount of money he could in
films—even mediocre ones—the stage at least offered him the opportunity to choose some more-textured roles.

Like Power, Greene left show business temporarily to serve his country in World War II, which he did admirably, even rising to the rank of
captain. When he returned to Hollywood in 1946, he found that he'd lost
whatever momentum he'd gathered, but gamely took whatever roles were
offered to him in film. He found himself cast as a swashbuckling hero in

a series of films, the most memorable of which was *The Black Castle*, in which he battled an evil, one-eyed Bavarian count.[2]

Hoping he could break away from this typecast as the spirited hero, Greene flew back and forth between Beverly Hills, where he owned a mansion with his British actress wife, Patricia Medina, and London, where he visited family and cast about for more serious roles in West End productions. Here, he found he had a different problem. Some fifteen years earlier, when he was barely out of his teens, Greene had modeled to support himself while he took acting classes and performed with a local repertory theater. He became the poster boy for a hair products company and soon was known as the "Brylcreem Boy," whose dimples and sheen-y hair were plastered all over buses and billboards. Somehow, Hollywood producer Darryl S. Zanuck took notice of him and his work and decided he could make Greene "the English Robert Taylor," and offered him a £200 a week contract. Zanuck couldn't suppress the advertisements, though he tried. In other words, Britain still thought of Greene as good-looking and talented but perhaps a bit superficial—even though he'd come from several generations of respected stage actors.[3]

Greene and his wife divorced in 1951, owing to what she claimed was his cold indifference to her. Greene had been carrying on an affair with a wealthy heiress, who gave birth to their daughter in March of 1951, but the pair had separated before this. In 1953, Greene and Medina flirted with reconciliation—the actor flew to Mexico to visit her on set, and they attended the Queen's coronation together. Regardless of their mutual respect, Greene and Medina decided re-marriage was not going to work and went their separate ways. Richard roamed around England, looking for a chance to prove himself as a serious stage actor and meeting with top British impresarios. Despite his movie work (*The Bandits of Corsica*, released in 1954, in which he displayed his usual competence in a role that was fun if not multifaceted), Greene was worried about his finances. He lived like a movie star, complete with boat ownership and the home back in Los Angeles—both of which he wished to keep, despite his alimony payments to Medina.

Greene made no secret of the fact that he was looking for personal investment in his works going forward. In 1954, he turned thirty-six, and he knew these "swashbuckling," athletic roles would start going to younger actors. In fact, Greene noticed that he was getting fewer offers for substantive roles of any genre. If he could take at least a partial ownership in a play or film, he might be able to control his own destiny to a certain extent, making his own starring role or perhaps learning how to produce. He even bought the rights to a comedy-western by writer Don Martin but could not get a studio to make it into a film.[4]

It's not clear exactly who approached Greene about Robin Hood, but it's likely that Weinstein made the overture, given their mutual friendship with Karloff. He could just as easily have played King Arthur, too, if the consortium decided to go that route. Until this point, Greene had not been terribly excited about the prospect of going into television full time. While he conceded that the medium could offer actors like himself the opportunity to play roles not available to them on stage, he thought the lack of an audience was a strange thing:

> *You rehearse for eight days and you give everything you have to the part. Then comes the great day of the show itself. And it's just like another rehearsal. No reaction, no laughter, no emotional outbursts of applause. Just the red beady eyes of the cameras to let you know that perhaps 10,000,000 are watching you.[5]*

Greene later admitted that he had some trepidation about playing a role that would most certainly typecast him. "But then I said to myself that other people had been typed and had managed to break out of it. Frank Sinatra is an excellent example. So I decided to take it on, reasoning that some future date I would be able to wriggle out of the green tights."[6] Weinstein's offer of a starring role for him was too good to pass up, especially since she offered him a third of any receipts Sapphire made on merchandise based on the show.[7]

Once Greene committed to a season of a Robin Hood series in the fall of 1954, Weinstein went to Lew Grade's office. The conversation most certainly took longer than what he recalled, which was: "Lew," she said, "I'd like to do a series called 'The Adventures of Robin Hood.' I want to do 39 half-hour episodes, and Official Films, an American TV distribution company, are confident they can sell it in America." Grade liked the idea a lot. He asked her what it would cost. She estimated that each episode would cost about £10,000, or $37,900 in American dollars. Not used to having to consult with others, he gave her the go-ahead without consulting other members of his board.[8] After he'd committed the funds, which totaled about £390,000 out of their capital of £500,000, he hastily called for a board meeting and asked forgiveness. The board was appalled; how could he make such a commitment? Commercial television was a brand-new venture—they should at least discuss it. And this deal was with an American, no less—for American viewership!

They were somewhat relieved when Grade revealed that he had only given a verbal commitment and had not actually signed any contract yet. "I liked the idea and honestly believed it could work," Grade recalled telling them. "We're supposed to be a production company," he reminded them. *Robin Hood*, and Hannah's vision of it, would be a great start for their fledgling company. To Grade's relief, the powerful Prince Littler overrode all objections and said, "Gentlemen, if Lew has given his OK, that's as good as a contract and we'll support him." Weinstein had her budget.[9]

Did Grade know that Weinstein intended to use American, blacklisted writers for the scripts? Maybe. Louis Marks, a producer who would become part of Hannah's "inner circle," once reflected that Grade was "almost certainly kept in complete ignorance" of her use of these writers. But this speaks to plausible deniability, not total ignorance. Despite his jovial and rakish exterior, the businessman was punctilious and shrewd. He was never cavalier with money, his or anyone else's. He got Weinstein to vouch for the quality of the scripts, and after all, Grade already liked the quality of *Colonel March of Scotland Yard*. And he knew full well that Hal Hackett, who had closed his side of the deal with Hannah just days before, would never have committed to the series without the guarantee of strong scripts to promise advertisers. "None but a fool makes television films for the British market alone," he said a couple of years later, after *Robin Hood* had been running on UK television. "Without the guarantee of an American outlet he will lose his shirt. How can you get, say, £10,000 from all the contractors, even with repeats?"[10]

The fledgling production company now just needed a physical space on which to produce a series. Southall Studios, where the first few episodes of *Colonel March of Scotland Yard* had been filmed, had been taken over by a British company that filmed commercials for products—a new business emerging within the country's new bigger business of commercial television.[11] The group decided to purchase Nettlefold Studios.

Nettlefold was created by actor, director, and producer Cecil Hepworth in 1899. He grew it to become one of the most prominent suppliers of film in the world. Nonetheless, it took a huge hit during and right after World War I and it had to declare bankruptcy. In 1926, Archibald Nettlefold, a theatrical producer and recreational farmer, purchased the studios. Though it was one of the last studios to convert to sound, it quickly caught up, and in 1932 it was the first studio in Britain with the new "high fidelity" sound system.

Nettlefold acquired more land at the rear of the studios and expanded Hepworth's original site. For the next few years, it concentrated on making "quota quickies." The British government mandated that a certain number of films per year had to be made with a certain number of actors, directors, cameramen, and producers from the Empire. The intentions were good—it was supposed to help an ailing British film industry—but the result was that studios began turning out short, cheap films that only barely met the requirements set for business as usual to carry on, all while they formed closer relationships with Hollywood.

This is exactly what happened with Nettlefold Studios. In November 1954, the Hyams brothers and Lew Grade used their considerable leverage within the British entertainment industry to make an offer to Ernest G. Roy, general manager and owner of the studio since 1947. They wanted to buy the studio in order to make *Robin Hood* and lease out space for other British and American companies that wanted to make television series. It didn't take long for the press to get wind of this offer and, for the most part, react negatively, mostly echoing the sentiments of *Kinematograph Weekly*: "News that the Nettlefold Studios have been bought by commercial television interests added a pre-Christmas gloom to people deeply interested in the future of film production in this country, though I believe no actual contracts have yet been signed."[12]

The contracts were signed in January 1955, and Hannah Weinstein became a director of both Nettlefold Holdings Ltd. and its subsidiary company, Nettlefold Studios Ltd., along with Grade, Official Films, producer Emmet Dalton, and left-wing attorneys Dorothy Rae and Hyman Stone. Stone's then young son, Victor, remembers one of the Hyams brothers slapping his father on the back, and saying, "Mazel tov! You are now a film producer."[13]

The board immediately commenced refurbishment of Nettlefold, spending £20,000 to modernize it and make it luxurious, along the lines of a Hollywood studio. It also changed its name to Walton Studios, a nod to its location in the village of Walton-on-Thames. The group added a new camera department and production offices and several cutting rooms. It equipped these with the latest recording, lighting, and filming equipment. They installed thick, gray carpet in most of the rooms and hallways and used a similar shade for painting the walls, with white for the floorboards, accents, and doors. The massive dressing room was gutted and repainted and carpeted, too, and the consortium added mirrored doors to the built-in wardrobe. Hannah oversaw the installation of wine-colored curtains and furnishings to add to its sleek, modern look, as well as a huge bathroom complete with shower—uncommon in British studios in those days. For the finishing touch, a full cocktail cabinet was built into an alcove beside the wardrobe room.[14]

None of this went unnoticed by J. Edgar Hoover. For Hannah to become a director with this new venture, the group had to get permission from the British Home Office, the ministerial department in charge of immigration, security, and anything related to foreigners working in the country. The office granted permission, and as soon as the Walton incorporation contracts were registered with the appropriate agencies, agent Cimperman was on the case.

***

By the age of forty-two, John Anthony Cimperman had already seen more than many intelligence officers saw in their entire careers. After graduating from law school in 1934, he worked in various FBI field offices all over the United States until late in the decade, when he went to work for the main headquarters in Washington, D.C. Here, among many other cases that required utmost delicacy, he worked on a Lindbergh-kidnapping copycat case that had a much happier ending than the one that inspired it. Soon, the Ohio native became involved with counterespionage, and his good work caught the attention of Hoover, who created a new position for him.

The basis for Cimperman's new job really began in 1940, when the bureau chief was irritated that Winston Churchill was able to install a bureaucrat in an office in Rockefeller Center, ostensibly as a British passports control liaison. This "British liaison's" job was to head up a covert operation to pressure the still-neutral United States to enter the war against Germany. The man's role expanded when the United States did finally enter the war, and soon he was overseeing British efforts to blunt Nazi espionage, sabotage, and propaganda activities from his office in New York.[15]

Hoover realized this organization could be helpful and, simply put, got Churchill to let him do the same in England. Of primary importance to Hoover was to get FBI men into the inner circle at Bletchley Park, the top-secret, Allied code-breaking center in Buckinghamshire. This he did in August 1943, when Cimperman was sent over. Formally, he functioned as the FBI's legal attaché, working out of the US Embassy in London. Informally, he led the bureau's efforts against Nazi Germany and, after the war, against the fascist efforts of Stalin and the Soviet Union's satellite nations.[16] He paid little attention to Weinstein's *Colonel March* efforts in 1953, but when she registered as a director of Nettlefold Holdings in 1954, Cimperman opened a file.

As he did with all American nationals visiting the UK, Cimperman recorded her basic information from the Home Office and her existing CIA file.[17] He put a "stop notice" on her file, which required an agency (such as a police department or immigration service) to alert the FBI if they had contact with her. Weinstein continued to fly back and forth to New York many times, with and without her children. Each time, the FBI and sometimes the CIA reassessed her social contacts and made reports on whether she might be planning something subversive. Like so many other gifted people in her circle of friends, she had left the United States because her political work made her a target of Hoover and HUAC and thus unable to work. Now, intelligence agencies filled pages about her employment and residence overseas, positing that she was working with the international Communist community. In one somewhat humorous if eerie incident in midsummer 1954, she landed in Boston instead of her usual destination of La Guardia. Customs officials hurriedly telephoned the bureau, which scrambled to figure out why she might have landed here. One agent surmised that since her hometown was New York City and the plane was ultimately headed there after this stop, she might have decided to get off to avoid an encounter with customs agents. He also noticed her waving to an "unknown man" at the airport. Agents subsequently discovered that the "unknown man" was Weinstein's father, Israel, and that she was meeting him there to drive to Augusta, Maine, and pick up her children at summer camp.[18]

***

One of Weinstein's first production hires was Peter Proud as art director. Born in Glasgow in 1913, Proud left school at age fifteen and soon found work as an assistant to art directors and set dressers. Within a couple of years, he was working as an assistant art director under Alfred Hitchcock on films such as *Murder!* (1930) and *Rich and Strange* (1932), and then as co–art director for Hitchcock's *The Man Who Knew Too Much* (1934), as well as assisting on many others. After several years at Gaumont-British Picture Corporation, he joined Warner Bros. First International as a full-fledged art director.

What Weinstein did not know—nor did most of the world until the information was declassified decades later—were the details of Proud's work during the recent war. He had joined the army and became second-in-command of camouflage in the Middle East. He is credited with the invention of battle camouflage, a new system of concealed entrenchment. His proudest and most ingenious achievement was to "hide" many ships in harbor at the siege of Tobruk in North Africa. Before the war, he worked on a series of "quota quickies"—short, rushed films financed by the British government to inject vigor into the UK film industry to better compete with the films arriving in droves from

Hollywood. Proud became renowned for his ability to make the sets look like they were designed on lavish production budgets.[19]

In normal filmmaking, studio technicians built huge sets, on which cameras are lined up for each sequence. This would have to change for *Robin Hood*, to meet its budget and need for speed. To cut out this delay and speed up production, art director Proud realized early that it would be most efficient to take the set to the camera instead of taking the camera to the set. Stock items of scenery such as a baronial fireplace, a serf's hut, a staircase and corridor, and entrance halls were built and then mounted on wheels so they could be quickly moved into position. He built house façades, castle corners, archways, and plain interiors and used these pieces over and over again but arranged differently so the viewer got the impression of many different corridors, rooms, and archways. If this ensemble approach could work for the stage, he thought, why couldn't it work for television?[20]

There was another reason for these mobile components. Walton Studios was more than sixty years old, and the *Robin Hood* crew inherited the oldest stage within it. Proud saw that the ceiling and its roof had no strength for hanging things. While thinking about what to do to resolve this setback, he remembered how his master carpenter was so enchanted by the floor, which was tongue-and-groove boarding. Proud realized that the floor would need to be the literal foundation for any set design. Despite the show's tight budget, he commissioned thirty-six mobile units in total, saving a few dollars here and there by sharing wheel sets and other metallic components for them. "It wasn't just a doorway, it might be a buttress that could be a doorway, if you used the other buttress," he later recalled. "So you got a doorway which could be two buttresses and so on."[21] Calling upon the ideas of his mentor, German-born production designer maestro Alfred Junge, Proud made every single piece fit together geometrically in some way, shape, or form.

By not having to build hundreds of sets from scratch, Proud and his team saved tens of thousands of dollars from the overall budget, even though the studio had to pay more stage hands to quickly move everything into place between each take. Standing by with the stage hands were a painter and plasterer, so they could quickly soften the edges of two or more pieces coming together and change colors, if need be. Sherwood Forest could be on stage at noon, and be replaced by a banquet hall by two o'clock in the afternoon.

Proud often used real trees and branches to dress up outdoor scenes and evoke the grandeur of Sherwood. He enlisted local residents to notify him about trees that had fallen on village greens. The production crew would drive over at night and pick them up. Proud reinforced them with tubular scaffolding, adding moss and extra branches if needed, and chicken wire and sod on top. This made a cool, camera-friendly canopy when they were shooting outside. It also made for an easily transported component if filming had to be done inside owing to the terrible weather London experienced that winter of 1955–56, after such a balmy summer.

Weinstein and Cole decided there would be a resident band of leading players, a stock company for supporting parts, and a small number of guest artists in each story. Before considering the rest of the leading players, they needed a Maid Marian for Greene's Robin Hood.

Lovely Bernadette Mary O'Farrell was thirty years old when she got the part of Marian. An exceptional actor in her own right, it did not hurt that she was married to Frank Launder, the prolific British producer who often worked in tandem with the equally prolific Sidney Gilliat. She and Launder met on the set of *Captain Boycott*, a film about the 1880 Irish tenant farmers' revolt—trivia that no doubt endeared both to Weinstein. What certainly sealed the deal was the fact that she was an accomplished equestrienne, and even had her own horse shipped from Ireland to the studio's grounds. "One wastes so much time with horses that are camera-shy," she said. Her horse, Windsor Cottage, had already appeared in a film and she knew he would behave.[22]

Cole decided that each half-hour episode would be planned with one hour of talk among himself, Proud, Weinstein, editor Albert Ruben, Marks, the director for the episode, and anyone else who necessarily had to be involved. Beer and sandwiches were served. Cole would sit in a chair and go around the room, letting everyone offer their input and bring up any problems.

Weinstein, Cole said, was an "exacting, 'hands on' producer." She energetically threw herself into every aspect of production—scripts, casting, design, costume, editing. No script was approved for production without deep discussion and, often, extensive rewriting. "She always challenged decisions," he said, "sometimes provoking heated reactions, but always aimed at making a better show." There were few dull moments when Hannah was around, he recalled. Despite this, there was never any question about the affection and respect the crews felt for her.[23] "I remember being shepherded into her office," then-child actor Helena de Crespo recalled. "I saw this lady with dark hair and dark eyes, dressed very smart. She said very little, but she was obviously 'the power' in the room. I should have been terrified, but I remember that she was very nice."[24]

***

Ralph Smart made a name for himself in 1946 by associate producing a movie called *The Overlanders*, an Australian WWII movie. He went on to become a director, helming a Christmas movie in Australia followed by a comedy in Britain. In 1954, the forty-six-year-old thought television might be a nice change of pace from film. "My main trouble was that a film used to start superbly, but after about thirty minutes it would go flat. I found that I just couldn't sustain the 90-minute film. That's why I turned to television."[25] Weinstein hired him to direct the pilot for *Robin Hood*, and he eventually produced batches of episodes of this program and did the same for *The Buccaneers* and *Adventures of Sir Lancelot*.

One of Weinstein's first directors was the stalwart Arthur Crabtree, who'd directed *Colonel March of Scotland Yard*. A veteran of the Spanish Civil War and World War II, he was keenly aware of the horrors of fascism and would have been very supportive of the content within the scripts coming in from the United States. Unlike much of his British film cohort, Crabtree felt strongly that television was truly the future of filmed entertainment. He was self-taught—in his younger years, he went around to movie theaters and got projectionists to give him worn-out film negatives to cut and paste into a notebook, then wrote detailed notes about that movie's director. He frequently took a pen to scripts, and crossed out and changed dialog and action scenes that could be improved with something he felt worked better. During his time at Sapphire, he frequently came home exhausted, at times in charge of up to about 150 people on the set. Crabtree was known for moving fast—getting scenes with one take—and this was incredibly important for *Robin Hood*, especially when setting an example in these early episodes.[26]

Director Lindsay Anderson, too, was indispensable. He had captured an Academy Award for his short documentary *Thursday's Children* just before starting work on *Robin Hood*. He admitted that he had to set his ego aside when directing the program—or, at least, compartmentalize his feelings. "I will not pretend that this hasn't its comic aspect," he told *Sight and Sound* magazine. "I have even felt a certain guilt to be writing severe strictures on de Sica and Zavattini in the evening, while knowing that next day I shall be struggling with a custard pie (or rather wild strawberry cake) routine between Tom the Miller and one of the Sheriff of Nottingham's men-at-arms." This was, he said, a kind of "schizophrenia" that one learned to live with.[27] He did, however, appreciate the fact that he could take advantage of equipment not available to him in his documentary work, like a dolly. "My only tracking shots had been made from a conveyor-belt, or by [cinematographer] Walter Lassally sitting on a chair, hand-holding the camera, while I pushed."[28]

Economy was everything. Each episode would run for just over twenty-five minutes. Each had to be shot in five days, with the goal of averaging five minutes of film time per day. Every director had to know how to take advantage of Proud's wheeled components. A main unit shot in the studio; a second unit—working mainly with actor doubles—shot exteriors.[29] Anderson recalled that Weinstein told him there was to be no deviation from this schedule, and that any director who did would never be employed again. He responded by singing, "Hardhearted Hannah, the vamp from Savannah." Fortunately, she found it amusing.[30]

While all these physical production plans were hashed out in late 1954, Ring Lardner Jr., Ian McLellan Hunter, and many others waited patiently for instructions, and wondered if they would be able to support their families. Weinstein's relationship with each of them was somewhat unique, owing to their varied shared experiences up until this point and the (mostly) strong personalities of all involved.

Ringgold Wilmer Lardner Jr.—better known as just Ring—was supposedly the first writer Hannah approached about writing for *Robin Hood*. The son of a great writer, too, Ring won an Oscar (along with Michael Kanin) for writing the screenplay for 1942's *Woman of the Year*, a comedy that marked the first teaming of Katharine Hepburn and Spencer Tracy. Like Hannah, he had started as a reporter, writing for the *New York Daily Mirror*.

After dropping out of Princeton his sophomore year, Lardner sailed to Hamburg and then caught a train to the Soviet Union, where he enrolled in the Anglo-American Institute of the University of Moscow, which encouraged young Americans to support the Soviet system. To eighteen-year-old Ring, the experiment in socialism there seemed like the answer to America's Great Depression. "It stuck in stark contrast to what was going on in the United States. People were outside, doing recreation, they were dressed and the streets were clean and everybody was fed, and at that point he felt it was a better way of governing," his son David recalled. "He later in life said that though he didn't regret his involvement, it clearly was not the perfect way of governing people, but he did feel that some form of democratic socialism was a better way."[31]

Upon his return, he went to work for the *Mirror* and then—by way of the father of his old Princeton roommate—got a job working in publicity for David O. Selznick, who was then in the process of starting his own company.[32] Within a year, Lardner started working as a "script doctor" for Selznick, and eventually began writing his own material. In 1937, he joined the Hollywood section of the Communist Party and participated in several political and labor activities. Sadly, the following year, his brother was killed by a sniper during the Spanish Civil War—a conflict he joined after traveling to Spain as a journalist with Ernest Hemingway and others. The war was, in part, an event that spurred Ring's devout left-wing politics and activism—he donated heavily to Republicans loyal to the Popular Front government, which fought against an insurrection by the Nationalists, led by the future dictator General Francisco Franco.

In September of 1947, just after Lardner had signed a contract with 20th Century Fox for $2,000 per week and purchased a new home in Santa Monica, a US marshal came to his door to deliver a subpoena to testify before the House Un-American Committee. Along with seventy-eight others, he was accused of injecting Communist propaganda into his films—though there was no evidence to back this up. During the October 1947 hearing, he was asked by committee chairman J. Parnell Thomas if he was then or had ever been a Communist, to which Lardner famously replied, "I could answer that question the way you want, Mr. Chairman, but if I did I'd hate myself in the morning." Enraged by that response, Thomas ordered Lardner removed from the hearing room, and Fox fired him within days.

In fact, Lardner did belong to the Communist Party at that time but believed that it was no one's business. He tried to list his film credits to the committee, emphasizing his work on anti-Fascist and civil rights–oriented subjects—it refused to let him read it. On November 24, 1947, he and nine others were cited for contempt for failing to cooperate with the committee. They were all convicted in federal court the following year. Though all these men really had little in common except that they worked in Hollywood and held various democratic ideals, they became known collectively as the Hollywood Ten. The others in this group were Herbert Biberman, Adrian Scott, Dalton Trumbo, Lester Cole, Edward Dmytryk, Samuel Ornitz, John Howard Lawson, Waldo Salt, and Alvah Bessie.

After court appeals failed, Lardner served ten months at the Federal Correctional Institution at Danbury, Connecticut, and was fined $1,000. When he got out, he (as with the other nine and many more) found that his prospects for making a living were gone.

Daniel Sandomire was one of a few lawyers and agents who made it possible for Sapphire Films writers to get paid.

Colonel March of Scotland Yard

Harry Alan Towers, Norman Collins, Richard Meyer, Val Parnell, and Lew Grade at first directors meeting for ATV. One of ATV's first commercial programs was *The Adventures of Robin Hood*.
ITV/SHUTTERSTOCK

Companies looked for shows to sponsor that exemplified family programming. *The Adventures of Robin Hood* fit the bill perfectly.
COURTESY JOHNSON & JOHNSON ARCHIVES

More than sixty TV critics were flown to England for a week-long junket for *Robin Hood*.

TV critics hobnob with producers and directors of *Robin Hood*. Writers were conspicuously absent.

A server indulges some press corps at the 1955 *Robin Hood* press junket in England.
COURTESY OF MARGARET STARK, STARK/DOHN FAMILY

Reporters flock to Bernadette O'Farrell, who played Maid Marian for two seasons of *The Adventures of Robin Hood.*
COURTESY OF MARGARET STARK, STARK/DOHN FAMILY

Richard Greene and Patricia Driscoll as Robin Hood and Maid Marian.

Weinstein's mansion at Foxwarren also served as the location for filming exterior shots. This castle was built for *The Adventures of Robin Hood*.

Weinstein's residence at Foxwarren
GEORGE ELAM/ANL/SHUTTERSTOCK

Robert Shaw starred in *The Buccaneers*.
PICTORIAL PRESS, LTD./ALAMY STOCK PHOTO

Weinstein, Richard Greene, Archie Duncan, and Patricia Driscoll celebrate the completion of 143 episodes of *The Adventures of Robin Hood*.
ANL/SHUTTERSTOCK

Louis Hayward and Hannah Weinstein joke around on the set of the pilot for *The Highwayman*.
REACH LICENSING/MIRRORPIX

One reporter dubbed Weinstein, "The Quiet Woman of Television."

After returning to the United States from Europe, Weinstein reinvented herself in the feature film world.

CHAPTER 8

My Friend Fran

THE FIRST SEASON OF *THE ADVENTURES OF ROBIN HOOD* GOT OFF TO A rocky start. Once Sapphire Films came into existence in late 1954 and had secured funding and a studio, Weinstein and Cole had to develop the series characters and long-range story arcs. Naturally, the writers had to do the heavy lifting in this regard.

Lardner was released from prison in April of 1951. Neither he nor eight other members of the Hollywood Ten were able to get any work. The tenth, director Edward Dmytryk, decided to testify to HUAC to rehabilitate his career, damaging several court cases filed by the rest. Other screenwriters, notably Richard Collins, also named Lardner, Lawson, Salt, Gordon Kahn, Lester Cole, Paul Jarrico, and others to try to resurrect their own careers, making it impossible for them to get work writing books or even to meet with non-blacklisted writers to doctor their scripts for cash under the table. Lardner managed to get one last job with his name on it before deciding he'd have to change his working identity. Director Joseph Losey hired him to take over for Hugo Butler as script re-writer for *The Big Night*. Butler had taken his family to Mexico when he heard HUAC was about to subpoena him.[1]

Within a year of his release, Lardner moved his family to Mexico, too, joining Dalton Trumbo, Albert Maltz, Gordon Kahn, Ian McLellan Hunter, and others and their respective families. After six months there, he and his family moved in with his mother in Connecticut. His wife, Frances Chaney, an established radio star and budding film actress, found her own career stifled because of her husband's ordeal and connection with the Communist Party. The pair managed to scrape by, and after living with his mother for two years, found an apartment in New York they could afford. Lardner finished a novel but needed to find work that provided more immediate funds.

Lardner's cousin "Dick" Tobin came to the rescue. He had worked for the *New York Herald Tribune* with Hannah in the early 1930s, and they were neighbors at the Peter Stuyvesant hotel. Rounding out this friendly cohort were Ring's brother John and their mutual friend from the *Tribune*, Tom Sugrue. Tobin and Weinstein were still close, so aside from the victims themselves, Hannah had an even more intimate view of the plight of the Hollywood Ten than most.

Lardner and writer Ian McLellan Hunter had been good friends since meeting in 1935, when they were young reporters on the *New York Daily Mirror*. The son of a British sea captain, Hunter came to the United States with his family as a teenager. He began working at the *Mirror* in 1935, but then left to enter Princeton later that year. Like Lardner, Hunter decided not to continue at the Ivy League school, left after his freshman year, and returned to the *Mirror*. Shortly after Lardner left New York for Hollywood, Hunter followed suit, in no small part because Lardner was earning $40 per week as opposed to the $25 he earned at the *Mirror*—clearly, there was a better living to be made in movies. Through a friend of his sister's, Hunter got work as a junior writer at Metro-Goldwyn-Mayer (MGM), and shortly thereafter, Ring managed to pull him over to Selznick's production home on the R.K.O. pictures lot. The pair worked with director Bernard Vorhaus, writing the Jean Hersholt-headlining *Meet Dr. Christian* and a sequel, *The Courageous Dr. Christian*.

After a short spell at R.K.O., the writers moved on to separate projects, one of which (for Lardner) was the treatment for a movie about a female newspaper columnist, for which Katharine Hepburn would be attached. MGM wound up making the movie based on it, the 1942 blockbuster, *Woman of the Year*, starring Hepburn and Spencer Tracy. Hunter, in the meantime, had gotten a job collaborating with lyricist Johnny Mercer on a film called *Second Chorus*. He also moved in with Ring and his wife. The Lardners introduced Hunter to his future wife,

Alice Goldberg, who was a head reader at Warner Bros. and a good friend. "By introducing Ian to Alice," Ring later recalled, "I not only helped him land a wife but laid the groundwork for his entry into the Communist Party, of which she was already a member." Other friends would gravitate toward this tight-knit core, including writers Trumbo, Butler, Maurice Rapf, and Budd Schulberg.[2] Lardner and Hunter were the closest of friends and writing partners. If Hannah wanted one, she would have to take the other, too—and she did.

Weinstein had to figure out the best way to communicate with and pay her blacklisted writers. She tapped New York attorney Daniel Sandomire. The lawyer was both principled and talented. He graduated summa cum laude from Harvard Law School in 1929 and was awarded the Fay Diploma, which was the highest honor in the law school. During World War II he worked at the Department of Justice as head of the Litvinof unit, which repatriated to the USSR assets deposited in the United States by Russian businesses attempting to avoid their seizure during Soviet nationalization. After leaving the DOJ, he worked mainly in tax and estate law. His wife, Esther Schultz Sandomire, convinced him to take Weinstein's work and that of blacklisted writers in general. During WWII, Esther had worked for the New York offices of the US Army to set up USO shows, during which time she made friends with many of the entertainers and was sympathetic to the plight of those who had been persecuted by McCarthy. The firm, Greenman, Shea, Sandomire, and Zimet, agreed to act as a clearinghouse of sorts for Lardner and Hunter.

While not overtly political, the partners in the firm leaned left and stood firmly on the side of justice. Greenman had written a book about the problems of wiretapping and civil liberties. Zimet sought to get attorney and Hoover-fixer Roy Cohn disbarred, and he and the other partners routinely tackled immigration and First Amendment issues.[3] Sandomire helped Hannah set up a US-based corporation that would hold funds from which payment to the writers could be dispersed. She named it Dilipa Corp., using the first two letters of each of her daughters' names. Weinstein and Sandomire settled on the use of telegrams when she needed to get faster show notes to Lardner and Hunter—but only if it was absolutely necessary, as the cost of cabling often was prohibitively expensive. They agreed that most often, they would write detailed letters.

This arrangement was knotty even without the extra burden of having to keep writer names a secret, and Hunter's and Lardner's stress about it is palpable even in their straightforward description of their plight:

> *There is just one other problem to all this from our point of view and that is money: when we get it and how. We had assumed the fact that you were working through a lawyer's office would make it practical for the loot to be delivered directly to us, or at least to a relative or close friend, and that there would be no particular problem about a formal contract. We have since been informed that we must produce either a writer of established reputation and spotless past or a literary agency through which money can be funneled; also that money will have to await the establishment of a corporate set-up to pay it out; and thirdly that drawing up such a contract presents a problem because it's an unfamiliar field. Now it so happens that we have a well-known Fifth Avenue agency which will serve as the funnel if necessary but it means bringing more people into the know and it has the additional disadvantage of lopping ten percent off our cut.[4]*

Unfortunately for Lardner and Hunter, Hannah confirmed that they would need such an agency. Hunter's friend, Sy Fischer, head of the New York office of Frank Cooper Associates, agreed to be the last stop along the winding route to both payment and updates in the contractual obligations.

The need for secrecy about the writers' names cannot be overstated. If even one blacklisted author was discovered to have penned a script for the show, it would never get picked up for distribution in the United States, and that would destroy Weinstein's funding arrangement and therefore her ability to make the programs. It would almost certainly spur harassment of the writers and their families, and the literary agents involved would not only lose their commissions for these artists but also subject their employers to an embargo of their other clients by Hollywood and New York.

While Weinstein had learned a lot from producing *Colonel March*, she knew she needed help setting up the processes by which *Robin Hood* would function as a mass-produced program, so to speak. The show would need character guides. Hannah had already tapped one black-listed writer who was already in England, Howard Koch, to help her implement a process by which she and Sid Cole could develop Robin Hood with Lardner and Hunter, the duo who would wind up writing the biggest portion of the episodes—some 40 shows out of a total of 143. The Koch family's experience merits some discussion, as it portrays the experience of a few of the blacklisted artists who made their way to Hannah's sphere—those few who were able to hold onto their passports and leave America. Their journey, as explained by Koch, also reflects the burgeoning television scene in England, and its acceptance of American talent woven into its filmed entertainment.

Koch and his wife, Anne, also a writer, were among the first casualties of the HUAC. In the 1930s, the extremely talented, versatile New York native wrote for the stage and radio, earning fame for adapting H. G. Wells's *The War of the Worlds*, which starred Orson Welles and caused widespread panic among its listeners in 1938. Koch was perhaps best known for his writing contributions to *Casablanca*, for which he received an Academy Award in 1944. In 1951 Koch was blacklisted for his work on the movie *Mission to Moscow*. Although the film was made at the request of President Roosevelt, and Jack Warner ordered Koch to write it, the work subsequently became viewed as pro-Communist propaganda. It was released in 1943, years before Budenz and McCarthy and HUAC coalesced for their reign of terror.

At the time, the movie received a great deal of attention, much of it generally favorable. Koch had no ideological agenda in mind when he wrote it. But it became controversial, since it presented many Soviet accomplishments in a positive light, even after the world had witnessed Stalin's purges of the 1930s and watched the horrifying results of the Nazi-Soviet non-aggression pact of 1939. Critics who opposed New Deal policies vigorously attacked it as pro-Communist, while many moderate scholars and anti-Communist liberals felt that the film whitewashed Stalinist policies. Splits within the existing Communist Party in America further complicated the response to the film.[5]

Koch may well have found himself in McCarthy and HUAC's crosshairs anyway, as he had worked closely with Hannah as the West Coast chairman for ICAASP and for PCA, and had worked on Wallace's campaign with her, performing research for his speeches. After brief residences in Rome, Paris, and Gruenwald, Germany, the Kochs (Howard, Anne, and young son Peter) found themselves abandoned by the mysterious businessman who had been paying for them to fly around the continent on behalf of a film company that reneged on a promise to pay Howard to write for them. Thinking it would be better to try their luck in England, the family made its way to London in 1953. Here, they were met by an American couple, Phil and Ginny Brown. Phil had been blacklisted too, after resisting one last effort by fellow actor Ronald Reagan to get him to name names.[6]

The pair had purchased a houseboat on the River Thames and made it a "landing pad" of sorts for exiled Americans until they could rent apartments.[7] The Browns and Weinstein spent a lot of time together, hosting and helping newly arrived exiles. "My mom embarrassed me and my brother by making us make little gifts for Hannah's daughters," the Brown's son Kevin remembered.[8]

The Browns counseled the Kochs on everything from where to rent an apartment and shop to where to look for writing assignments. The first step, Phil Brown advised, was to find a strong agency to represent them. Howard remembered the following exchange with him—one that was surely simplified from memory, but representative of what all the exiled American writers wondered when they decided to leave the States:

> *"But do they want Americans?" I [Koch] recalled asking. "There are good English writers."*
>
> *"In films they prefer Americans. I suppose because Hollywood movies play everywhere and make the most money."*
>
> *"How about the blacklist? Doesn't that make us suspect?"*
>
> *"The English, at least those we've met, despise McCarthyism."*

I thought of our recent experience in Munich. "It's funny—in Germany I wasn't sure who won the war. They seem in better shape than our allies. Now I'm not even certain who won the revolution."

Phil laughed. "Forget politics. Go get a movie job. With your credits, it should be a cinch."[9]

It was not a cinch. The Home Office still called the Kochs in and queried them about his work on *Mission to Moscow*. The British officer demanded they turn in their passports, as requested by the US State Department. The pair managed to guilt the man into letting them go without surrendering their documents, but the incident strengthened their resolve to stay in England and make a living, perhaps permanently. Their young son, Peter, liked their newly rented home, with its large, coal-burning fireplace and the big park nearby, where he lobbed horse chestnuts with other children. Hannah was a big part of their social lives, and a calming presence for the transplanted family. Peter concocted the nickname "Sillydumb" for her, and she gamely let him tease her every time she came over.[10]

Koch signed with a prestigious British agency and quickly got a job writing a screenplay for a major British movie production company, with Elizabeth Taylor attached to star. His rate was much lower than his established ones in the United States, but he was glad to have the work. A month later, though, the production company canceled its contract with Koch. United Artists, which was set to distribute the film in the United States, decided it could not sell it with Howard's name on it. "The blacklist had a long arm," Koch later wrote. He and Anne decided they would have to rechristen themselves with different names. Howard became "Peter Howard," and Anne became "Anne Rodney."[11] And though they were able to write some feature screenplays for independent British producers, money was still tight. And so, they looked for other opportunities.

It was Anne who wound up writing many scripts for *Robin Hood*. In the beginning of the series, though, Howard loaned his services as a development executive and editor, to run interference between Sapphire and Hunter and Lardner back home in the States. Koch knew how to marshal the capabilities of his fellow blacklisted writers, even from across the ocean. In October of 1954, Koch darted back into New York City for just five days to deliver some basic outlines to Lardner and Hunter of how Hannah and Sid envisioned the first few episodes of *Robin Hood*. These first three were crucial, not just because they set the tone and introduced the characters and larger story arcs for the TV series, but because they could be sewn together for a feature shown in the UK, like with *Colonel March*.

On January 26, 1955, Koch wrote Ian and Ring, to explain some of the realities of editing scripts from three thousand miles across the ocean. Poignantly, their names are scribbled out on some of these communications, in case they were intercepted by the wrong person, and replaced with "WS/FT," which stood for Will Scarlet (Hunter) and Friar Tuck (Lardner).[12] Lawyer Sandomire was now just "S."

In any era of television, a typical production schedule requires long days and long nights of reviewing scripts and getting approvals on every little thing, even before the actors read one word and rehearse. It's hard work even with writers and producers and directors in the same room or a phone call away. Looking at the situation through a modern-day lens, when the process includes writers who are some three thousand or six thousand miles away (New York and Los Angeles, respectively), in different time zones, with no fax machines or email, the operation seems impossible.

Accordingly, Koch's letters were apologetic, noting that under normal circumstances, his accomplished friends were perfectly capable of making revisions on their own. But, he said, the distance and Hannah's needs created the need for flexibility, and he would make the smaller changes himself. For example, he and Hannah and Sid had to make some substantial changes to the pilot, "The Coming of Robin Hood," but he again noted their professional standing: "You'll see what we've done to it—and either you'll approve or shout 'Koch is murdering our scripts!' And if you feel values are being lost, by all means shout it right across the Atlantic, because these are your stories and you have every right to protect them from any dilution of their values, both for Hannah's sake as well as your own."[13]

They may have had the right to protect their stories, but Weinstein made it clear throughout all her correspondence that she had the first and last word, and deftly managed expectations on both sides of the Atlantic, occasionally injecting her sense of humor: "You scared the hell out of us with the eye-gouging," she wrote Lardner and Hunter about one of the initial scripts. "This, if you don't mind, we'll moderate."[14] She admonished them to be a little less cerebral. "I think we must as a matter of policy keep the series an adventure series with all the action, sword play, horse play, quarter-staffing etc. and very much within the feeling and mood of the period."[15] Albert Ruben recalled that Weinstein was very secure in what she wanted, infused with confidence after successfully producing *Colonel March*—confident enough to defer to Cole when it came to translating story ideas to the limitations of physical production.[16]

Koch also told the scribes of some practical problems that arose with producing scripts for filmed entertainment from so far away, where the writers could not see the limitations set by the studio and geography and budget. For example, Sapphire had long-term contracts with some of the main characters: Robin (Greene), Little John (Archie Duncan), Friar Tuck (Alexander Gauge), Maid Marian (O'Farrell), and the Sheriff of Nottingham (Alan Wheatley). These actors should be used as much as possible, he wrote, but others should be used sparingly so Sapphire would not feel compelled to add them as contract players. And so, for example, the brother of Will Scarlet had to be dispensed with after his usefulness was over in episode three. "The upshot of it is," Koch explained, "that we killed off poor Scatlock and thus, with one fell stroke, disposed of both him and the actor."[17]

Koch passed along some concerns by Sid Cole, too. Cole and Weinstein felt that some of the scripts were too expansive. For example, six people on screen (meaning, six people on set) was enough to give the impression of a crowd scene, he wrote. Another concern was the English weather, at least for the shooting of the first thirteen episodes in winter and spring. The certainty of plenty of rain and fog, he told Lardner and Hunter, made it necessary for them to be more sparing with outdoor dialog scenes—the ones that remained could be dealt with using stock footage of the outdoors along with Peter Proud's fake boulders and walls inside the studio, using tight shots. Cole also warned the duo of a problem that would remain an ongoing issue with production in all of Sapphire's programs, but particularly with Robin Hood: four-legged animals. "Another point is that horses, let's face it, are a nuisance and a problem unless absolutely essential to the plot."[18] Ruben followed up with a caution about giving wildlife any agency in their scripts, noting that yes, they had access to deer at nearby Richmond Park. "Let me urge you, however, to require nothing more of them than what comes naturally. No deer in bogs or proffering tin cups please."[19]

Lardner's and Hunter's frustration with such cloak-and-dagger communication from so far away is evident in their letters about the first four episodes. In one letter with Hannah, they noted that if just one person in the chain of communication went on vacation, they would be so far behind that they would have to accelerate their tempo far beyond what was reasonable. They pointed out that they were seemingly the last to know that Robin Hood, as opposed to King Arthur, had been decided upon as the show, after they had "steeped themselves in Arthurian legend" and started outlining a series based upon it.

They also complained about the punctilious nature of Weinstein's attorney, Sandomire, who would not hand out any money until "real pressure" was "brought to bear," presumably by their agent, Ingo Preminger. As Lardner and Hunter soon discovered, this chain of communication was composed of many people who necessarily had to weigh in on both the content of the episodes as well as the budget and payments—and keep quiet doing it.

Besides Weinstein, Cole, Koch (later Al Ruben), the writers, the lawyers, and the agents, there was Hal Hackett, whose criticisms included that there were too many scenes that felt familiar. Hackett's input prickled the writers, who were not used to having to mold their work for a financial backer—the feature film world was a lot different than this new era of television. They found his commentary confusing and pushed back: "We simply do not know what times he's talking about," they wrote. "The fight on the bridge between Robin and Little John, for instance, has been used in every version and is a traditional illustration in the books, but is that a reason not to use it in a television series? We think, on the contrary, that people will be looking for familiar incidents they associate with the name."[20] The writers acknowledged that this was all new territory for them, and not the same as feature films, but stood up for themselves. Though they had no personal knowledge of Hackett, they wrote to Hannah, Lardner and Hunter felt quite confident that they were better able to tell what would be effective on film than he was. Still, they understood where their bread was buttered: "We will always try to conform with whatever reasonable demands by such necessary evils as Mr. Hackett, but we hope that you, in return, will assume that we are continuing to exercise the faculties which led you to engage us in the first place."[21]

As for Hackett, he had to be kept completely in the dark about the real identities of the writers. He was a very astute man and a shrewd businessman, and may have had suspicions, but there is no doubt he would have had to pull the plug had he known for sure. He had too much to lose if the advertisers or networks found out about the writers of *Robin Hood*.

After a few months, Ruben took over for Howard Koch, who left to make a movie. Ruben and Weinstein carefully implemented a more formal system by which the writers—a group mostly consisting of just Lardner and Hunter for the first season—could contribute to the show. Lardner's description of his "elaborate precautions" taken during this time was virtually the same for all blacklisted writers who worked for production entities under an assumed name:

> *It would have been preferable to keep on using the same name, so that it would become familiar to potential purchasers of our material. We learned, however, that if a writer appeared to be doing more than a few scripts in the same series, there would be a demand for personal contact with him from investors, sponsor representatives and network executives who wished to communicate their views on how to improve the program.*[22]

There was also the distinct possibility that network or film executives would want to hire the writers for other projects based on how much they liked their *Robin Hood* work. Naturally, this was not an opportunity the writers could pursue. By creating a heavy rotation of names, Sapphire could keep any one writer from attracting too much attention.

Lardner and Hunter were so prolific that they had to be assigned many different names. Over the course of this first season, they would have at least half a dozen, using pseudonyms like "Oliver Skene," "A. D. Hunter," "Lawrence McLellan," and "Eric Heath," to name a few. This kept advertisers and studio heads in the dark, but it added another layer of complications to the men's ability to retrieve payment:

> Cashing a check made out to an imaginary person is not a simple matter when your own name cannot appear as an endorser. You have to open a bank account under your alias, and my recommendation is that you start in the savings department, where no attempt is made to verify your identity. Checking accounts, in New York at least, require credit information, but once your savings account is well established, you can transfer money from it to a new checking account in the same bank without going through the rigmarole.[23]

They also had to pay very close attention when filing their taxes, because it was not possible to go so far as to invent an entirely new human being who paid taxes:

> On your tax return you simply report all income as if it had been paid to you in your own name. You may expect, of course, that at some point the Internal Revenue Service will note that so many thousands of dollars have been paid by a certain corporation to a man who has apparently filed no tax return. They will then trace your bank account through the canceled checks you have deposited and very likely conclude they have a hot lead on a shifty bit of tax evasion. This can result, if you are careful about keeping your records straight, in the rare satisfaction of demonstrating to an eager investigator that no illegality has been committed.[24]

The men used their legitimate social security numbers, but they could assign any number of aliases to them.

There are two distinct arguments about writers' pay on *Robin Hood* and subsequent Sapphire dramas. Some "in the know" thought Weinstein was taking advantage of writers, because they were the best in the business and their blacklist status meant they had to take what they could get. This point was underscored in Michael Eaton's 1989 film *Fellow Traveller*, in which the fictional protagonist Asa Kaufman eked out a living writing for *Robin Hood and His Merrie Men* while living in a "dingy bedsit" in austerity-era London. Eaton acknowledged that, though a work of fiction, *Fellow Traveller* drew loosely upon the experiences of real, living people. Others thought Weinstein was a lifesaver—literally—by providing the means for a scribe to put food on the table for his or her family.

The truth was it was both. No one disputes that the American writers by and large worked for much less than they would have if the Red Scare never existed. The first season of *Robin Hood* was the worst for Lardner and Hunter because they received a per-script fee based solely on Hannah's and probably Cole's evaluation of them, which must have been demeaning even if they were glad to have the work. But everything was relative in this case: The budget for production (and therefore writing) was lower, so it necessitated these lower rates. Also, television in general in those days was still considered "mini-theater," paying lower rates than feature films. Louis Marks later explained it this way:

> *To see Robin Hood, as Eaton does, as the fruit of exploited and underpaid writing talent implies a more damaging charge—that professionals like Sidney Cole and Hannah Weinstein were consciously taking advantage of other people's misfortune in order to defraud them of their proper fees. On the contrary, they were on the side of the victims. Both were staunch supporters of union principles, and the respect and esteem in which writers were held—especially highly talented blacklisted writers who had suffered for the principles—was unquestioned.[25]*

By his own admission, Marks had conflicting memories of this time, noting that when he joined the *Robin Hood* writing team as a young, aspiring British screenwriter, the fees paid to the American writers were three to four times higher than those paid to him and his UK colleagues.[26]

Weinstein's friend, Australian novelist Christina Stead, revealed her darker thoughts on Hannah's employment of the American writers when she used her as a model for one of her stories. Stead, who could generously be labeled as "complicated," pulled no punches. In this passage, "Catchbone" represents an unidentified blacklisted writer who speaks of "Fran," who is based on Weinstein:

> *Because of her past which, because of her connections with the great radicals, people thought of as a radical past and because she was a clever convincing talker, talents like Catchbone and many others, with better names, saw their future and fortune in her. She enjoyed creating her own society, was charming, gave parties and was believed to have helped many people: at least she helped them in little ways, or at least in her company they met "useful" people. The poor, degraded, frightened could for the first few months find a sort of welcome with Fran: at that time she was feeling her way, she had an idea; she would build a new theatre empire out of the free-floating and high-paid talents of the radical world. The persecutors had done her a favour and denied them all employment: they had once worked for fantastically high wages, now they must work for nothing and find doors shut, or must work under assumed names. . . . These highstarred gentry found in her a foster-mother; they were anxious to work for reduced wages.*[27]

Like Marks, Stead had a close view of Weinstein's operations, and perhaps could not help but look at Hannah's growing stable of blacklisted writers as artists who were getting a comeuppance of sorts. After all, Hollywood represented some of the world's most gifted writers, but it also represented real or perceived excess and bloated salaries.

Anne Edwards, who was blacklisted and would also go on to write several episodes for Hannah, fondly remembered Weinstein as a "mother hen" to all her persecuted American writers stuck at home and, eventually, to those who found a way to move to England. As their numbers increased—as McCarthy's targeted campaigns increased—she offered "her home, her counsel, and her heart" to them. "I was fortunate to be one of the American writers who received Hannah Weinstein's aid when I came to England in the turbulent 1950s," she recalled. "She was a savior to many who—in lean times—were hired by her to work on her successful *Robin Hood* TV series that starred actor Richard Green[e]. She was a remarkable woman and a mentor to many."[28]

CHAPTER 9

First Season

WEINSTEIN SET UP OFFICES AND A RESIDENCE AT FASHIONABLE 63 Cadogan Square, a tall redbrick building in the center of London that housed the Colombian Embassy along with several other entities.

By way of single-spaced, typewritten letters sent back and forth across the Atlantic, the writers and producers ironed out most of the problems in story arcs and character do's and don'ts. It wasn't perfect—Lardner and Hunter reminded Hannah that it wasn't fair to keep asking for major revisions after approving the bulk of the script, especially since their rate of pay was already so low and the distance made it hard to keep up with the smaller revisions made by staff in England—revisions that could create continuity problems for later episodes. Also, there was a brief couple of weeks' panic about whether Howard Pyle's book, *The Merry Adventures of Robin Hood*—was in the public domain (it was), as many of the scripts had been built around scenes in that book.

There was also the issue of the writers not being able to meet the actors who gave life to their characters. Lardner and Hunter originally wrote Friar Tuck as a sort of bumbling, oafish figure, more along the lines of how he is represented in Pyle's book. Hannah, though, felt Alexander Gauge was "a first-rate" actor and wished he could be emphasized in future episodes more often, and written as having more agency as a strategic partner to Robin Hood and perhaps more sophisticated.[1] Hannah, and likely Cole, found some of the secondary actors lacking after shooting scenes, but because time and money were so tight, felt it necessary to kill off the character entirely rather than replace the actor.

In addition to Scatlock, Hannah decided to scuttle the actor who played the Count of Severne and thus the character altogether. "As to the Merry Men," Ruben wrote Lardner and Hunter, "their ranks have indeed been decimated by the withering fire from the executive suite." They decided to hold auditions for these roles going forward, as opposed to taking them sight unseen from a repertory company.[2]

***

The main character of Maid Marian was still in flux even as cameras rolled on the first four episodes, with Hannah and Ruben still trying to decide how O'Farrell and Greene might best play off each other. Finally, on February 11, 1955, Weinstein wired her final thoughts on Marian: She would be on similar social standing to Robin; she would not live in the forest; she would use (her) sex and guile in social situations; she would be a good athlete and could be mistaken for a forester at times; and she should look "fine" in tights and a plunging neckline and be "bright and quick." Though Robin and Marian would always have romantic undertones and play between them, Weinstein warned, the writers should avoid all clichés for the time being.[3]

Whatever the writers worked out with Weinstein financially must have been agreeable to both parties. The first day of shooting was February 7, and just a little over a week later Weinstein notified Sandomire that she wanted to hire Lardner and Hunter to write thirteen more episodes in addition to the original six for which they were commissioned. As with most of her communication for the writers going forward, Hannah wrote Sandomire, who passed this perfunctory note on to Sy Fischer at Frank Cooper Associates, who then passed it along to Ingo Preminger, who then notified the writing duo.[4]

Around this time, Howard Koch pleaded with Weinstein to find another story editor. He had gotten Sapphire off to a good start but was overwhelmed and desperate to move on to his movie commitment. He recommended his good friend, screenwriter Ellis St. Joseph, but he was committed to other work. Hannah decided to approach someone who had not worked in filmed entertainment but was an exceptional writer and someone they could trust.

***

At the end of 1954, twenty-nine-year-old Albert Ruben sat at his copy desk at International News Service in London and worried about his job. There were rumors that INS was going to shut down or merge—and in either case, he'd have to find something new or move his family home. Founded by William Randolph Hearst in 1909, INS was always a distant third to bigger rivals Associated Press and United Press, but its fortunes had temporarily lifted with coverage of Queen Elizabeth II's coronation in 1953. In fact, Ruben was hired to cover this, fulfilling his goal of moving back to Europe and seeing more of the region where he'd fought in World War II. The last thing he wanted to do was leave England and take a job at a boring, suburban newspaper in the States.

Ruben's wife, Judy, discussed her husband's troubling job situation with her parents back home in New York. Her father, Dr. Samuel Rosen, was an internationally renowned ear surgeon; just a few years earlier, he had discovered a procedure to restore the hearing of many who relied upon hearing aids. Her mother, Helen, was his surgical assistant. The pair was active in leftist and civil rights causes, and they may have been aware that they were under nominal FBI surveillance for having signed documents supporting freedom of expression by Communist causes—documents signed by hundreds of other doctors, lawyers, and educators. The Rosens suggested to their daughter: Why didn't Ruben reach out to their friend Hannah Weinstein? She was in England, and she was looking for writers for some new television venture she was spearheading.[5]

Ruben had already met Weinstein through mutual friends at a party in London some months earlier. Besides being acquainted with his in-laws, Weinstein knew his stepfather, William Morris Jr., now president of the premier agency founded by his father, who, seven years earlier, had served as vice chairman on the National Council of American-Soviet Friendship, for which Hannah had served as national executive secretary. Soon after they met, she told Ruben she planned to make a television series based on the Robin Hood stories, and did he want to come set up a story department for her? "I remember very clearly saying," said Ruben, 'I haven't the slightest idea what you're talking about. I don't know anything about television movies. I'm quite content doing what I'm doing.'" Ruben later decided to circle back to Weinstein and called her. "Do you remember that conversation we had?" he asked. Sure, she said. "Is it still something that's going to happen?" Yes, she said. In fact, she added, she was in the process of purchasing a motion picture studio outside London to make the series. "If the job offer is still there," Ruben said, "I'm your guy."[6]

Ruben arrived at the Cadogan Square production offices in early March of 1955. Here, he met several core people who would become the creative nucleus of Weinstein's television empire: Sidney Cole, Ralph Smart, and, of course, Hannah. There was also Marie Miles, Hannah's assistant, whom she'd hired while back in the United States in the spring of 1955. Miles was the sister-in-law of composer and lyricist Harold Rome, who had been on the FBI's watch list at least since 1947. He'd served on organizations suspected of being Communist fronts, such as the New York Committee for the Preservation of the First Amendment, along with just about every other luminary in entertainment at the time, including all the writers who would eventually write for Hannah. While Marie was not particularly political, she was intensely supportive of her sister and brother-in-law, and loved to travel. She was uncommonly intelligent and vivacious, and excited about working overseas.[7]

One of the first things Ruben did was to commit to writing regular updates to the writers. Weinstein told him who they were and swore him to strict secrecy. Initially, the writers weren't supposed to know that Ruben knew who they were. This quickly proved unworkable owing to the sheer amount of paperwork involved and Ruben's need to be fast, thorough, and discrete. The way it worked, he later explained, was that he and Hannah and Sid Cole would meet in London when they got an outline from a writer for an episode or few episodes. "My job," he said, "was primarily to take copious notes as Hannah and Sid discussed the problems. It was a regular story conference, except that the writers weren't there. Then, immediately after the conclusion of the meeting, I would go to my office and sit down at my typewriter and write a letter to the writers with all of the material that had come out of the story conference."[8]

Though this young, new-to-script-editing executive knew of the enormous talents he was working with, it did not faze him in the least, and did not detract from the task at hand. He was not afraid to be direct with them. On one episode, for example, he wrote, "This one has, frankly, been tough since the outset. I think the principal difficulty lay in the general tone which was more that of a modern detective yarn. The plot only seemed to relate casually, if at all, to the problems of 12th Century England."[9]

Nervously, Hannah and her crew awaited the rushes—raw footage—for the first days of filming. To their delight, everything looked great, if a little short. They decided they'd have to quickly write a few more scenes to fill out the third episode, "Dead or Alive," in which Robin meets Little John and invites him to join his band of outlaws. Greene, too, decided he wanted to give some input on his role going forward. He was jealous of the role of Friar Tuck, so eloquently delivered by actor Gauge in episode four, and, as Hannah joked, wanted to look less like an "early Christian martyr," disliking all his sermonizing, and wanted to be more "gay, lively, and full of bright remarks," with the ability to flirt with more women than just Maid Marian. He also wanted more physicality, telling Hannah that he wanted to do more jumping on and off horses and more fencing. "I want to see all this for our Richard," she told Lardner and Hunter, "because at the end of a three hour monologue the other night on what he thought his part should be like, he turned to me and said, 'You are the most attractive producer I have ever had.' When I dizzily enquired who his last one was, without blushing he told me Otto Preminger! So let's be nice to him!"[10]

Greene got his wish. It was Greene who got Sapphire to hire the enormously talented, London-born Gabriel Toyne to choreograph all the Sherwood fights, swordplay, and archery that would be required on *Robin Hood*. The actor had met Toyne at a fight studio set up by for him by Douglas Fairbanks Jr. in Chelsea.

Toyne was an accomplished stage actor and producer throughout the late 1920s and 1930s, but his first love was swordsmanship. In 1935, he competed in the British Empire Games for England's team and earned silver in the rapier category. As his fighting and athletic prowess for the stage became better known, he was tapped to choreograph more productions for the West End and for films. In 1935, he befriended Errol Flynn, and in 1939, actor John Gielgud asked Gabriel to mount the fights in his 1939 Lyceum Theatre production of *Hamlet*—considered by many to be the definitive production of the century. Notably, Adolf Hitler (by way of an intermediary) banned Toyne from competing for Great Britain at the 1936 Berlin Olympics—at the time, the authoritarian German chancellor thought left-handed people were inferior and suspicious.

***

On March 20, 1955, TV critic Steven Scheuer got into a chauffeured car waiting for him outside the new Westbury Hotel in London. Jet-lagged but excited, the twenty-nine-year-old craned his neck to look at the sights along the hour's drive to Walton-on-Thames. When he got to the studio, he was greeted by Weinstein, whom he noted as a "bouncy, energetic American in her late 30s."[11] Scheuer was happy to be back in England, having graduated from the London School of Economics just five years earlier. Since then, he'd worked for CBS as an assistant director, working on live cooking and talk shows. He always read critics' reviews of programs after they aired, of course, since there was no pre-recorded television to speak of, and certainly no home recording devices. He later claimed that sometime in the middle of 1952, he woke up in the middle of the night with an epiphany, which was that the whole approach to TV criticism was backward. "It was being covered the same way as books and plays and movies. You were told on Thursday by a newspaper critic that there had been an interesting program on Tuesday. It was live. So you couldn't see it if you missed it."[12] This midnight "ah, ha!" moment gave him a career idea.

At the beginning of 1953, Scheuer quit CBS and started a newspaper column called "TV Keynotes." Using the contacts he'd made at the network, he got himself invited to watch rehearsals of shows, and then wrote reviews that appeared in a syndicated write-up on the day the show was scheduled to run. He made recommendations of what to watch and, sometimes, what to avoid, using diplomatic comments like, "This is a good evening to catch up with a good book or a good movie."[13] Television executives, hungry for advance coverage, not only welcomed him at rehearsals but also gave him scripts. A contact tipped him off about

Official Films' discussions with television station groups and the three networks (CBS, ABC, and NBC). Already obsessed with Britain's foray into commercial television, he got himself an invitation to the *Robin Hood* set at Nettlefold.

Filming had been underway for about a month when Scheuer arrived. There was no need to hide the identities of the writers from the critic, because, in fact, he already knew who they were, or at least who they might have been. Scheuer was intimately involved with the blacklist, having worked with many of the writers on their CBS shows. He was close friends with Sam Wanamaker and knew of Hannah and her endeavors with *Robin Hood*. The young critic typically was not easily impressed, but he was blown away when escorted past Proud's fixed-set pieces, like Nottingham Square, complete with drawbridge and gallows. He was especially interested by some of the new equipment technology, like the special glass the cameramen used to shoot forest scenes, which gave Proud's movable tree pods the impression of having greater depth.[14]

Scheuer waxed about the shrewdness of Sapphire's production schedule, which kept costs down. All the scenes from three episodes involving the sheriff's dining room, for example, were being completed, so the crew could avoid having to prepare the dining room table repeatedly. And Scheuer couldn't help but write a veiled nod to the lunacy of the blacklist: "A lighting man reminded me that twentieth century urban morality can still be applied to twelfth century village life," he said in his column. "At the conclusion of one brief scene he was heard to remark amusedly, 'That's charming. A man is charged with murder and the sheriff says it's up to him to prove he's innocent.'"[15]

Sapphire's executives hoped that Scheuer would tease *Robin Hood* to the American public and help with negotiations with broadcasters and advertisers. In the 1950s, the "alphabet soup" networks sold inflexible advertising. In effect, advertisers bought an entire block of airtime or a series of programs on behalf of one or two corporations. Cigarette companies, personal hygiene manufacturers, and auto manufacturers became associated with a particular program and often controlled content within the program itself.

As soon as shooting on *Robin Hood* began, Official Films began compiling presentations for all the major Madison Avenue advertising firms: Young & Rubicam, Foote, Cone & Belding, Ogilvy, Benson & Mather, Ted Bates & Co, and Batten, Barton, Durstine & Osborn (BBDO), to name just a few. The goal was to make these presentations beginning after Washington's Birthday in February, when corporations would start buying sponsorships of programs that could air the following fall season. Advertisers were tied to specific shows, and in essence owned those programs. It did not hurt when Scheuer praised the stewardship of this pioneering series being shot so far away: "If Robin's marauding band had been as highly organized as the film crew shooting the series, Robin would surely have retired in those pre–income tax days—as one of the richest men not only in the forest but in the entire county as well."[16]

Around this time, too, Weinstein and Ruben realized they'd have to come up with names for Lardner and Hunter for the screen credits and didn't have time to gather input from the writers. Weinstein came up with "Lawrence McClellan"—one name for two people, with a nod to at least the real name of one of them—but had Ruben ask the pair for their preference going forward. He got a quick response: "On the subject of the billing," Lardner and Hunter chastised, "we feel that there is no positive value in using names that combine portions of ours. There might be a negative value, if some oaf started muttering about us, since the composite name would serve to confirm the rumor." They suggested using the bland "Eric Heath" for the next few.[17]

While the scripts were coming in cleaner, owing to Lardner's and Hunter's fast learning curve and Ruben's narrative acumen, Weinstein stressed over payments to her friends. "I must tell you I am in a constant bind with the accountants," she wrote. "They have the greatest reluctance to pay money out which does not belong to them." She complained that the procedures and forms needed seemed to change with each episode. Still, she took full responsibility for getting them paid as quickly as possible. And, in an indirect way, she apologized for Greene's continued input into the creative aspects of the show, which often required Lardner and Hunter to indulge the whims of its star, who had no idea about the identities of the famous scribes providing his material, at least in the early days. In one instance, Ruben passed along a note about Greene's screening of a movie called *Vera Cruz*, with Gary Cooper and Burt Lancaster. After seeing a similar motif in the movie, the actor harangued Weinstein and Ruben to provide a script in which someone makes a friendly but serious challenge to Robin's leadership.[18] Ruben thought this was a good idea to consider, as it would provide fodder for future episodes, too.

The writers were not as intrigued. They had already outlined an episode called "The Highlander," in which a strange Scotsman arrives in Sherwood with an as-yet-unknown agenda. More importantly, though, they did not wish to be hamstrung by the creative input of an actor, however integral to the production he might be. "We are pleased that 'The Highlander' solves the crisis brought on by Mr. Greene seeing 'Vera Cruz,'" they wrote. "On the whole, however, it might be just as well if you could keep him away from the movies."[19] To this, Hannah pushed back:

> *Flattery is from where you get it. Most of the script points Greene made which we passed on we did so because we felt they were valid. You must understand about him—he has a feeling—not unfounded—that in a sense this is his last chance to grab an audience. He works very hard, and on the whole has been sincere enough to get into an ice-cold river last week in his scene with Little John. He keeps constantly going around saying 'Why can't we get those writers who wrote The Knight Who Came to Dinner and The Archery Test over here.' So who's being flattered now?*

Going forward, all writers incorporated Greene's notes as they were passed along by Ruben, if the latter approved of them.

Animals—specifically horses—were still a problem. One director always desperately hoped he could get the next shot before lunchtime, praying that the horse would not shift moodily just as Maid Marian was delivering her line. Horses were "the devil in the studio," but if actors always dismounted in the second-unit exterior and walked into the studio shot, the production would seem very bland.[20] On April 20, 1955, spectators—mostly children—arrived at Walton to watch the location filming of the episode "Checkmate," in which Robin hears of a plan by an evil count to conscript three thousand men to terrorize Sherwood. Actor Archie Duncan, playing Little John, was leading a horse and cart piled high with spears and suits of armor on the back lot. The rattling of the props frightened the animal, causing it to bolt. The horse headed straight for the crowd watching the scene. Duncan threw himself on the horse's neck, pulling on the bridle hard enough to eventually stop the horse from plowing into people. Unfortunately for Duncan, the cart collapsed on his knee, injuring him badly and sending an errant wheel into the baby carriage of a watcher.

The baby was fine, but Duncan required several days in the hospital, and actor Rufus Cruikschank had to play Little John until he healed.[21] Dogs didn't act much better, especially in a rejected episode titled "The Miracle." In his tongue-in-cheek way, Ruben explained that their canine actor simply refused to stand in a fine bog they had built for him and pretend that he was struggling for his life. A suggestion to tie him to a stake in the bog, he added, was met with a frown by the Society for the Prevention of Cruelty to Animals.[22]

Hal Hackett made a trip to Walton in April and was very pleased with the footage he saw of the first four episodes—so much so that he tried to hammer out a deal for another series with Hannah right away.[23] Once back in New York, he started trying to sell the show to both advertisers and a network. It was a laborious process. He pulled his salesmen together in a smoky conference room to show them the footage. The company made one or two duplicates of the 16mm films—an expense the company was used to absorbing—and then its sales team, led by vice president Herman Rush, brought them to all the Madison Avenue giants.[24]

Ultimately, two advertisers picked up sponsorship of *Robin Hood*. Agency Young & Rubicam made a winning bid to support its client Johnson & Johnson, for its line of baby products and surgical dressings. J & J, however, wanted to mitigate its risk and only support half a season of *Robin Hood*. This left the problem of who would pay to air the other half.

CBS Television president Jack Van Volkenburg was on the prowl for a program that could dampen ABC's foray into family programming at the 7:30 p.m. timeslot. In 1954, the alphabet network had contracted with Walt Disney to produce a new series called *Disneyland*. As part of the deal, the network provided funding toward the construction of Walt's amusement park of the same name, which opened in July 1955. The series was an instant hit and marked the beginning of the networks allowing Hollywood programs into their schedules. Other CBS executives previewed *Robin Hood* and thought it had the potential to resonate with everyone in a typical American household.

Once it received notice that J & J had signed on the dotted line, CBS decided to purchase the remaining half directly and sell it to another advertiser. In early May, it sold its half a sponsorship to Wildroot Cream Oil, by way of the latter's ad agency BBDO. And so, every other week, *Robin Hood* would shill Wildroot's line of hair products for men, alternating weeks of support with J & J.[25]

This was the best possible news to Weinstein and everyone else at Sapphire, because it solidified the program's financial viability. In these early days of television, a full "season" of a series meant that thirty-nine episodes would have to be produced to show a new episode every week of the year minus the summer months, when networks and syndicators showed reruns.

But this celebratory news added new layers of stress. Weinstein quickly realized that certain creative themes in the episodes had to be carefully constructed and monitored, so as not to risk criticism from educators and religious groups in the United States who might pressure the networks to disavow the series. Her letter to Lardner and Hunter about school groups is lost, but the writers responded with suggestions for making the episodes more historically accurate and thematic so educators would promote the series. If they could make the series even more historically accurate, the writers noted to Hannah, perhaps this would ward off any efforts to criticize Robin as "egalitarian"—in other words, Communist. Weinstein and Ruben, however, cautioned the writers to revise two episodes and be wary of future portrayals of the church. Hannah wrote them that the sponsors lectured her at length about "crackpot organisations" and how they never really influenced the viewership of the program, but they could influence the sponsors, and Sapphire could not risk the attention.[26]

From this time forward, they could expect the ad agencies and their corporate clients and the network to examine their books and production schedules at will. And they could, of course, expect more people to examine each script, and to wish to know more about the writers—whose ranks were increasing. Howard and Anne (Green) Koch wrote at least a couple of episodes, to help keep pace and earn some extra income. James Aldridge, the credited name on "The Sheriff's Boots," may have been the leftist novelist of Australian birth who lived in Britain and knew the episode's credited co-author Ralph Smart quite well. Austro-British writer Peter Lambda undertook one episode. And Waldo Salt, using "Arthur Behr" and other pseudonyms, wrote several episodes of this first season.

Salt became an integral part of the undercover Sapphire team. In 1951, decades before winning Academy Awards for penning *Coming Home* and *Midnight Cowboy*, Salt was, in fact, a long-standing member of the American Communist Party, though, like all the other victims of HUAC and McCarthy's persecution, never remotely thought about overthrowing the government of the United States. In 1947, during the "first wave" of HUAC-compelled testimonies, Salt claimed his First Amendment rights and declined to discuss his political beliefs. He, along with eight others, managed to avoid being charged with and jailed for contempt. But in the second, more vicious round of HUAC hearings less than four years later, the thirty-seven-year-old married father of two was once again targeted. Several witnesses turned "friendly" and gave up names of their colleagues. Salt refused.

With the circle of people "in the know" and quantity of scripts growing larger, Sapphire partners on both sides of the ocean grew more uneasy about the writers' identities being discovered. In mid-April of the first season, for example, one of Ruben's detailed letters got lost somewhere along the sequence of delivery stops. At this early point, Ruben may have been more worried by the two-week delay in delivery of three scripts that this caused, but his alarm is evident even when cloaked in his dry humor: "Your failure to receive this letter is cause for concern. In fact, I could conceivably lose sleep over it if I weren't such a sound sleeper." And he was placed in the uncomfortable position of having to ask their allies—the offices of Sandomire and Frank Cooper Associates—how their instructions might have disappeared. Lardner and Hunter answered Ruben with an equally dry summation, after describing their discreet investigation:

> *We can offer our theory, noting that the letter began "Dear Eric Heath," that a secretary opening mail, in one or the other offices, figured that the letter was addressed to the wrong party and threw it away, which would have been an anti-social act, it is true, but this hypothetical secretary might have had a hangover or some thing. In any event, we were able to raise this possibility to the Cooper office, and the girls there say it would have been impossible.*

The pair decided not to press too hard on the Sandomire office, they wrote, "because it is a law firm and we do not want to be sued for insolence."[27] As if Ruben thought about the anxiety this would cause, and the need to keep the artists on track, he tempered his concern in a subsequent letter, suggesting that perhaps the lost missives were simply because of the vagaries of the mail. He suggested a post office box, but this idea proved to be untenable with the lawyers.[28]

The details of what transpired in the first week of May are not clear, but Ruben grew more alarmed about discovery of the scribes' identities and chastised Hunter: "We received a letter this morning from your agent. It was disturbing for the manner in which it jeopardized all our past attempts at discretion. He seems unaware of the nature of your silent partnership. Suggest he be briefed on the facts of life."[29]

Weinstein fired off a letter to Sy Fischer, and while that letter is lost to history, its effects are not. She was not pleased, and after Hunter and Lardner read her letter and conferred with Fischer, they wrote her immediately to explain and apologize. They had, they reminded her, picked an agency that could fulfill the role of an additional relay station along with the various law offices involved, but was small enough that they could minimize the risk of too many people becoming familiar with their affairs. However, they said, publicity about Weinstein's plans for Sapphire had been in some of the trade magazines, and one of the associates naturally wondered: Shouldn't Frank Cooper Associates take advantage of its connection with her? This associate, the writers explained, had been kept somewhat in the dark about Weinstein's relationship with the office, and went ahead and recommended another client to her, using their names as a greeting and point of entry. The agent, they explained further, was contrite and deeply apologetic about his thoughtless actions, and assured her that there was no deviousness or concealed purpose in his mind. "Since then," the writers wrote, "such fear has been instilled into that office on security matters that they don't dare speak to each other."[30]

They also asked Weinstein if it wasn't too soon to be optimistic about the blacklist, that perhaps an agent's forgetfulness of identity measures just six months into this venture was a good sign:

> *If it is not too early to be objective about such an annoying incident, it does have the added significance that it is a symptom of a slow change for the better here. A man like that can forget a security precaution for the reason that he is much less aware of an evil atmosphere than he was six months or a year ago. The warm are cooling off and even the hot are only warm.*[31]

This sentiment, of course, was wrong. Sandomire warned Weinstein that the film studios and government alike were ever on the prowl for subversive writers and producers, and that security measures must be tightened, if anything. Weinstein's assistant, Marie Miles, was shifted to a production assistant role and replaced with thirty-three-year-old Sonia Marks, who became the gatekeeper to Hannah's office. Marks's husband Louis recalled, "Her first instruction on arriving at the Cadogan Square offices was not to accept any registered letter lest it be the dreaded subpoena to appear before the HUAC."[32]

As if to underscore this fear of discovery, two senior advertising executives from Johnson & Johnson and Wildroot notified the production office that they intended to come visit the set, which they did in late June. Thankfully, at this early stage, these men had to justify their trips' expense by visiting other overseas clients, so they were only in England for a few days. In the mid-1950s, Weinstein was not the only American shooting TV outside the United States. Douglas Fairbanks Jr. and

Don Thorpe were producing *Douglas Fairbanks Presents* in England, and American directors and producers were involved with *Captain Gallant* in North Africa, which had its first airing on NBC, and in England for *Errol Flynn Theater*. There was Sheldon Reynolds's *Sherlock Holmes* in Paris, and America-based Guild Films was shooting *Brother Mark* in Germany. Besides Reynolds, Hannah was the only one using American writers—blacklisted ones, at that. But it was easy enough to keep the ad men distracted by the stars, Greene and O'Farrell. This time.

Meanwhile, even with the Kochs and Salt helping, Lardner and Hunter needed to crank out scripts even faster, and the flurry of notes and rewrites increased over the spring weeks to make sure there were enough scripts to keep pace with filming. Daniel Birt, a respected director who had already done one of the episodes, died suddenly in May, leaving Weinstein to scramble for some of the upcoming, un-filmed half-hours. However, she already had Bernard Knowles and Ralph Smart, two highly respected movie directors who would take turns commanding the bulk of these first episodes, until their ranks could be joined by Terence Fisher, Lindsay Anderson, Arthur Crabtree, and Leslie Arliss.

That these acclaimed directors helped create *The Adventures of Robin Hood* is significant, and a feather in Weinstein's cap. All of them took a certain amount of criticism for switching to television instead of features, owing to the infancy of commercial television and a certain amount of snobbery that accompanied that transition. The men themselves, at times, had to put their egos in check. Anderson thought *Robin Hood* deserved some thoughtful critique. He could not pretend to be objective about the program, given his time and effort. "But I would say without hesitation," he elaborated, "that here is at least one series which entertains in a *good* way; which does not take itself too seriously to be humorous; yet is serious enough to insist on a decent moral, to forbid violence and human falsity." The "cheapjack policy" of so many producers, Anderson said, was shortsighted. "It's only TV" was often said as a justification for shoddy workmanship, poor scripting, and cramped schedules that left no room for anything but getting clichés onto celluloid. "*Robin Hood* is made for TV," he said, "but it is made as *cinema*. Its success proves that quality can pay." And pay it did.[33]

CHAPTER 10

Who's Davy Crockett?

JACK ANDERSON, ENTERTAINMENT COLUMNIST FOR THE *MIAMI HERALD*, posed for a picture with one of the blonde models at the steps to the airplane. The young women were dressed in fishnet stockings and a green, velvet "Robin Hood" dress, which stopped short at their upper thighs. After the obligatory shot with the young woman, Anderson was ushered along so Wendel John of the *Seattle Post–Intelligencer* could have his turn, then Herb Rau from the *Miami Daily News*, and then the rest.

In all, sixty-seven reporters and a few advertising executives gathered to board a Pan Am flight at Idlewild field in New York, an airport that would later be renamed after President John F. Kennedy. The manifest read like a "Who's Who" of entertainment writers. It included representatives from all the major metropolitan papers, and even one from the women's magazine *Redbook*. Cocktails, flashbulbs, and representatives from CBS and the advertisers surrounded the lucky passengers invited onto the "Robin Hood Charter Flight" bound for London on August 30, 1955.[1]

Many of them were incredibly hungover. Since the writers came from all over the country, the advertisers had put them all up at a midtown hotel the night before to make sure everyone got on the charter at Idlewild. They also sponsored a cocktail party. Columnist Rau joked that many members of the group had already been "flying around" the New Weston Hotel Bar, drinking giant martinis all night and demolishing several cases of scotch and bourbon, too. "I hope we get there before they start the commercials," one television editor joked, "because I've dreamed about commercial-less television for years." A young agency executive defended his job. "But if it weren't for commercials, you wouldn't be making this trip." The editor admitted the truth to this, as they both gulped another drink.[2]

This junket was the source of incredible stress for Weinstein. She wrote to Lardner and Hunter that at this time, Sapphire and the advertisers were "on the same team," but make no mistake—the sponsors had to be kept happy in order to keep the money flowing and attention drawn away from the writing team. She told them about the critics set to arrive on September 1. "This from where I sit is not a happy prospect, obviously. I am hoping [attorney] Dan [Sandomire] will get here within the next week so I can tell him in detail how we will handle this."[3]

Johnson & Johnson and Wildroot Cream Oil paid about $75,000 for this junket—about $1.2 million in modern money. It was, without a doubt, one of the biggest and most elaborate press tours of the era. During the thirteen-hour flight, with stops in Canada, Iceland, Finland, and Sweden, passengers smoked, drank, ate, slept, played poker, and pored over the thick binders of press materials they were given before boarding the flight.

The messages in these materials were clear: *Robin Hood* was to be the first British-filmed TV series that would appear on an American network, and the first that would appear simultaneously in three countries: the United States, Canada, and England. The time of their visit would coincide with the inauguration of commercial television in the British Isles. And if toy and clothing executives were to be believed, Robin Hood merchandise would be the hot ticket at Christmas. A Robin Hood juggernaut would replace the Davy Crockett craze, and bow and arrow sets would supplant the toy rifles and coonskin caps.

In London, newsreel cameramen and photographers and official representatives of the press and the BBC greeted the contingent. After they were interviewed and treated to drinks at a seventeenth-century pub, a coach service took the exhausted writers to the Westbury Hotel, which would be their lodging for the week. Each night, after a day's worth of activities and cocktail hours, the bunch was expected to (literally) write home to their papers about their experiences, which they did. Shortly after their arrival, they might have learned that actor Philip Loeb, Hannah's friend and a *Red Channels* victim, had taken his own life that day, owing to his loss of ability to make a living.

The main event was the screening of episodes of the TV show. Weinstein took questions about production costs; why they picked Richard Greene and the other actors for their roles; and . . . why Robin Hood? No one was better with press than Hannah, and she gave an answer easily digestible and printable. Naturally, she made no mention of her personal convictions or anything messy like politics or being terrified of financial failure as a single mother. When she arrived in Europe in 1950, Weinstein said, she became convinced of her theory that Americans were developing a vital new interest in the "Old World." The reason for this, she thought, was that European films were becoming very popular in America, and also, travel to Europe was soaring. Why not capitalize on this postwar interest and film European tales against locales in the same?[4]

Before and after this Q and A with Sapphire, the press corps was treated to several choreographed outings. They were shepherded to a show at the London Palladium, featuring the popular Hungarian dance team of Nicholas and Julia Darvas. They enjoyed a formal lunch at the Mitre Hotel, built by King Charles II in 1665 to house some of the king's courtiers who could not find accommodation in the palace. There was another luncheon, buffet-style, at the American Embassy on Grosvenor Square. Guides took them to some usual tourist haunts, like the changing of the guard in front of Buckingham Palace, the Tower of London, and Hampton Court Gardens.

Naturally, the advertisers planned a trip to Nottingham and the actual Sherwood Forest, a 120-mile train ride north of London, about a three hours' journey. The *San Francisco Examiner*'s Dwight Newton found it a charming way to spend the day, comparing California's drought-burned hillsides to the English countryside, which he glibly noted consisted of "green pastures, green meadows, green hedges lining every fence, green trees." He was also charmed by the graciousness of Nottingham's modern-day sheriff and mayor, who hosted a luncheon for the writers.[5]

There were some uncomfortable moments for both Brits and Americans. After a long cocktail hour, the Americans—for the most part—reached for their cigarettes. The first one to fire up was Mary Wood, TV critic for the *Cincinnati Post*. When the first spirals of smoke hit the air, a uniformed steward pounded his gavel, scaring the daylights out of her and the rest of the press corps. "M'lord Mayor and Lady Mayoress, Sheriff and Sheriff's Lady, and ladies and gentlemen!" he shouted. They all jumped to their feet, confused as to what was happening. The steward announced that the mayor would offer a toast to the Queen, and then the president of the United States. After these toasts, the steward announced that the room now had permission to smoke. "You can mention my name to the Lord Mayor of Nottingham, friends," Wood later quipped to her readers, "but please don't tell him where I am. He's trying to forget and so am I."[6]

The mayor and sheriff and their contingent and staff were equally jarred by an unscheduled announcement by the journalists for the *Houston Chronicle*, the *Fort Worth Star-Telegram*, and the *Dallas Morning News*, who decided to make the High Sheriff of Nottingham an honorary deputy sheriff of Texas. Ira Cain, of the *Star-Telegram*, had been wearing a ten-gallon hat the entire trip and took the honor of giving the sheriff his new badge.[7]

The acerbic Will Jones of the *Minneapolis Tribune* was less charmed by these lessons of British etiquette than most of his fellow journalists. No one told them that dress should be casual instead of fine Sunday attire, and because the lunch and toasting took so long, there wasn't much time left to see the forest itself. And it wasn't much of a forest at all, he complained—more like a park, complete with some random, old, gnarled trees and picknickers. Robin Hood's oak, he wrote, was held together with a network of steel braces and cables and had to share space with an ice cream vendor's truck. "If the sheriff couldn't catch Robin Hood in here," one of the other writers said, "he goofed." For his part, the warden of Sherwood wasn't happy about the American tourists, and came out shaking his cane at them and their director. Many of the critics were smoking on the grounds, which was verboten, and the buses were apparently supposed to park some distance away, not drive right up to the ancient tree.

All in all, they spent a mere fifteen minutes looking at the greenery. But the worst offense, Jones griped, was that the American advertising men forgot to tell the mayor and sheriff why all these columnists had descended upon their town in the first place. The lord mayor turned to him at one point and quietly asked, "Why are you here?" Jones quickly filled him in.[8]

The "TV writers' safari," as one reporter called it, continued with few breaks over the week. In accordance with the "rules" of the trip, the group progressed through a light fog of publicity, carrying bundles of releases that they sometimes tossed in a trash bin, but only when out of sight of their chaperones. The group stayed together, except for Fairfax Nisbet of the *Dallas Morning News*, who insisted she had to diverge to get exclusive stories. This was silly, quipped one New England writer, because every experienced junket-traveler knew it was more fun to make the rounds together and simply make up exclusive pieces.[9]

The crew was taken to Earls Court just outside London, where a huge radio and television trade show was being held. Not unlike today's media confabs, TV writers and broadcasting executives hurriedly ducked in and out of temporary meeting rooms built in an expansive conference hall. People could watch snippets of British television shows that the BBC planned to air over the coming year. They could also see previews of American programs slated to air in Britain, thanks to the easing of restrictions and the ability to offer more fare. Ernie Hill of the *Oakland Tribune* joked that viewers in the United Kingdom were in for a "rude shock" when they saw what they were getting: *Roy Rogers, Hopalong Cassidy, I Love Lucy, Lassie*, and "other programs with little or no cultural message." Hill acknowledged that this could be a nice change from only having dry fare like museum documentaries. "Wait until the dear old ladies of Cheltenham and Kensington see Liberace," he overheard another American say.[10]

There was also new technology. The BBC offered a new test pattern, which was similar to the geometric designs seen on American sets before and after shows and throughout the night when broadcasting ceased until the next morning. The sets already in the homes of British viewers weren't numbered yet—there was simply a dial marked "BBC," and possibly "Commercial Band" if they were only a year or two old. People would have to buy converters and adapters of various sorts to make their sets able to receive multiple channels of programming. In addition to the show at Earls Court, the corps toured the thirteen-acre White City media district and Lime Grove studio—a complex built for the British film industry in 1915.

The most important events, though, were the screening of two completed half-hour episodes of *The Adventures of Robin Hood* and a visit to the set afterward. Someone forgot to have the hotel place a wake-up call, so the cadre of reporters was hurriedly roused and then rushed by bus to Walton-on-Thames, about twenty minutes from London. Here, they were ushered onto the grounds of Nettlefold and seated inside a theater for a sneak peek at the program that would debut in America in just a few weeks.

First, though, Sapphire and advertising executives from both countries wanted to see what media critics and officials from both sides of the Atlantic thought of the commercials that would be shown within the program. This was a big deal, particularly for the Britishers, because viewers in the UK had never had commercials with their programming before. Now, there would be commercials, but the Independent Television Authority (ITA) had very strict rules for their purchase and placement. Advertisers were not allowed to sponsor programs in the direct sense; they would purchase spots and ITV would decide when and where they would air, within or between any shows it chose. Also, the ITA would allow up to six minutes of commercial time per hour of television, but it insisted they be placed within natural breaks of programming—not after cliffhangers, a device that American television typically used to keep viewers tuned in.

Some Walton-on-Thames residents wandered into the theater to watch. Well-mannered, but unused to sales pitches or commercials, they scoffed and whispered about the glossy advertisements. They also snickered that it was ironic that a hair pomade company sponsored the show because Richard Greene's hair was a rumpled mess in the program. One man was overheard saying he would never get used to the idea of this slick television programming interspersed with all those commercials.[11]

For their part, the Americans didn't even flinch when the opening of the first episode showed Robin Hood's arrow flying through the air and landing in a tree with an image of a box of Band-Aids superimposed over it—but the Brits giggled nervously. Blatant commercialism—so intertwined with the content itself—wasn't something they were used to seeing. Everyone in the theater laughed at the clever Band-Aid commercial that showed one of the plastic strips holding an egg, even in boiling water. But the entire presentation had to stop for a few minutes when a commercial for Wildroot hair tonic appeared and made the British media executives explode with laughter. The ad advised everyone to use the product and make a good impression, "socially and on the job." The idiom "on the job" meant having sex or, sometimes, that one was on the toilet.[12]

From Nettlefold, the group was taken to lunch nearby, and Richard Greene stopped in for some informal mingling with the writers. There was some gentle sparring between British and American executives. One gentleman, who was investing in a competing show, badgered his colleague who was investing in the Sapphire production: "For years in this country we've been trying to forget Robin Hood!" After this, they were whisked off to the main part of the studios, where scenes from *Robin Hood* were being filmed. "The average Hollywood producer would think he had been banished to Siberia, were he to see this old and sparingly equipped studio," Hal Humphrey quipped. "Nonetheless, the British crew brings a smoothly produced show from such relatively crude surroundings."[13]

Humphrey was perhaps jaded, coming from Los Angeles, but in fact, Sapphire pulled all the stops and it showed. They were led around, in part by Greene, and also got to spend time with the gracious Bernadette O'Farrell, who let them ask endless questions about playing Maid Marian. There was some unanticipated drama when Alan Wheatley as the Sheriff of Nottingham and Rufus Cruikshank as the (replacement) Little John filmed a sword fight. As the critics watched them clash their weaponry, Wheatley suddenly dropped his sword and grabbed his chin. Blood began to pour over his fake beard. The crowd broke production protocol and started to murmur and move closer as it realized this was not in the script. Wheatley fainted and was taken to a hospital where he got five stitches in his chin.

The most surprising and elaborate part of this day was at night, when they were served a "medieval feast." The production company struck a huge, green-and-white-striped banquet-hall tent and plastered signs that said "To the Wenches" all over the grounds. At the entrance to the tent, the TV writers were given a quill pen and asked to sign a guest book. Once inside, they stepped on a floor that was a thick layer of straw, just like the kind used in medieval castles. At one end of the long tent, there was a minstrel's gallery where musicians plucked bowed instruments from undefined periods of time during the Middle Ages, and a strolling one with an ancient guitar sang among the guests. A brightly clothed jester pranced around and danced.

Young women dressed as the indicated "wenches" seated them along long, wooden tables. They filled the writers' large, wooden plates with food from side tables, which had delicacies that reflected no small amount of planning, expense, and research into royal menus of the twelfth century: baked peacock (complete with its colorful tail repositioned on it), swan, boar's head, sturgeon, a "royal salad" (cabbage, horseradish, apple, and cinnamon), a chopped fruit-and-vegetable "salmagundy salad," and both castrated and non-castrated baked roosters. The *Providence Journal*'s William Keough thought the dinner resembled a taxidermist's shop but had to admit that the entirety of the setting was really wonderful.[14]

To wash this all down, Sapphire had its maidens serve "mead," an ancient drink made from distilled honey and apple juice. "It's real potent stuff," Greene warned the writers, "so be careful." Some were, but most weren't. "Shoot the honey to me, honey!" one New York editor shouted as one of the servers tapped a fresh keg of it. Greene also explained to the guests that if this had really been hundreds of years earlier, dozens of long-haired dogs would be running around so diners could wipe their greasy hands on them—napkins were a more recent invention. There were no dogs here, but some of the writers did get into the spirit, especially after the mead had been flowing for a while. They dug their fingers into their portions of cooked animals and flung the eaten or uneaten bones behind them into the straw.[15] At some point in the evening, someone explained that centuries prior, it was customary for men to pinch the rear of a "serving wench" after she delivered a tankard of ale. A couple of the Americans tried this and were verbally and soundly rebuffed.

For his part, Richard Greene went above and beyond to make the TV critics feel like they were part of something special. He drove to the various events in his green Jaguar and gamely took photos with the writers to show their families back home. When asked how he liked doing television as opposed to feature films, he glibly assured reporters that this first season of *Robin Hood* would be like doing thirty-nine films—so he did not miss it at all. But he did miss California—he was fond of saying that his house was in London, but his home was in Hollywood.

Greene's effusive behavior was somewhat self-serving in the sense that the actor had everything to gain from making sure the program was a huge success. But he also provided a huge service to Weinstein in helping distract the critics with his celebrity, and by showing them the technological achievements of the filmmaking process itself. Some of the journalists asked about the writers of the show, and they must have wondered why none were available to meet with them. Albert Ruben cut his distractive teeth on this visit, coming up with ways to tell them, "look over here," literally and figuratively, to help keep the topic from becoming the subject of investigation by any more-curious scribes.

***

Two days before the end of the press tour, the Independent Television Authority (ITA) hosted the American critics and British writers for lunch at Claridge's Hotel. According to observers in both the British and American press, it got very heated. The chairman and director-general of ITA presented statements about the future of British commercial broadcasting, in which they stated that advertisers were never going to run UK television "any more than an American publisher would let them dictate their editorial policy," for example. This led to loud grumbling by the Americans—perhaps more because of the slight insult than the idea. Soon after, American and UK writers and executives began shouting at each other about the pros and cons of sponsored programming, and commercials and show content in general. At some point, the British contingent turned its wrath onto the ITV executives, demanding to know why Americans had hundreds of stations while the UK only had two. Furthermore, some US cities had as many as seven stations, with color, no less. Harry Rauch, head of Young & Rubicam, yelled, "Let's call it a draw." The ITA chairman conveniently remembered that Claridge's had another engagement for the room, and quickly emptied it.

The only problem with *Robin Hood*, one American critic wrote—and many agreed—was that it was aimed somewhere between children and adults, with no clearly defined demographic target. Some of the more comedic scenes, he thought, would go over the heads of the youngsters, while appearing slapstick to their parents. Still, he wrote, the "rogues of Sherwood Forest" came off as likable characters even in their villainy, and their Norman oppressors were "properly crooked." Richard Greene would, no doubt, become the idol of early evening viewers. Overall, American audiences would like the show just fine, he thought. But the character featured on *Robin Hood* could not surpass America's current screen idol. "It is doubtful," he wrote, "that he will become the national hero Davy Crockett was, but some smart merchandisers should be able to clean up through the show for a while." The *Miami Herald's* Jack Anderson disagreed. "It wouldn't surprise me, in fact, if the Davy Crockett hat weren't eventually supplanted (God help us) by the Robin Hood bow and arrow."[16] How right he was. "On the location site at Foxwarren, only one thing has changed since the 12th Century," noted *San Francisco Examiner's* Dwight Newton. "Nowadays, Robin Hood robs the rich and gives it to a TV producer."[17]

CHAPTER 11

Robin's Nest

IN APRIL OF 1956, AS *ROBIN HOOD* GAINED STATUS AS A TOP TWENTY show in America, Official Films announced that it had sold the show into Japan and Australia.[1] It reached the equivalent of a number two in Nielsen ratings in the UK, where it stayed for two years. Over the next few months, it also sold to markets as diverse as Syria, Iran, and Puerto Rico.[2] The show's international appeal seems to have been due in part to its British pedigree, but also because its content differentiated it from American series. So did its presentation. "We have been highly praised by schools in America," Weinstein told *TV Times*, "because the English spoken in my films is infinitely more literate than the kinds of stuff the kids hear around them at home." Better yet, *Variety* noted, Weinstein wisely eliminated British accents in her casting of the secondary roles in the program, which "should overcome alleged Midwestern resentment toward British-made pix."[3]

All the while, Al Ruben and, eventually, Peggy Phillips kept the writers' identities top secret. "I had to keep doing this tap dance," Ruben remembered. "Hannah or Syd would say, 'Al, I don't want to talk to these guys. You show them around.' I had to answer their questions. Sometimes it got dicey. I'd say something like, 'They're not in town right now.'" There was fear, too, that the FBI would provoke action by the Home Office, which could revoke visas for American staff and also cause trouble with technical unions.

Alone, the first season of *Robin Hood* brought $1.25 million in initial profit back to Sapphire and Lew Grade's consortium—about $15 million in today's purchasing power and a huge sum for TV at the time. This was for sales in the United States and Canada only; more profit poured in as the series was sold into other countries and in syndication worldwide.

Hal Hackett later reflected that British historical-costume subjects had wider appeal in the world market than contemporary US subjects:

> *Historical costume adventure types of programs which pre-date the American Revolution and have more or less to do with the British Empire at its height, find a responsive audience in all English speaking countries of the world, as opposed to contemporary programs of the American "cops and robbers" type, which are not as well understood by countries remote to the United States.*[4]

Before this benefit of hindsight a year later, Hackett and Official no doubt breathed a collective sigh of relief and then cheered when their gamble paid off. By the end of 1956, *Robin Hood* was garnering an estimated seventy million viewers per week worldwide—one of the biggest audiences ever by that time.[5]

Mel Heimer of the *Miami Herald* offered perhaps the funniest mea culpa among critics for not spotting the appeal of the program back in September 1955:

> *It was only a year ago that the writer of this piece, who has been watching Tonto get the L. R. out of trouble regularly for many years now, drifted over to England and spent some days watching the obviously young and foolish British filming a video series called Robin Hood. Very pleasant, the writer thought, but, of course, no solid competition for America's swashbuckling cowboy heroes. Anybody in the house got a cork, for the hole in the writer's head? The startling truth is that Robin Hood, success-wise, is a veritable smasher in the U.S.A. on CBS-TV.*[6]

The program was just as popular in the United Kingdom. By January 1956 it had become the second most-watched program in the ITV London region. Here, too, it was deemed appropriate for both kids and adults, as evidenced by both broadcast patterns and reviews. The program was originally broadcast in a Sunday teatime slot at 5:30 p.m., a time when the whole family would be watching, but it was repeated at different times, too, including Tuesdays at 7:05 p.m., Thursdays at 8:45 p.m., and Fridays at 10:00 p.m. That it was repeated in a late-evening slot suggests that there was a significant adult audience for *The Adventures of Robin Hood.*[7]

***

In the fall of 1956, Richard Greene and Bernadette O'Farrell did a press tour in ten American cities. Weinstein crafted a brilliant public relations campaign with the Boys' Clubs of America, in which both Greene and O'Farrell attended receptions for the organization and further yoked the show together with wholesomeness and youth. After addressing the New York affiliate, Greene planted two trees on top of the Empire State Building, which—as one stateside publicist pointed out—made them the "two tallest trees in America." Afterward, he and O'Farrell were special guests of two hundred children and their mothers at Tavern on the Green in Central Park.[8] In cities like Minneapolis, Boston, and Los Angeles, the celebrities met with young members of the Robin Hood Club and anointed them as loyal followers and showed them how to better aim their bows and arrows. In addition to turning up at various youth organizations, the pair also stopped into local children's hospitals.

The main cast of *Robin Hood* spent so much time together that they became sort of secondary family to each other. Choreographer Gabriel Toyne and his wife, Diana Beaumont, who acted as various noblewomen in *Robin Hood*, began hosting Sunday lunches at their Drayton Gardens flat. As their son Christopher (one of many child actors in the show) remembers, the main actors used these weekly gatherings to relax after a grueling workweek. They also used this as an unofficial self-critique opportunity, crowding around the Toyne's fourteen-inch, black-and-white screen at 5:25 p.m. to watch that week's episode. Cast members Victor Woolf, Alan Wheatley, John Arnatt, Ronald Hines, Alex Gauge, and editor/writer Al Ruben came for Diana and Gabriel's roast beef. "None of them could rub a couple of shillings together and the bottles of cheap Spanish plonk presented to the table were, by all accounts, terrible! Richard (Greene) attended occasionally, and everyone was on best behavior—for about five minutes!"[9]

There was some bad behavior, too. "My father spoke fondly about his time working on *Robin Hood*, and told us a lot of anecdotes," said Oliver Hansard, son of actor Paul Hansard, who played several roles in all five Sapphire series. "One of the themes drawing many of these stories together was how everybody seemed to be busier jumping in and out of bed with each other rather than focusing on actually filming!" These stories, Hansard said, were always told with a "tinge of missed opportunity," though his father was a happily and faithfully married man. Maggie McLean, widow of actor Shaun O'Riordan, remembered that if not necessarily sexual, there could be too much closeness overall. "His greatest complaint," she said, "was the 'chain mail,' made from string and painted silver. It itched badly. As I understand, it was often shared among the company and people used to get 'crabs'! It was very uncomfortable."[10] The more prominent stars were invited to be very, very careful by "spending the weekend" at Nettlefold, away from the public eye.

While Weinstein, Cole, Ruben, the writers, and certainly Lew Grade and everyone else at Sapphire was overwhelmed by the success of *Robin Hood*, they were far too busy to do much celebrating. With Grade having committed nearly 70 percent of Associated Television's budget for this one show, and Sapphire's purchase of Nettlefold, both entities needed to amortize their costs as much as possible by filling the studio's other filming stages with productions and use the stock company of actors that they had contracted with after the problems with repertory players. They needed to get other filmed entertainment into production in those stages.

As for Official Films, Hackett wanted to capitalize on his sale of *Robin Hood* to CBS—he didn't want to wait for the show to air. His philosophy was, why not target more network sales in one sales season: the spring. He would prepare three or four properties to present for each television season. If they weren't sold by midsummer, the shows would be taken off the market and either reformulated or scrapped for new properties to show the following year. By outlining shows almost a full year in advance, he thought, Official could offer its prospects a huge advantage: If the client was interested in the property from the outset, it could keep on top of the show through its preproduction stages and thus, to some extent, tailor it to its own needs. In turn, this might attract larger, wealthier product companies who were able to offer sponsorship far in advance.[11]

Hannah was obviously motivated by these financial goals, but she had a more personal reason to keep firing on all cylinders, which was her desire to keep as many blacklisted writers employed as possible. She peppered Lardner and Hunter to keep supplying names of colleagues in dire need and willing to work fast. Thus, Gordon Kahn and Waldo Salt were added to the New York–based Sapphire writing and development roster, while Hollywood-snubbed screenwriter Adrian Scott was tapped to informally head up a Los Angeles team, pulling in writers like Robert Lees and Fred Rinaldo, who'd created the Abbott and Costello movie franchise for Universal before being blacklisted.

These efforts came none too soon, because Hannah promised Official Films an outline for a new series loosely based on Sir Henry Morgan, the Welsh pirate who plundered Spain's Caribbean colonies during the late seventeenth century. The series was titled *The Buccaneers* and starred future *Jaws* icon, Robert Shaw, as Captain Dan Tempest. Lardner and Hunter would develop the series with her and Ruben's guidance while they continued their *Robin Hood* episodic duties.

Weinstein, always looking for ways to stretch a production dollar (or pound sterling), found an actual seagoing outfit consisting of a 160-foot sloop, two longboats, three dinghies, and a 30-foot model of the sloop for interior shooting. She bought it from a theatrical production company that had just finished making John Huston's $4.5 million *Moby Dick*, starring Gregory Peck. Proud and his assistant set artists and designers quickly converted the sloop from a nineteenth-century whaler to a seventeenth-century frigate, while Hannah made arrangements to use a castle in Cornwall overlooking the harbor for shooting purposes.[12] A real crew pulled the three-masted vessel past hundreds of cheering people at the Customs House Quay in Falmouth, and the mayor of that town made an official onboard visit, dressed in his scarlet robe, heavy gold collar, and three-cornered hat. Weinstein aptly named the ship *Dilipa*.[13]

The Buccaneers, too, had plenty of subtext. Those paying attention could see the parallels between blacklistees and graylistees trying to subvert the anti-Communist climate of the early Cold War and the actions of protagonist Dan Tempest:

> *The show's action centered on the eighteenth century British colonial port of Nassau in the Bahamas, and featured a protagonist named Dan Tempest, a reformed pirate now in the service of the crown as a privateer and hired guardian of the island of New Providence. Tempest, like Robin Hood, is a roguish individual who tends to buck authority, although he ultimately bears allegiance with the orderly forces of good, who in this case, are the British colonial government. His enemies are the Spanish, and pirates like Blackbeard, and to a lesser extent, bureaucrats and colonial governors with which Tempest might bump heads.*[14]

In other words, a citizen could disagree with his or her government and not be planning to overthrow it. Notably, an early episode of *The Buccaneers*—"The Slave Ship"—took on the issue of race.

Weinstein also commenced development for *Sir Lancelot*, which could use all the Arthurian material that Lardner and Hunter had pulled together prior to *Robin Hood* and research Hannah had commissioned from Oxford University. It marked star William Russell's introduction to American audiences, and, though slightly less of a splash than *Robin Hood*, audiences in Britain, the United States, and Australia loved the weekly dramatic exploits of the Knights of the Round Table, Merlin, Queen Guinevere, and, of course, Lancelot. This program, too, had its fair share of sociological commentary. One episode, for example, dealt with women's rights, tucked behind the age-old story of inheritance and agency: After their father dies, two sisters inherit his tiny, impoverished kingdom. Their guardian is eager to set up a rich marriage for the older girl, but she rebels.

There was little separation of work and personal life for Hannah. She and her daughters, and their governess, Hattie, had been living in an apartment on South Audley Street, in London, but needed more room.

Also, by the fall of 1956 Sapphire was the new jewel of entertainment society in Britain, so she needed to be able to entertain guests and have a place for visitors and friends to stay. And last, but not least, *Robin Hood* and, to a lesser degree, *Lancelot* and *The Buccaneers* needed more land to choose from for their outside scenes. When naturalist Alfred Ezra died in 1955 and left his massive zoological gardens and estate at Foxwarren Park, Surrey, Sapphire's board approached his widow and bought it, both for Hannah's private use and for the use of its grounds for production. One film reporter called the purchase a "dream of many an independent production company." The main house had fifteen bedrooms, five living rooms, and six bathrooms and stood on a hill overlooking an estate of about eighty acres, which included terraces, cottages, gardens, meadow land, woods, and a lake.[15] British director Cyril Pennington-Richards bought one of the cottages and a different partition of the acreage. His swath had no water rights—those stemmed from Hannah's portion of Foxwarren Park. After speaking to Weinstein, the pair agreed that she would provide ready access to the water, in return for Pennington-Richards directing a few episodes of *The Buccaneers*, which he did.[16]

The mansion and estate—referred to collectively as Foxwarren—was situated near the village of Wisley, and just a few miles away from Nettlefold. Being able to shoot here would save valuable time and cost in ferrying equipment around to other locations. Peter Proud oversaw the construction of a faux castle on the crest of one of the grassy rises. The property had excellently maintained stables, so Weinstein and Cole decided to purchase and keep horses there instead of renting them for every episode in which they were needed. This also solved the problem of the horses sometimes being too spooked or tired to perform after being transported to the set from elsewhere. The horses also served as athletic activity for all the children of the producers, directors, friends, and lawyers in Weinstein's circle. Jennifer Read, daughter of leftist friends, remembered riding there on weekends with her brother. "The main contradiction I think was that Surrey is a very conservative area and here were left wing people living in its heart, an irony." The animals and the set props served as a de facto playground for all the kids, like the young son of Paul Robeson's lawyer: "I recall being put on a horse with a knight and being disappointed that his armour was rubber rather than metal!"[17]

At her new estate, Weinstein installed a swimming pool and a recreation pavilion complete with repaved squash and tennis courts and a sauna. After refurbishing and making some necessary repairs, Weinstein moved her family and governess from her luxury Mayfair apartment into the mansion. The extra rooms soon overflowed with European friends, political expats from home in the States, artists, famous married men and women (and their girlfriends and boyfriends), and "surrogate uncles" like Dashiell Hammett and Robeson.

Several women joined Sapphire in 1956, including editor Thelma Connell and story editor Peggy Phillips. Though not the only women to work on the productions, these two technicians were perhaps the closest to Weinstein personally and worked the longest on the Sapphire ventures.

Hannah and Peggy met while working on FDR's 1936 election campaign for his second term. Both were working as public relations specialists at the time. Like Weinstein, Phillips was born in New York City and attended New York University. Her parents owned a theatrical agency and, in part, inspired her to read and write stage plays. Phillips left NYU for stage writing classes at Columbia to better hone her skills in writing plays, but needed a job to pay for these classes and living expenses in general. She took a job writing press releases for the Park Central Hotel, which had a somewhat unique problem: It was the destination for those who wanted to take their own lives by jumping off upper-story balconies. Peggy's job was to crank out press releases that highlighted the hotel's occasional weddings and promote its viability as a venue for bar mitzvahs and other happier events. She was promoted a couple of times but quit when her boss demanded she help him push a live turkey wearing roller skates and a sandwich board advertisement down a hill in Morningside Heights.[18]

Thankfully, one of Phillips's school playwriting assignments caught the attention of a Paramount Pictures scout, who offered her a job as a junior writer through a flagship program in Los Angeles. The program didn't last, and—dejected—Phillips came back to New York. On a trip to Vermont with a ski club, she met a journalist named Pete Kalischer.

It was Kalischer who helped her crystallize her feeling that the recently ended Great Depression was the result of a failure of capitalism, and that FDR's New Deal was the only reasonable response to the devastating unemployment it caused. By 1938, Kalischer had introduced Phillips to fundraisers for Loyalist Spain's resistance to Franco. Like Weinstein and so many other young professionals at this time, Peggy felt that Kalischer's analysis of the Spanish Civil War was an apt one: that it would be the last war in their lifetime in which a man could fight and have no doubt as to what he was fighting for.[19]

To make ends meet, Phillips took a day job in the Shubert Press Department while continuing to volunteer for political causes in her spare time. Because the Shubert job paid so little, Phillips jumped at the chance to do some extra press representative work when a friend offered it to her. In April of 1939, she became press representative for the Soviet Pavilion at the New York World's Fair. It was here that she again ran into Hannah.

At a dinner for VIPs at the fair, Peggy and Hannah sat at a table with director/producer Joseph Losey, who would come to figure prominently in the lives of both women. Also at this table was Losey's wife, Elizabeth Hawes, a major force in the fashion industry who was also a well-known writer and labor organizer. And there was Lillian Hellman, author of the prizewinning play *The Children's Hour* and noted for her uncompromising stand on civil rights. Besides working as a publicist with the Institute of Public Relations, Hannah was campaigning heavily for FDR's third term. The entire group spent the evening talking excitedly about social reform, the rights of labor, working conditions for all races, and the abuse of power. Hannah enlisted Peggy to work with her on the latest FDR campaign, too. The two became very close, to the point where Hannah tried valiantly (and unsuccessfully) to set Peggy up romantically with her younger brother Albert.

When FDR passed away in April of 1945, the two women stood together in Times Square, watching the moving electric sign announcing his death scroll along the Times Building. "What do we do now?" Peggy recalled asking Weinstein, as tears rolled down both of their faces. With a determined look on her face, Hannah said, "We make sure Truman carries the torch."[20] Ten years later, Weinstein begged Phillips to come over to England and help her. As it turns out, Peggy became an integral part of both the creative process of all of Sapphire's shows and the shielding of its writers' identities.

British-born Thelma Connell met Weinstein in 1954, through Sid Cole and others in the film industry. The same age as Hannah, Connell started her film career at Ealing Studios in 1942. She began as a secretary to producer Sir Basil Dean, and then as an assistant to film editor David Lean. Connell quickly moved up to senior editor and worked on films for the writer/producer team of Frank Launder and Sidney Gilliat—Launder would later marry Bernadette O'Farrell. She was meticulous and a perfectionist, highly desirable traits for a job that required someone to look after myriad technical details. Connell once described her role as "rather like a weaver, who is provided with the various coloured threads which form the warp and woof and from them has to design and execute the finished pattern." She was extremely bright, too, having picked up proficiency in several languages without any formal education or travel. When Sapphire reached out to her to be supervising editor for *Robin Hood*, Connell jumped at the chance to work in the new field of commercial television.[21]

There were many other women who were not in Hannah's "inner circle" but who contributed mightily to the success of the Sapphire shows. Brenda Dabbs, Joan Bridge, Doris Martin, Joan Warwick, Kathryn Dawes, and many others served as costumers, colorists, continuity artists, and script supervisors. Many got their start on Sapphire programs and went on to long and successful careers in production.

Hannah's younger brother Seymour flew over to help with the productions. Like his sister, Seymour attended NYU. He had been a Gimbels department store executive, although he was working in St. Louis as a teacher when Hannah was first getting established in Europe. Sy's wife, Ruth, was already on the FBI's watch list because of her membership in the Progressive Party of Missouri. Because he served in the Navy Reserves during World War II, the FBI requested a report on him from the Office of Naval Intelligence in London. Brother Albert also flew over with his family and stayed for extended periods of time to help, and for his trouble, fell under nominal surveillance by the bureau's office in England.

By the middle of 1956, it was clear that Weinstein's operation was exceeding the wildest dreams of anyone involved. Dick James's recording of the *Robin Hood* theme song was a Top 20 hit. *Sir Lancelot* garnered high enough ratings on America's NBC that the network offered to subsidize a budget increase to produce it using colorized film. It became the first British-made program to be broadcast in color. By January 1957, Weinstein's name appeared as executive producer three times per week on three different programs, in the UK, United States, and Canada. American talent and literary agents—besides the chastised ones at Frank Cooper Associates—clamored to find jobs for their clients on her productions.

This was a catch-22: Sapphire needed more and more writers but could not open the floodgates to just anyone and risk exposure by an unsympathetic agent or writer. Weinstein assigned most of these scripts to help her friends who were blacklisted or graylisted: Lees, Rinaldo, Norma Barzman, Scott, Salt, Kahn, the Kochs, Rapf, Arnold Perl, Kraft, Manoff, Sam Moore, Howard Dimsdale, George and Gertrude Fass, Arnaud D'Usseau, Anne Edwards, Frank Tarloff, and possibly a couple more. And so, a trusted few emerged who funneled appropriate clients when possible. One of these, of course, was Ingo Preminger, brother of Otto. Then there was "Blazin'" Blanche Gaines, who represented a hot new TV writer with very strong opinions about censorship and the problem of racial inequality in America; his name was Rod Serling. There was Mark Hanna, whose more famous clients included several members of FDR's family, Gypsy Rose Lee, and Helen Hayes, but who also represented some of Weinstein's blacklisted writers using pseudonyms, like Hy Kraft and Gordon Kahn. It was Hanna who helped Kahn come up with the pseudonyms "Hugh Foster" and "Norman Best" for his scripts. When an entity in the States wanted to use Kahn's photo in connection with work he'd done under a pseudonym, Hanna told them they could not. "He's getting a divorce," the agent said. "If his wife sees the piece, he'll owe her money."[22]

Flush with cash and confidence, Weinstein very quickly wanted to branch out into feature films. She enlisted her best friend, Lillian Hellman, to help her get the film rights to the story of Anne Frank. Fresh off a successful opening of her adaptation of *The Lark* on Broadway, starring Karloff and Julie Harris, Hellman could do (and did) reconnaissance for Weinstein by way of her play's producer, Kermit Bloomgarden, who had produced the stage version. Hannah desperately wanted to get into the feature film business and thought she could do so with Columbia if she could bring the right property—the Frank story would be a home run—and she could do it the same way she had been doing television. That is, she could film it in England using cheaper labor and credits to keep the cost down, use American writers to do the script, and then sell it worldwide.

Hellman demurred from any further interference, politely saying that she thought the Frank story "a tough one" for her friend to want; it would be expensive, and it would bring too much attention to the people used to make it, whether because of their political leanings or the perceived second-tier labor or both. She was noticeably irritated about Dan Sandomire calling her to discuss the idea while she was at Martha's Vineyard:

> We had an unsatisfactory conversation because I was unwilling to take his word for who he was and because I was at a borrowed telephone. . . . Incidentally, I know you don't mind me saying so, if you are going to bid on anything like Anne Frank or have any other large theatre deals I strongly suggest that you get one of the big firms of lawyers to do it for you. Whatever you think of them as people, their involvement in such a deal has a prestige of its own.[23]

Ultimately, the movie rights at this time went to George Stevens Productions. Weinstein redoubled her TV efforts, but never stopped planning to get into features.

In February 1957, the popular *Sunday Mirror* called Hannah "the smartest woman in ITV." In addition to the three programs on-air at that time, it noted she was preparing to film a TV movie called *The Highwayman* and trying to develop a series that would be set in historic

Florentine, Italy. She jovially told the reporter she would finish this work over a weekend in Paris. "I can't lock a door here without some-one knocking—I fly to Paris just to talk in peace!" She did stay in close contact with her exiles in Paris, the Barzmans and the Webers, a group that now included *Salt of the Earth* and *Bridge on the River Kwai* writer Michael Wilson and director Jules Dassin.

Two weeks after this interview, *Kinematograph Weekly* announced that Weinstein's company was responsible for a full 40 percent of ITV's total receipts brought into Britain by its exports since the inception of commercial television eighteen months earlier.[24] And though it's not clear what the retail merchandise split was among all the parties, this merchandise was licensed into thirty-three different manufacturers and earned $42 million in contemporary dollars between 1955 and the middle of 1957. And this was just show-themed merchandise; it did not account for generic Robin Hood items.[25]

There was a hiccup in Sapphire's production engine in March of 1957. Bernadette O'Farrell, who had been playing Maid Marian and who was beloved by audiences worldwide, decided she had to leave the show. Thousands of letters poured into Sapphire's offices when rumors of her dilemma leaked. Each begged her not to leave Robin. "The trouble is that while I'm making Robin Hood films," she told one reporter, "I haven't had time to do any other stage or film work." This was only partially true. She wanted to spend time with her two young girls, and she also worried about getting typecast, unable to get any other role besides Marian. By the mid-1950s, an estimated thirty million people each week watched her in this role—an actor's dream, but one that ironically could typecast a person. She told one reporter that her decision was made when shop-keepers began addressing her as Maid Marion.[26]

It sounds trivial, but Weinstein and the other main producers wor-ried about making the decision: Should they do away with the Marian character altogether, or try to find a new one? If they found a new one, and she didn't resonate with audiences as much as O'Farrell, the series could be irreparably damaged.

To the relief of millions of viewers (and Sapphire's investors) Wein-stein, Cole, and casting director Basil Appleby found the perfect person to replace O'Farrell. From 1955 until she auditioned for *Robin Hood*, Patricia Driscoll had appeared as the host of *Picture Book*, an after-school crafting program for small children, so she already came with a reputation for wholesomeness. The thirty-one-year-old, born in England to Irish parents, was married to Duncan Lamont, who appeared in some minor roles on the show. The talented and scandal-free Driscoll was innocently beautiful and as equally adept at equestrienne skills as O'Farrell. She was a seamless replacement.

At about the same time Sapphire announced its new Maid Marian, it announced Weinstein's program set in sixteenth-century Florence: *Sword of Freedom*. Unfortunately for the company, Hannah's lieutenant Peggy Phillips decided to move back to the States, owing to her pregnancy with her son and the wish to be back home for the birth. Press agent-turned-talent agent George Baxt arrived to help. The energetic Baxt had a reputation for going to the ends of the earth for his clients, feeding both true and made-up gossip to Walter Winchell about them (and about himself). Always on the hunt for new clients, he would ride the elevator in the Algonquin Hotel in New York City to find out who was staying there. He was a talented dialog writer himself, and in the early 1950s started writing TV scripts, many of which he sold on the side. But by the mid-1950s, several of his clients were blacklisted because of suspected Communist affiliations, and Baxt was looking at a subpoena, too.

Sword of Freedom featured British actor Edmund Purdom as a Renaissance artist and freedom fighter against the intrigue of the Medici family. Weinstein helped Purdom and his second wife rent an apartment in Cadogan Square, which they promptly trashed with parties and fighting and had to make restitution.

Weinstein initially signed Baxt to a three-month contract, but he wound up staying for five years, writing ten of the thirty-nine episodes and working for Sapphire on other productions. *Sword* was not as well received as *Robin Hood*, *The Buccaneers*, and *Lancelot*, likely because the costumed dramas were starting to wear a little thin after so many had flooded the airwaves so quickly. Baxt himself later conceded, "I used to call it *The Sword of Boredom*."[27] To be sure, the program gamely filled open spots in UK and American schedules, but reviewers panned it in both. *Variety* called it "mediocre" in tone and story. "The apparent shoestring budget may enable Official and the producers to make some coin out of this entry, but its audience appeal is close to nil." One critic for *The Stage* pulled no punches: "Somebody's making a packet of money out of these half-hour filmlets. Good luck to them. They are to be congratulated for being able to sell such rubbish." *The Stage*'s other columnist, Margaret Cowan, though, printed support for her friend Weinstein, acknowledging that even though the program had not been as successful as *Robin Hood* and that Sapphire's formula was "wearing a little threadbare," Weinstein herself was "far too intelligent" not to pivot in time.[28]

Despite the sniping over *Sword*, the world of television had to concede that Weinstein had pioneered all the success it now enjoyed. It may have been his former Communist Party membership that inspired TV writer Tony Gruner to write favorable ink for Hannah, but his summary was well supported by other papers, too, and it was the truth. "In 1955," he wrote, just thirty-six months after the debut of *Robin Hood*, "only Hannah Weinstein appeared to be serious about making films for television. Today, every leading studio without exception is likely to be the home of one or more television series being planned."[29]

In November of 1958, Weinstein announced that she was developing a show to be shot in Australia. Called *Stingaree*, it was going to be about the development of the country in the 1860s—a "Commonwealth Western." Raymond Bowers, a script editor for *Robin Hood*, wrote a pilot script, and Hannah made plans to visit Sydney in a few months' time to scout for locations. Sapphire pushed several other shows into development, too; Weinstein had long wanted to do a series about the French resistance during World War II. In other words, Sapphire wanted to branch out from its foundation of costumed dramas. There were even plans to do full-length feature films, a series based on the controversial book *Women in Love*, and taped musical programs—a precursor to today's musical "specials."

In 1958, she completed negotiations with the Edgar Wallace estate for the film rights to his novels of the same name. The premise of *The Four Just Men* was four men acting in unison to combat injustice on a world scale. Their assistance was requested by those unable to ask for it from normal law enforcement agencies. The vast scope and number of locales used in the books, Sapphire thought, made it the perfect vehicle for an international co-production, and to attract more buyers from around the globe. In a coup for the studio, it signed British actor Jack Hawkins and Italian actor Vittorio de Sica to play two of the principal roles. Hawkins had appeared in TV movies and specials but never a series; de Sica had never been on TV at all. Both thought the quality of the premise and scripts made *Just Men* a safe bet with which to step into the medium.[30]

There were some other firsts associated with the show, which made it particularly attractive to Sapphire's investors on both sides of the Atlantic. In addition to Hawkins and de Sica, American actor Dan Dailey joined the cast, making it the first time three big, international stars from three countries took part in one series together—not just in Britain, but in the TV world altogether. It was the first time that two top British directors, William Fairchild and Basil Deardon, deigned to step over from the feature world and lead a series for the small screen. It was also the first time such hugely expensive sets were built for a half-hour series, a good part of the show's enormous total cost of £50,000 per episode. American broadcasters had to carefully consider the opportunity, given their history of success with *Robin Hood* and *The Buccaneers*, but this cost was hard to reconcile, no matter how well the show was produced.

In early spring 1958, Weinstein flew to New York to meet with all the networks and assuage their fears in time to put *Just Men* into production with a US buyer.[31] With her three previous series, there was no need for such assurances, but the US market was evolving so rapidly that Sapphire had to keep up with all the new companies jostling for space on the landscape. It didn't land a network, but it was picked up in syndication—profitable in the long run, but much less money up front.

The series was also unusual in that except for the first episode, the four main actors appeared in alternate episodes, though occasionally one or two made a brief appearance in each other's episode, albeit using a telephone. Sid Cole and Jud Kinberg divided up producer duties. Future *Midnight Cowboy* director John Schlesinger served as second unit director.

All the principal actors in *The Four Just Men* asserted that it was the quality of scripts and how the characters were brought to life that convinced them to take a risk with their careers by doing the series. "They are stories with a certain style," di Sica said. "And in them I appear in a dignified and sympathetic role—as an Italian gentleman. I think this makes a change from the impression one gets from most American films, that all Italians are crooks or ice-cream vendors!"[32] Hawkins assured his fans (and future employers) that he understood that doing television in these early years could affect his feature career either positively or negatively. Regarding *Just Men*, he said, "I took the precaution of scrutinizing every script before I agreed to take the money."[33] The British press highlighted some of the writers because their excellence was a selling point: Wilton Schiller, Jan Read, Barbara Avedon, William Fairchild, and others were some of the very best in the business. Ian McLellan Hunter and Ring Lardner Jr. wrote many episodes of the program, so their names were hidden behind that of Louis Marks and some others. In 1959, some blacklisted writers' names were slipping through the proverbial net; British papers printed Frank Tarloff's name, though it doesn't seem to have harmed the program, perhaps because it was distributed by the UK's ITC and not Official Films.[34]

Sapphire's flagship program, *The Adventures of Robin Hood*, came to the end of its network run in the United States in December of 1958. For three full seasons, *Robin Hood* was CBS's Monday 7:00 p.m. lead-in, and was only bettered in 1958 by NBC's *The Price Is Right*. However, it had already been sold into syndication in the United States for its fourth, 1958–1959 season, and remained an ITC staple for the same, as well as having new and repeat episodes sold to distributors all over the rest of the world.

Its popular opening theme, heralded by its nine-note trumpet fanfare, helped launch the career of composer Edwin Astley, whom Weinstein also hired to create the music for *The Buccaneers* and *Sir Lancelot*. For these three Sapphire series, he wrote original music for every episode, recording three episodes per four-hour session at Beaconsfield Studios. As other composers did for other series at this time, he wrote original music specially for the first dozen or so episodes, to build up a library of incidental music for reuse in later episodes.[35]

Meanwhile, Sapphire kept spending. She produced a short with her blacklisted friend Zero Mostel, called *Zero*, based on Samuel Beckett's *Act Without Words*. It wound up becoming the British short entry for the Venice Film Festival in the summer of 1960.[36] In February of 1960, Hannah concluded a deal with Adrian Doyle, son of Sherlock Holmes creator Sir Arthur Conan Doyle. Sapphire gained the rights to produce both movies and TV shows based on all his 170 novels and short stories, except for *The Lost World*, a book that was already adapted into film by another company. The studio planned to start with both film and TV adaptations of *Brigadier Gerard* and a broadcast anthology tentatively titled *The Conan Doyle Theater*. The dollar amount wasn't made public, but it must have paid handsomely for the rights, given that many other media companies were interested in the library, too. But Sapphire wouldn't commit to making Sherlock Holmes, feeling that the 1960s public, especially younger viewers, might not be interested in the Holmes and Watson adventures.[37]

Sapphire's expansion proved to be part of its undoing. Its successful costumed drama series depended on reuse and economies of scale and, more broadly, a worldwide market that hadn't seen these dramas before. Now, four years later, those dramas were wearing thin among audiences in the States and Britain, but a program like *The Four Just Men* was too costly for an independent without a network sale. Without network pre-sales for the concepts of *Stingaree* and *Women in Love* and others that required more expansive production work, the studio could not put all its stages to use, even as it rented those stages out to other productions companies. Sapphire lost a good amount of time and money developing *Women* in particular. After reaching the stage where three-quarters of the scripts for a first season had been written or commissioned, casting director Appleby recalled, the call came that "half-hour stories were out." Then, after scrapping those and starting all over again with hour-long ones, they got the call that hour stories were not popular either, except for a handful of Westerns.[38]

Consequently, the studio announced that it would go into the feature film and commercials business. Seymour Dorner produced its first feature film, a supernatural horror titled *City of the Dead* and starring Christopher Lee. Written by George Baxt, it was about New England witchcraft and demons. Its British actors used American accents and filmed on Walton soundstages over four weeks using many of the usual Sapphire interiors that had been used for its TV shows. Despite Baxt's good script, its budget-friendly production values didn't raise it to hit status among horror aficionados, and its subject matter was still shocking to some mid-century audiences. It did not recoup its production costs. A feature called *Kick-Back*, written by Louis Marks, never made it into production.

By the end of the 1950s, both the British and American television markets had rapidly changed from just five years earlier. American networks began to buy more programming made at home. The major Hollywood studios, which had previously walled themselves off from the competitive threat of television, decided to dive into the business: Disney, Warner Bros., and MGM all started supplying TV-only fare, and at a quality that could not be matched by independents like Sapphire. Also, the then-major networks, NBC and CBS, formed their own in-house production divisions, and ABC combined with Paramount to do similarly. Conversely, British production companies and networks were increasingly wary of shooting series that were subject to the uncertainties of foreign taste. Despite the UK's quota requirements, there was considerable fear of "cultural Americanization" of its television.

Despite all these changes in the media world, Weinstein and Sapphire could have survived and thrived; she had enough social, political, and financial currency to pivot. However, the second part of Sapphire's demise came in the form of Jonathan Fisher, Weinstein's second husband.

CHAPTER 12

The Fishers of England

IN MID-JANUARY OF 1959, BRITISH TV COLUMNIST CATHRYN ROSE cornered Weinstein at a reception for *The Four Just Men*. "Nine months ago," she said, "Mrs. Weinstein (first marriage dissolved years ago) married American lawyer Jonathan Fisher. Characteristically, it was a quiet wedding. Only a few observant viewers will have noticed that lately the name Hannah Fisher has replaced Hannah Weinstein in the credits." Rose found herself waylaid by Fisher while trying to walk over to Weinstein. She asked him about his experience in television or show business, to which he admitted he had none. What do you do, she pressed? "I was a lawyer in Washington. But I don't practice now. What do I do? Well, there's real estate. Do you have any real estate? That's the thing to be in you know."[1]

Weinstein had divorced her husband Pete in absentia, three years earlier. Soon after, she began a romantic affair with Fisher. At forty-eight the tall, lean, gray-haired Fisher was just a year older than Weinstein, and a lawyer by training. It isn't clear how they first met. Many of Weinstein's friends felt that he just appeared one day, without any formal reason for leaving his wife and daughter in the States. An assistant, who took over for Sonia Marks when the latter was put on bed rest for pregnancy, remembered the rumor that Fisher came to Britain specifically to see the producer. "He brought with him a huge sausage, which was her favorite type of sausage, apparently, and she fell in love with him."[2]

There was certainly more to their history than food products. Fisher told reporter Rose that they'd known each other for "aeons and aeons," and that they should have gotten married long before—a difficult prospect since he already had a wife of two decades. People described him as "dashing," and he was very handsome and charming. "Imposing and forceful," writes one media historian, "he was the kind of man who could make the tough-talking studio chief feel like she was being taken care of."[3] When he was younger, he'd had an interest in acting and still harbored a fascination with show business. For almost two years, he gave the impression—and outright told people—that he was untangling assets held in Florida and would be investing in Sapphire. He had, in fact, in the early to mid-1950s amassed a large fortune in real estate dealings. "He was extremely bright, and he had a photographic memory," his granddaughter remembered, "and certainly well educated. He was also larger than life and very handsome and charismatic."[4] He loved handmade suits and Piaget watches and other jewelry—he also had a fondness for fur coats.[5] All of these things he would sometimes simply hand over if the right person complimented them.

What Fisher did not tell people was that he had spent most, if not all, of his money before ever setting foot in England. Some of this was due to bad business dealings and investments; some of it due to manic behavior. "He could be very generous, giving money and even building space to artists or really, anyone who said they needed it. But he just liked to buy things on top of things," his granddaughter recalled.[6]

The problem was his first wife and daughter were the ones who suffered when there was nothing in the bank. One of Weinstein's daughters later heard that he coerced his daughter's mother into giving him a divorce by telling her he was dying of cancer and had found a rich woman to take care of him. Weinstein's lawyer, Hyman Stone, grew very concerned. His son, Victor, remembered that in 1958, as a brand-new lawyer at his father's firm, he learned a lot about the business from watching him handle Weinstein's affairs. He'd met her on numerous occasions, both legal and social. "We got on with her very well, enjoying her hospitality and parties for a number of years, that is until she became romantically involved with a Jonathan Fisher." The Stones found Fisher a "creepy character," nearly always dressed from head to foot in black. It was not difficult to discover Fisher's international past. "In spite of our warnings to Hannah about Fisher, she took no notice," he said.[7] The pair married in a quiet, small ceremony in April 1958, with Hy Kraft, Israel Dorner, and Hannah's eldest daughter serving as witnesses.

Immediately after they wed, Hannah made Jonathan a director of Sapphire. In keeping with the times, British press began referring to her as "Mrs. Jonathan Fisher," and Foxwarren as both his and hers, or just his. Though he came with no knowledge or work experience in the television world, she entrusted the business details to him and concentrated on the creative side of programming. Jonathan immediately began to spend, leveraging trust in productions that were not nearly ready to turn a profit and, in most cases, had not even made it to the camera stage.

Hannah may or may not have known that her husband submitted to an interview with the FBI. On February 16, 1960, Fisher told Agent Cimperman that although his wife had been the "guiding force" behind Sapphire Films, she had decided to relinquish control to him. "The company has not been too successful financially in their recent productions," he said. In taking the helm of the company, Cimperman reported:

> Fisher has dispensed with the services of some of the former employees who were identified as members of the Communist Party or closely associated with the Party. Fisher himself is an accountant and does not share the extreme views of his wife. He is primarily interested in improving the financial position of the company and removing any suggestion of political implication from the films which the company produces. This way he hopes to recover the lost market in the United States.[8]

Fisher's first major spend was to buy a controlling interest in an entity called the Television Writing School (TWS), in London. Founded three years earlier by two writer/producers, the school had a thousand students. Its mission was to train people to write for the relatively new medium of television. It had approached the BBC and various ITV contractors to invest, but as of 1960, they had not, until Sapphire stepped up to the plate. Jonathan invited the press to Walton Studios, where he told them how the school would re-chart its course under his direction. No longer would it look for talented writers, nor teach them how to write. "What we are offering," he said, "is facilities for writers, including established writers, to learn about, and gain experience in, the needs of television, and especially the TV market abroad." It would be, he continued, a sort of "post-graduate course" for writers. Both Fishers joined the board and added their managing director of Walton Studios. Columnist and friend Anthony Gruner remained as principal of the school.[9]

It's likely the Fishers thought this endeavor would be a way to have people pay to use the studio equipment and facilities that were increasingly lying fallow at Walton. As of May 1960, the studio was not filled to enough capacity to pay its bills and was already showing a year-to-date loss of £78,000. There were also other liabilities, including bank overdrafts and damages for breach of production contract, which brought the total to about £145,000 of debt or anticipated debt.

To be sure, much of this debt could be tied to the expense of running and maintaining Foxwarren, both as a living space and a filming space. Despite the precarious position of the British-American co-production horizon, Fisher built state-of-the-art soundstages at the studio, indulging in new technologies and lavish sets. All of this he did without the upfront monies that Sapphire had betted on with a potential network sale, which it did not get, and its inability to meet some of this debt with feature films, the costs for which take longer to recoup. There was also the rent on the large office and living space at Cadogan Square, one of the most expensive buildings in London.

Weinstein tried to get ahead of this slowdown, knowing that with its current schedule the company could not afford to subsidize Foxwarren and its other buildings. She contracted with a real estate company to find a suitable renter—not an easy task given how large Foxwarren was. A perfect solution presented itself in the form of Elizabeth Taylor and her then-husband Eddie Fisher, who were moving to England to make the film *Cleopatra* for 20th Century Fox. A deal was struck for these other Fishers (no relation) to rent the estate.

Just two days before they were set to move in with their three children, Taylor and her husband canceled. Her producers said she'd received two threats to kidnap her children, and that Surrey police had refused to keep sightseers from the borders of the estate. Some British papers gave another reason, which was that the two Fisher families could not come to an agreement on the length and dates of rental. And Hannah's husband gave his own reason for rejecting the would-be Foxwarren renters. "I understand that the owner, Jonathan Fisher, a director of Sapphire Films, has been so shocked by the invasion of his 35-acre home by rubber-necking, camera-toting fans that he is worried about the security of his property while the star and her family are living there." Whatever the reason, the Jonathan Fishers lost an opportunity to stave off financial woes for a bit longer.[10] And by the end of 1960, Sapphire (and the Fishers) were supplanted on the TWS board, and the school stopped advertising its Walton connection.

Fisher was spending a lot of money on personal items, too. He purchased even more expensive new clothes, and lavish dinners and jaunts out of town. Their neighbor, director Cy Pennington-Richards, recalled that he insisted on driving a Bentley, to appear as though he was British gentry of some kind. He purchased one from a local doctor for a hundred quid, but it didn't start very well. The studio grounds had a little diesel-engine cart, which was used for carting equipment from set to set. Fisher hired a chauffeur, a gray-haired old Englishman complete with boots and gloves. "He used to tow this thing down the drive to get it started. 'Boom . . . boom . . . boom . . . boom..!' Off would go John down to the local pub where he was lording it you know, and then at two o'clock the chauffeur had an order to go and collect him. So he'd go down in the diesel dumper, you'd see this diesel dumper going down the A3 with a chauffeur on it!"[11] Indeed, Fisher's drinking was already a problem even before their marriage. By 1960, it had become acute—he was often in bed, explained as "ill" but, in truth, recovering from binge drinking. Likely, he was self-medicating; he sometimes left suicide notes and disappeared for a day or two.

Investors approached the couple and the other directors repeatedly, asking what could be done about the mounting debts. Weinstein announced that the company would soon form an in-house distribution arm for both its own and other people's productions, but this never materialized. Jonathan put up a good front, traveling to and from Florida, explaining that he was working on a capital reorganization plan and also trying to disentangle his personal fortune to help bankroll the company. Neither endeavor produced any money, and Weinstein had no choice but to shut down the studio altogether, pink-slipping some two hundred surprised workers. The Federation of Film Unions lobbied the government to help British Lion make an offer for the studio, so it could fill it with work and thus hire its workers, but this didn't come to fruition.

On or around January 15, 1961, while Hannah dealt with creditors, Fisher disappeared, leaving a bizarre trail of suicide notes in various English hotel rooms. Some three or four days later, Weinstein found him at the Edinburgh Royal Infirmary. Shortly after, television personality Chan Canasta decamped to the Hotel George in that city, ostensibly to lend support to Hannah. "I am not here in connection with the studios or as Mrs. Fisher's spokesman. I have come so that I can help in any way as I can as a friend." Hannah likely told Canasta to keep quiet—she refused to speak of Fisher's condition as anything but bronchial pneumonia.

In March of 1961, a property development company purchased Walton Studios for about £700,000. This sale so closely on the heels of public notification that anything was wrong shows just how precarious her situation had become in such a short amount of time. But it also reflects her reported desire to put everything into receivership quickly, so investors could get their money back. Close friend Joseph Losey wrote their mutual friend Vladimir Pozner and offered this summary of her situation:

You have, perhaps, seen, that even as we were speaking about Hannah, something of what we feared was happening. Her empire has collapsed totally, apparently through the mistakes (not to give them an uglier name) of Jonathan. He had apparently disappeared from the house and was finally discovered in Edinburgh; though I don't know the details, I gather that he has still not regained consciousness. Meantime, the studio has been taken over by receivers, as was also her house, her cars, and apparently everything. They are keeping it as quiet as possible, and she is in Edinburgh so I have not yet spoken to her. The children are being wonderful, and are being taken care of, so I think

there is really nothing anyone can do at this moment excepting to hope
that something will be rescued for her.[12]

There was a huge outcry from the unions and would-be media investors that having homes and a shopping center built on a perfectly viable studio spot would be detrimental to the industry at large. On April 24, at London Bankruptcy Court, there was standing room only as creditors of Walton Studios met to discuss next steps. The official receiver told the assembled crowd that according to his information the studio had lost nearly £250,000 between its empty stages, bank overdrafts, and breach of film contracts. Its total liabilities were more than it could generate from its output. Creditors voted for the appointment of an official liquidator, and the sale went through.[13] One year later, Foxwarren mansion and its grounds sold to a businessman for £40,000.

***

As Weinstein grappled with running a studio and the machinations of her husband, the FBI continued to keep tabs on her. It repeatedly queried Douglas Fairbanks Jr., through the Office of Naval Intelligence, to see if he knew of anything subversive with Sapphire, given that both he and Seymour Dorner were former US Navy, and because of his membership in the upper echelons of the entertainment world in England. Though he claimed not to know Weinstein or her brother, he promised to make discreet inquiries. All he reported was that Weinstein and Cole appeared to be "sympathetic" (presumably to Communists or left-wing groups) but not trying to hide anything.

The agency asked the same chore of Samuel Eckman, an American who, until a few years before, had been head of MGM in Europe; it got the same result.[14]

During the last days of 1960, the FBI did a perfunctory but thorough review of citizens listed on its Security Index who might better qualify for its Reserve Index. The Reserve Index was a secret list of individuals that Hoover conceded could not qualify for inclusion in the Security Index but "who, in a time of emergency, are in a position to influence others against the national interest or who are likely to furnish material financial to subversive elements due to their subversive ideology and associations." The primary difference between the two groupings—besides the color of the index card on which they were typed—was that the Reserve Index listed all left-wingers and people suspected of being a Communist, while one's appearance on the Security Index meant that he or she could be arrested upon order of the president invoking the Emergency Detention Program. Agents in the New York office interviewed confidential informants who purportedly were familiar with the doings of the Communist Party.

A month-long investigation didn't turn up any data on Weinstein's activities, Communist or otherwise. A couple of months later, in the spring of 1961, at least one agent concluded that because she had married Jonathan Fisher, whom he mistakenly determined to be a British citizen, she was no longer a threat to the United States.[15] The irony, of course, was that Fisher was the biggest threat to Weinstein.

Fisher went back to the United States to try to regain his health. Weinstein flew back and forth for the next year.[16] With the help of friends who loaned her money, she was able to keep the Cadogan Square townhouse, and she took a board seat in Britain's new pay TV venture, "PayVision," a precursor to cable television—a technology she had been interested in since arriving in Britain. Jonathan installed himself at the fashionable Hampshire House, at the edge of Central Park, where TV and stage stars often stayed between homes or while working in the city. The FBI frequently interviewed the manager of the hotel and the bell-hops, asking them to be on the lookout for any letters or notes directed to Hannah and notify them, and to try to ascertain her travel plans as they arose.

On November 17, 1963, Jonathan checked himself into the Waldorf-Astoria and washed down a bunch of pills with scotch. He was rushed to Bellevue Hospital. Five days later, he passed away, surrounded by members of the Weinstein family. When Hannah contacted their bank in Switzerland to get more money, it wrote her back that her accounts, along with those of her children's trust funds, had been cleared out.[17]

CHAPTER 13

Goodbye to Greenwood and the Blacklist

AFTER FISHER PASSED AWAY, WEINSTEIN MOVED HER FAMILY BACK TO the United States for good. Because of Sapphire's sudden and volatile ending, she was not allowed to work with any talent from Equity, the actors' guild there, nor was she allowed to contract with members of several behind-the-scenes workers' unions. It became clear that company money had been, in large part, diverted for household expenses, and luxury ones at that. Author Hazel Rowley posed the question that naturally emerges when looking at Weinstein's saga at the end of this decade:

> *Hannah Weinstein saw herself as a communist; was she being philanthropic or exploitative in the Foxwarren days? According to Ring Lardner, Jr., she was both. Howard Koch, another blacklisted writer in London at the time, observes that if Weinstein provided employment for blacklisted writers, "the benefits were mutual."*[1]

Rowley, though, was using the same assumptions about Weinstein's alleged party membership as the press and intelligence agencies and her political rivals did. The question about her motives, though, remains the same. And the conclusion remains the same.

While Fisher began to dismantle Sapphire, and the TV industry on both sides of the Atlantic started to shift, the institutional mechanisms of the blacklist began to crumble in the late 1950s. The absurdity of the blacklist was heralded in large part by Dalton Trumbo's Academy Award for *The Brave One* in 1957, which he'd written under the assumed name of Robert Rich. Two years later, the writer, weary of being coy and using fronts, announced that he was Rich. In August 1960, star and producer Kirk Douglas told Trumbo that once their film *Spartacus* was finished, he would announce Trumbo as the writer and demand his name be put on the film. The studio acquiesced. It was the highest-grossing film of the year, and in large part, symbolized that the blacklist had been broken.[2] In 1959, Hunter and Lardner were able to get their passports back, though Polonsky did not for several more years. The rest of Weinstein's stable of blacklisted and graylisted writers had different experiences with returning to work under their own names—or not. For example, Lardner was hired to write the screenplay for *The Cincinnati Kid* (1965) under his own name, and in 1971, he won his second Oscar for adapting Robert Hooker's comic novel, *M*A*S*H* (1970), cementing his return to his own moniker. Hunter and Lardner went on to write the smash Broadway musical *Foxy* (1964) and myriad other big- and small-screen contributions, like *Dr. Jekyll and Mr. Hyde* (1968) and a TV movie version of *Roman Holiday*, the feature for which he'd fronted for Dalton Trumbo in 1953. Arnold Manoff passed away in 1965 but wrote several other TV episodes of various shows using his pseudonym, "Joel Carpenter." Adrian Scott was hired as a production executive with MGM-British in 1963. Robert Lees continued to write for other, non-Sapphire programs for a time under his pseudonyms, but once the blacklist was over, was not able to recover that career.[3] His one-time writing partner, Fred Rinaldo, went into another career altogether. And so on.

It should be remembered, too, that Weinstein got work for not only blacklisted writers, but others who just desperately needed the work, or at the very least, wanted to try to break into that new technology of the 1950s: television. Many had similar stories to Shirl Hendryx, who wrote an episode of *Robin Hood*: "I was starving to death in the Village . . . I had only written for live shows when Blanche (Gaines) came to me and said I had to write for this woman in England. I was so poor I had to type my script on the back of an older script . . . she and I stayed up all night, her helping me get it right for the show." Carol Gluck, who wrote at least one episode of *Robin Hood*, wasn't blacklisted either, but was trying to transition from radio to television, and do so while suffering from the effects of polio.[4] Left-winger Brit Leon Griffiths was trying to segue from newspaper journalism to TV scriptwriting when Cole and Weinstein hired him, based on one episode of another series, and assigned him several episodes of *Robin Hood* and *Just Men*, establishing his career.

Weinstein even hired at least one Canadian writer to work on her programs. The long arm of McCarthyism had spread north, where the Royal Canadian Mounted Police had started trying to root out "subversives," too, working in tandem with the FBI. When writer Ted Allan realized a play of his was about to be pulled on the second day of rehearsals just on the nod of an advertising executive, he packed and left for England with his wife. He later claimed he wrote episodes of *Robin Hood* and *The Four Just Men*. His pseudonym has yet to be identified.[5]

There are at least a dozen more instances of how Sapphire created opportunity for struggling writers. Separate but related to all these individual, life-changing examples is the tens of millions of dollars Weinstein and her company injected into Britain's fledgling TV landscape, employing thousands of British workers between 1953 and 1962.

Upon her return to the States, Weinstein went back into political work. Alongside best friend Lillian Hellman, she worked for Eugene McCarthy's campaigns, particularly his 1968 one in which he vied for the Democratic Party nomination. Weinstein arranged for two of her Madison Square Garden rallies to promote this McCarthy—both sold out, as was her custom. This time, though, two decades after the heyday of her Wallace rallies, her second McCarthy speech was televised via closed circuit to 160,000 people attending similar rallies in twenty-two cities across the country. That one evening, as co-chair, she helped raise nearly $2 million for the anti-Vietnam War candidate.[6] In 1970, Weinstein produced an anti-war rally at her beloved MSG to raise money to elect senators who called for a quicker withdrawal from Vietnam and bigger spending on environmental improvement.

The following year, she was back in the film business, developing a feature based on the memoir *Whose Heaven, Whose Earth?* about a pair of political activists. She tapped Walter Bernstein to write the script and Jane Fonda and Donald Sutherland to star. She also optioned the rights to the book *The Khaki Mafia*, about alleged corruption in US Army service clubs in Vietnam.

Neither of these true-life stories made it to production, but Weinstein wasn't deterred. At the beginning of 1972, she and a friend, actor/director/activist Ossie Davis, announced the fruits of a company they'd set up the year before. It was called Third World Cinema Corp. Its mission was to increase the number of opportunities for Blacks and Puerto Ricans "on the movie scene." 20th Century Fox agreed to distribute several TWC films, and the company announced an ambitious slate that included writers, directors, and actors such as Millard Lampell, John O'Killens, Rita Moreno, John Berry, and Davis. What made TWC stand apart from other studios was that it created a training program for actors of color to find roles in film and television and to help create films produced and directed from minority perspectives. It obtained the backing of several film and TV unions, as well as federal grants, including $200,000 and $400,000 grants from the US Manpower and Career Development Administration and the Model Cities Program, respectively.

The first feature TWC got to theaters was *Claudine*, a comedy-drama featuring James Earl Jones and Diahann Carroll (who replaced an ailing Diana Sands) and directed by John Berry. Filmed in Harlem and other New York locations, *Claudine* was the story of a romance between a sanitation worker, who was the divorced father of three, and a welfare mother of six children. A far cry from the costumed fun of *Robin Hood* and the other Sapphire dramas, *Claudine* represented the work of a woman who could now produce filmed works that directly spoke to the issues in which she so passionately believed: equal opportunity for people of color and women, and a social safety net that covered all Americans. These ideals weren't just given screen time. They were put into practice by the company itself: Third World trained many of the technicians who, since the 1980s, have worked on other films made by actors of color.

A few years later, Weinstein produced *Greased Lightning*, starring Richard Pryor, Beau Bridges, and Pam Grier, about the life of Wendell Scott, the first (and for a long time, the only) black man to race stock cars professionally in America. It underperformed at the box office but went on to be a cult favorite and enduring video and streaming rental.

The never-sleeping producer put a Cher feature into development, which didn't get made, but soon after, Weinstein produced *Stir Crazy*, starring Pryor and Gene Wilder, with Sidney Poitier directing. It was one of the biggest box office smashes of the era and, until recent years, the most successful film made by a black director.[7]

When Weinstein passed away of a heart attack in 1984, her friends and colleagues and family gathered at several ceremonies and galas in her honor, setting up scholarships and voter registration drives in her name. She posthumously received that year's Liberty Hill Upton Sinclair Award, given to inspiring community leaders and donor-activists who make change possible through their commitment to social justice.

Afterword

By the time I finished this manuscript, the January 6, 2021, insurrection at the US Capitol had long been in the rearview mirror for millions of Americans, if it ever concerned them at all. Despite the diligence of some Democrats and a few Republicans to provide a truthful accounting of that day and the days leading up to it, the nation at large has failed to punish those who masterminded it. It has all but ignored Section 3 of the Fourteenth Amendment of the US Constitution, which allows for the removal of such a lawmaker that engages in rebellion or insurrection. Not only have these insurrectionist politicians avoided accountability, but they have been reinstalled in the highest levels of government. I think many of Weinstein's circle of friends and colleagues would agree that trying to negotiate justice within a system of democracy that ignores major fractures within itself to preserve the privilege of relatively few is a daunting task.

This and so many other major examples of dereliction of those in power lend an understanding of Hannah Weinstein's political efforts both before and after her time in England. That is, if not enough lawmakers on any spectrum of either party can enshrine basic rights for its population, maybe there needs to be a disruption on that spectrum. Though Weinstein and her colleagues failed to build a permanent third party, and to remove the specter of HUAC and McCarthy investigations and general discrimination, she *did* help move that needle. ICCASP and the PCA forced both FDR and Truman to reckon with Democrats who began to stray from New Deal ideals. They reenergized those who were tempted to succumb to the apathy found in post-war comfort. As her one-time colleague Helen Keller said, "The world is moved along, not only by the mighty shoves of its heroes, but also by the aggregate of tiny pushes of each honest worker." Weinstein aggregated thousands of honest workers. And as daughter Paula once recounted, she taught her that there was great happiness in the trials. "She didn't say it wasn't important to succeed—it was—but she said whether you win or lose, you still have to do it anyway. There is deep joy in engaging in the struggle, deep joy in it."[1]

Hannah Dorner Weinstein played an important role in the history of the blacklist, and in the history of progressive media production. As media historian Carol Stabile recounts:

> *Under Weinstein's direction, Robin Hood in particular proved a powerful vehicle for progressive political views. In this show blacklisted authors like Ring Lardner, Jr., and Adrian and Joan LaCour Scott explored these themes of betrayal and social justice that were very much on their minds. In an episode written by the Scotts, for example, titled "The Cathedral," the mason in charge of building the structure is falsely accused of "being a tool of an international conspiracy, anti-Church and anti-Christ." In "The Charter," also written by the Scotts, Robin located a lost document that protected the rights of progressive nobles who wanted to reform the aristocracy and redistribute land and other forms of wealth."[2]*

Some of the writers had been terrorized to such a degree that they recognized the themes they wrote about in the context of a television show that took place hundreds of years ago might still be too subversive for anti-Communists. "Today," Adrian Scott told a friend in 1957, "when you characterize the rich as stingy, this is subversive."[3]

As Stabile also writes, we share this "historical amnesia," focusing on the heroism of blacklisted men like the Hollywood Ten and forgetting the double and sometimes triple vulnerability of the professional women who would be singled out not only because of their political views, but because the lives they led did not conform to conservative prescriptions about gender.

Weinstein understood better than most that it was fruitless and time-wasting to respond to labels like "pinko" or "dupe" or even official designations such as "concealed communist." It also appears that she ignored—or, at least, deflected—the misogyny of the times. Sometimes these external pressures worked in tandem, when she accomplished her monumental tasks, such as a rally, or helping get FDR reelected, or co-founding a new political party, or making a film or TV show. With these, she was not seen as successful because of her hard work, or exceptional writing, or organizational skills—it was because she was being manipulated by Communists or using her "feminine wiles" to do the same to others. Her intelligence files are peppered with statements like, "She knows all the leading fellow travelers and is supposed to have had [writer and progressive leader] Norman Corwin wound around her finger for quite a while," and label her female colleagues as "misled" or "scatterbrained." She earned some of this from people she employed, too. Director and neighbor Pennington-Richards called her this "little typist from America" who suffered from "megalomania,"—though some of these insults can be attributed to anti-Americanism, too.[4]

Most in her circle, though, knew her strengths and appreciated what she did to help friends and the country at large. "She was just a huge help," remembered Joseph Stevenson, son of blacklisted writer and civil rights leader Janet Stevenson, who wrote some scripts for Weinstein under a pseudonym:

In the 50s, my mother was a very talented screenwriter—one of the few women teaching at USC. The school wanted her to sign a loyalty oath; she refused, so the school fired her. One of her plays won this huge prize, but she couldn't get it produced. She desperately needed jobs like writing for Robin Hood. I distinctly remember her asking me—a little boy at the time—about something on which she could hang a plot point. She asked if it would be plausible for someone to hide in a lake or pond and be able to breathe through a reed or a hose. I thought that meant garden hose, and I reasoned that Robin wouldn't have a garden hose. So, I told her "no." Anyway, those were heavy times and I know my parents really appreciated the work.[5]

While some writers like Lardner and Hunter were able to return to lucrative Hollywood careers, some were not. Regardless, Weinstein helped lessen the terrible effects of the "Red Scare" for many incredibly talented people, at least for a time. Joan Scott later recalled the risk she took: "She was hiring every blacklisted writer in town. Hannah Weinstein was very gutsy."[6]

The children of John Weber, who helped Hannah get her film career started through his own mutual aid network, remembered how some victims of blacklisting—official or unofficial—like Weinstein, risked their own health and livelihoods to help each other as best they could. They recalled how they kept tabs on each other:

> *I have a vivid memory of staying put in my seat in a movie theatre while the credits rolled and everybody else was leaving their seats to exit the theatre. Mom and Dad would get excited when they saw the name of someone they knew, expressing their pleasure that so-and-so was able to get work in the industry. The Robin Hood series was particularly beloved by many families of the Left for the meaning of its story as well as the people who created it. For our parents an added joy was that they knew the producer, Hannah Weinstein, and were happy for her success.*[7]

Millard Lampell wrote that without Hannah, "there would have been no food on the table to feed my children." Hyman Kraft was even more effusive: "No single individual did more for the personal and professional sustenance of condemned American writers and directors during those grave years than the Weinstein lady. As a result, she built a colossal enterprise. All of which must prove something."[8]

Ailing Lillian Hellman, who died just a few months after her dear friend, wrote a letter that was read aloud by actor Jane Fonda. It said, in part:

> *My own belief is that she was the only person in the world Joe McCarthy was afraid of. . . . One of the most remarkable things about Hannah is that in this shabby time, in a time when either nobody*

believes in anything or have long given up hope, she does believe and
she does carry out what she believes in.[9]

***

I tripped over Weinstein's story when I was researching the twelfth- and thirteenth-century Robin Hood myths for a potential work of fiction. This effort, in turn, was to be an homage to my beloved grandmother. She was born with the name Sophia Blanche, which she changed to "Dale," in honor of "Alan-a-Dale," the wandering minstrel in Robin Hood lore (and played by John Schlesinger in Sapphire's production). Grandma Dale died when I was only nine, but I remember my time spent with her much more vividly than just about anyone else in my life. She gave us her undivided attention, doing things with us like building popsicle stick houses and letting us pick anything we wanted from her garden. And that garden was magic. She gamely stayed up late with us, all of us racing around her backyard with mason jars trying to capture lightning bugs. I can still hear her laugh—a sudden, staccato burst punctuated with absolute joy and vulnerability lasting for about ten seconds.

Grandma Dale's life was never easy, but her youth was particularly hard. Money was always in short supply, even before the Great Depression. Her father, even though he'd been well educated in Belarus before immigrating, was a housepainter, and health issues prevented him from being a particularly busy one. Her mother was bitter because money had to be diverted from her household to that of other children he'd fathered in the old country who had moved nearby—children that she may or may not have known about before they married. Moreover, their tiny daughter, Dale's little sister, died of polio in 1916, when she was just two.

Grandma coped with her tumultuous family life by immersing herself in the far more romantic world of books. Howard Pyle's *Robin Hood* was her favorite—so much so that later in life, she not only gave herself the name of a character, but also those of her children. My father's name is Richard, after King Richard the Lionheart, the alleged rightful ruler of England who, according to the outlaw story, was hypnotized into going off on crusade while his brother John tried to usurp his throne. Film buffs call him "Richard of the Last Reel" because he appears at the end of every Robin Hood film as the heroic, and supposedly victorious, crusader monarch returning to punish treacherous Prince John and the wicked Sheriff of Nottingham.[10] (My father is a wonderful and brilliant man; he has no interest in ruling, though, and does not ride horses.) One of my aunt's names is Marian, after Robin's love interest. Dale was a bit subversive about the naming of my other aunt, Frances. As the first daughter, as per Jewish custom, she was carefully named after another grandmother who had died twenty years earlier in a car accident. But this was also a nod to Friar Tuck, who belonged to the Franciscan order of monks, and who was integral to the story of Alan-a-Dale in Pyle's *The Merry Adventures of Robin Hood*. I always wondered about what my grandparents might have named their kids if they'd had any more of them.

I'd like to be able to say that my grandmother went on to become an activist, taking all the elements of Robin Hood lore that encapsulate justice and equality. My grandparents even lived down the street from some of the leftist families interviewed for this book. She did not, but she did something more beneficial for us. She fell in love with my thoughtful, kind, intelligent, quiet, punny, very tall grandfather and married him in 1936. Eventually, they purchased a house on a tree-lined street in Westchester and started a family.

Grandma's struggle was not with class distinction or nationalism, but rather teaching full time, raising toddlers, and managing her and Grandpa's elderly parents, who lived with them. The only "red" in the family was my Aunt Frances, called "royt khedad jeraf" by my superstitious and suspicious great-grandmother. In Yiddish, the term means "redheaded giraffe," a derogatory reference to her long legs and gorgeous red hair.

In any event, I'm grateful to Grandma for posthumously introducing me to Hannah Weinstein.

ACKNOWLEDGMENTS

Many of the people in this story have long passed away, as have many of their children. And some of the children of major figures had no interest in talking with me—their parents' stories have been told repeatedly in film or television or biographies from previous generations, and they felt they had nothing to add. Some barely knew their parents—in the case of several writers or actors, these children, now in their eighties or nineties, were raised by nannies or relatives and had little exposure to what their parents were doing thousands of miles away or even down the street at the studio, if they were taken along to Europe. The daughter of Richard Greene, star of *Robin Hood*, for example, graciously tried to help me but was simply too young at the time of her father's heyday to recall anything pertinent. And naturally, those working under pseudonyms did not speak of their work to other adults outside the Sapphire circle—never mind speak to their children—for the obvious fear of being detected.

It's because of this gap in oral histories that those who did share their time and stories with me shine even more brilliantly. Norma Barzman, the blacklisted screenwriter and gifted novelist, with her infectious laugh that punctuates every fourth sentence, generously shared her time and insights with me about a long-ago time in Paris with Hannah and many other creators. John and Tara Bucci, son and daughter-in-law of the late Peggy Phillips, a close friend of Weinstein's and a pioneering television writer, were a huge help in contextualizing the life of single, working moms on the *Robin Hood* and *The Buccaneers* sets. Herman Rush, former producer and chairman of Columbia Pictures and, during the heyday of *Robin Hood*, head of Official Films—the show's distribution company—helped me understand the business model of costumed dramas coming out of Sapphire.

Albert Ruben took the time to explain to me his feelings about running correspondence between Weinstein's Sapphire Films production offices in Britain and blacklisted writers in the United States. Angela Babin was able to help me gain a better understanding of her grandfather, Hannah's second husband, Jonathan Fisher. British film producer and financier Gavrik Losey, son of famed blacklisted writer Joseph Losey, let me pick his brain to my heart's content about his father's friendship with Weinstein and other exiled artists in their sphere. Several FBI historians graciously and patiently walked me through the seemingly nonsensical markings and verbiage found in Weinstein's files—and the files of some of her friends and colleagues. I'd especially like to thank Bob Rinaldo, Herman Rush, Dr. James Chapman, and Jeanne Romano. They know why.

Many, many more helped me in my quest to paint a portrait of an incredible woman who squeezed together an ensemble crew of writers, producers, and directors to make a product that became popular around the world. Almost every single person mentioned in this book has had enough experiences in their lifetime to write a book or ten. Thankfully, many of them have.

Thank you to the following people, in no particular order: Tom Devine, Jon and Tara Bucci, Jeffrey D. Bader, Ann Prather Foster, Wendell Foster, Norma Barzman, Tony Kahn, Vivian Kahn, Rebecca Prime, Loren Gold, Lynn Dimsdale, Julie Deering, Maggie McLean, James Kahn, Matthew Kerns, Robert McNally, Patricia Schiller, Simon Broadley, Shirl Hendryx, Nancy Flanagan, Sally Wood Thomson, Maggie Stark, Michael Rogers, Richard Arnatt, Dr. Robert Crabtree, Joshua Avedon, Jim Colman, Brian Neve, Jennifer Anne Compton Wills, Peter Koch, Carlos Read, Elaine Koelmel, Judy Barnett, Jeremy Weintraub, Carissa Weintraub, Erik Tarloff, Joseph Stevenson, Helena de Crespo, Helen and Ed Tosch, Eden Endfield, Sam Slote, Mark and Dan Risner, Jennifer Risner Read, Victor Stone, Ann B. Graham, John C. Cimperman, Dyanne Asimow, Alexander Citron, Rachel and Sue Seifert, Kevin Brown, Alida Brill Scheuer, Nicole Miller at Syracuse Library, Ivan

Sandomire, Katie Sandomire, Simon Broadley, Stephen Brickel, Paul Nicholas Boylan, Esq., Cornelia McNamara, Dr. Zach Zahos, Sara and Linda Weber, Dan Stotter, and Dr. Danielle DuBois, NARA.

Notes

Introduction

1. Very special thanks to Daniel Stotter, FOIAdvocates.com.

2. *The Nation*, November 29, 1980, 587.

3. Central Intelligence Agency, Information Report, Biographical Data on Persons Connected with the Cultural and Scientific Conference for World Peace, distributed May 2, 1949, obtained under the Freedom of Information Act from US Information Agency, requested as "Materials regarding Hannah Dorner Weinstein," received November 4, 2022.

4. Hannah Weinstein memorial speech, Ring Lardner Jr. file, Margaret Herrick Library.

5. Brian Neve, *The Many Lives of Cy Endfield: Film Noir, the Blacklist, and Zulu* (Madison: University of Wisconsin Press, 2015), 105.

6. Karl E. Meyer, "Hoover Intolerant of Criticism—Clark," *Los Angeles Times*, November 18, 1970, 1.

7. Leah Finnegan, "Living with Ennui in Trump's America," *The Outline*, July 11, 2017, accessed April 5, 2020, https://theoutline.com/post/1887/ennui-in-trumps-america?zd =1&zi=4am2k26t.

8. Louis Marks, "Hannah Weinstein: Film and Television Producer," *The Times* (London), March 16, 1984, 16.

Chapter 1

1. *The Count of Monte Cristo* was airing in syndication and *The Three Musketeers* debuted the following year, also in syndication.

2. Ben Gross, "Let's Be Honest About Pre-Recording for TV," *New York Daily News*, September 30, 1955, 57.

3. Thank you to Sumithra Barry for her ratings expertise.

4. Catherine Johnson and Rob Turnock, eds., *ITV Cultures: Independent Television Over Fifty Years* (Berkshire, England: Open University Press, 2005), 75–77; James Chapman, *Swashbucklers: The Costume Adventure Series* (Manchester University Press, 2015), 25–26. The author thanks Dr. Chapman for his extraordinary help and patience in understanding British television in the 1950s.

5. Chapman, *Swashbucklers*, 24.

6. Scott Brand, "*The Adventures of Robin Hood*: Outlawed in Sherwood, Banned from Hollywood," Chapter 3, in *The Cold War and Entertainment Television*, ed. Lori Maguire (Newcastle upon Tyne: Cambridge Scholars Publishing, 2016), 39.

7. Chapman, *Swashbucklers*, 26.

8. Andrew Paul, "Reassessing Blacklist Era Television: Civil Libertarianism in *You Are There*, *The Adventures of Robin Hood*, and *The Buccaneers*," *American Studies* 54, no. 1 (2015): 40–41.

9. Letter from Ring Lardner Jr. and Ian McLellan Hunter to Hannah Weinstein, dated December 16, 1954, Ian McLellan Hunter Papers, 1938–1989, Margaret Herrick Library, Academy of Motion Picture Arts and Sciences.

10. Ring Lardner Jr. interview, "The Interviews: An Oral History of Television," Television Academy Foundation, accessed November 23, 2022, https://interviews .televisionacademy.com/interviews/ring-lardner-jr?clip=60091#interview-clips.

11. Ancestry.com, Year: 1920, Census Place: Bronx Assembly District 3, Bronx, New York, Roll: T625_1135, Page: 21A, Enumeration District: 214; Year: 1930, Census Place: Bronx, New York, Page: 2B, Enumeration District: 0189, FHL microfilm: 2341204, all accessed October 7, 2022, https://macaulay.cuny.edu/seminars/lobel08/articles/b/o/o/ Boom_Times_(1900-1920s)_81d3.html. Excellent summary of emergence of the Bronx.

12. Daniel Katz, *All Together Different: Yiddish Socialists, Garment Workers, and the Labor Roots of Multiculturalism* (New York University Press, 2011), 100.

13. "Garment Trades Out Communists in New York City," "Communist Methods of Infiltration," US House of Representatives, Subcommittee of the Committee on Un-American Activities (Washington, DC: US Government Printing Office, 1953), 1409.

14. Rachel Abramowitz, *Is That a Gun in Your Pocket? The Truth About Female Power in Hollywood* (New York: Random House, 2000), 19.

15. Vivian Gornick, blog, accessed December 5, 2022, www.versobooks.com/blogs /4688-what-endures-of-the-romance-of-american-communism. Other sources place its membership at 85,000 at its height.

16. Vivian Gornick, blog.

17. Louis Marks, "Obituary, Hannah Weinstein: Film and Television Producer," *The Times* (London), March 16, 1984, 16; Registrar's Office, New York University.

18. For example, Hannah Dorner, "Manhattanville Widens Courses in Girls' Sports," March 20, 1932, B7; "Lisa Lindstrom to Devote Aquatic Skill to Teaching," April 10, 1932, B6; "Miss Locke, Fencing Champion, Pointed for Career in Chemistry," May 29, 1932, B9, all in *New York Herald Tribune*.

19. Hannah Dorner, "Little Liberia Faces Foreign Intervention," *New York Herald Tribune*, September 20, 1931, A5.

CHAPTER 2

1. NCASF was successor to a group called the National Council on Soviet Relations. In most contemporary references, the group was called CASF, without the "National" in front of it. For continuity's sake throughout this book, the more modern name is used. Also, the descriptor "Congress" was often used for Weinstein's events sponsored by the

group, leading to some contemporary mislabeling or more casual use of the group's formal name.

2. See Ronald Radosh and Allis Radosh, "The Nazi-Soviet Pact and Its Aftermath," Chapter 4, in *Red Star over Hollywood* (San Francisco: Encounter Books, 2005).

3. See Radosh and Radosh, "The Nazi-Soviet Pact and Its Aftermath."

4. See Radosh and Radosh, "The Nazi-Soviet Pact and Its Aftermath."

5. "Salute to Our Russian Ally: Report of the Congress of American-Soviet Friendship, New York City, November 7 & 8, 1942," (New York: Congress of American-Soviet Friendship).

6. FBI file 100–371293, Hannah Dorner Weinstein, NARA; Central Intelligence Agency, Information Report.

7. Bella V. Dodd, *School of Darkness* (New York: P. J. Kenedy & Sons, 2017), 71.

8. Dodd, *School of Darkness*, 69.

9. FBI file 100–371293, Hannah Dorner Weinstein.

10. "FULL UNITY URGED WITH THE RUSSIANS: Congress of American-Soviet Friendship Stresses Need of Spiritual Understanding DAVIES ISSUES WARNING Fears German Peace Offensive Here in Which 'Knaves or Fools' Will Take Part," *New York Times*, November 8, 1942, 36. A good resource is William L. O'Neill's *A Better World: Stalinism and the American Intellectuals* (London and New York: Routledge, 2018). Note that "congress" refers to events sponsored by NCASF. For simplicity's sake, the author uses the umbrella organization NCASF when discussing these.

11. For example, "Soviet-Friendship Day Designated by Mayor," *Times-Tribune* (Scranton, PA), November 8, 1943, 5; "American-Soviet Friendship Day Set for Nov. 16," *Pasadena (CA) Post*, November 9, 1943, 3.

12. "Ickes Sees U.S. Fate Bound to Soviets," *New York Times*, November 9, 1943, 1.

13. "Red Army Is Praised for Victories by U.S., British, Chinese Officers," *New York Times*, February 22, 1944, 4.

14. It's not clear if they were.

15. Jo Davidson, *Between Sittings* (New York: The Dial Press, 1951), 341–43.

16. Davidson, *Between Sittings*, 343.

17. Radosh and Radosh, "The Nazi-Soviet Pact and Its Aftermath," 111.

18. For an in-depth analysis of Wallace's political life, see Thomas W. Devine's *Henry Wallace's 1948 Presidential Campaign and the Future of Postwar Liberalism* (Chapel Hill: University of North Carolina Press, 2013); "Artists, Writers Pledge Aid to Roosevelt," *New York Times*, October 6, 1944, 15; "Broadway Stars Aid Roosevelt at Fete," *New York Times*, October 23, 1944, 11.

19. "Artist Group Gives Roosevelt Pledge," *Los Angeles Times*, October 6, 1944, 7.

20. Elinor Siegel, "More Women Than Ever Are Campaigning in Partisan or Independent Groups This Year," *New York Times*, October 30, 1944, 12.

21. "Bette Davis, Fannie Hurst Ask Women to Vote," *Brooklyn Daily Eagle*, October 9, 1944, 11.

22. Henry W. Clune, "Seen and Heard," *Democrat and Chronicle* (New York), November 7, 1944, 31.

23. FBI file 100–50870, Florence Eldridge.

24. FBI file 100-HQ-371293, Hannah Dorner Weinstein, NARA; *Communist Members of Infiltration (Entertainment)* US Congress House Committee on Un-American Activities, 1953, 3871–72. Sloane admits that his memory is somewhat fuzzy, and says he thinks the Bretton Woods conference and the preceding conversations with Weinstein, White, et al. were when they were ICAASP. However, White was not in New York in July of 1945, but was in 1944, and was known to have met with Sloane.

25. For an interesting read on the underreported brilliance of Harry Dexter White, and incisive discussion of his supposed treachery, see James M. Boughton, *Harry White and the American Creed: How a Federal Bureaucrat Created the Modern Global Economy (and Failed to Get the Credit)* (New Haven, CT: Yale University Press, 2021).

26. FBI file, 100-HQ-371293, Hannah Dorner Weinstein; *Communist Members of Infiltration (Entertainment)*, US Congress House Committee on Un-American Activities, 1953, 3872.

27. "World Peace, Reconversion Studied by Artists' Group," *Miami Daily News*, November 26, 1944, 7-B.

28. See *National Health Program: Hearings before the Committee on Education and Labor, United States Senate, Seventy-Ninth Congress, Second Session on S. 1606, A Bill to Provide for a National Health Program* (Washington, DC: US Government Printing Office, 1946), 419.

29. "Show Biz Playing Its Part," *Daily Variety*, February 21, 1945, 38.

30. *Daily Variety*, February 24, 1945, 38.

31. "Political Notes: Glamor Pusses," *Time*, September 9, 1946, online archives, accessed September 19, 2022, http://content.time.com/time/subscriber/article/0,33009 ,855380-5,00.html.

32. The HDC had no formal connection to the Democratic Party.

33. Radosh and Radosh, "The Nazi-Soviet Pact and Its Aftermath," 111.

34. Letter from Hannah Dorner to George Pepper, dated June 12, 1945, State Historical Society of Wisconsin, Madison, Box 4, Folder 21; Nicolas Lewkowicz, *The German Question and the Origins of the Cold War* (Milan, Italy: IPOC di Pietro Condemi), 23.

35. "Ickes Landed in the Money When He Jumped from the Cabinet," *Passaic (NJ) Herald-News*, March 29, 1946, 9.

36. Helen Walker, "Playing Politics—For Keeps," *Mademoiselle*, October 1945, 185.

37. Radosh and Radosh, "The Nazi-Soviet Pact and Its Aftermath," 111.

38. "The Union: One if by Land, Two if by Mistake," *Newsweek* 28, no. 13 (September 23, 1946): 26.

39. "Political Notes: Glamor Pusses."

40. "Political Notes: Glamor Pusses."

CHAPTER 3

1. For example, "Cites PAC School Pro-Red Faculty in Congress Talk," *The Tablet* (Brooklyn, NY), June 22, 1946, 1.

2. Arthur M. Schlesinger Jr., "The U.S. Communist Party," *Life*, July 29, 1946, 93; "Letters to the Editor," *Life*, September 16, 1946, 21.

3. "The Union: One if by Land, Two if by Mistake," 25–27.

4. "Wallace Opposes Hard Policy Toward Russia and Ties with Britain," *Buffalo News*, September 13, 1946, 19; "The Union: One if by Land, Two if by Mistake," 26–27.

5. Devine, *Henry Wallace's 1948 Presidential Campaign*, 17.

6. "In the Matter of J. Robert Oppenheimer: Transcript of Hearing before Personnel Security Board," Washington, DC, April 12–May 6, 1954, 105–6.

7. "Ickes Challenges Liberals on Atom," *New York Times*, October 8, 1946, 3.

8. Alonzo L. Hamby, *Beyond the New Deal: Harry S. Truman and American Liberalism* (New York: Columbia University Press, 1973), 158.

9. "Standard of Living at Stake in Election, Pepper, Murray Say," *Pittsburgh Press*, November 4, 1946, 5.

10. "What Are U.S. Communists Up To?" *Newsweek*, June 2, 1947, 22–29.

11. Joseph and Stewart Alsop, "Tinker to Evers to Chance," (syndicated) *Birmingham News*, June 29, 1947, 63.

12. "10 Liberal Groups United to Form New Political Movement," *Gazette and Daily* (York, PA), 1.

13. Joseph and Stewart Alsop, "Third Party Movement," *Fort Worth Star-Telegram*, July 5, 1947, 6.

14. "Progressives Bar None on Political Faith—Jo Davidson," *Seattle Daily Times*, January 28, 1947, 2.

15. As summarized by Curtis Daniel MacDougall, *Gideon's Army* (New York: Marzani & Munsell, 1965), 109.

16. MacDougall, *Gideon's Army*, 129.

17. MacDougall, *Gideon's Army*, 129.

18. By most credible accounts, Michael Whitney Straight spied for the KGB, but stopped in 1942. Most posit that by the time of Wallace's "ascension," Straight personally believed his editor was good for the *New Republic*, but not the country.

19. William Harlan Hale, "What Makes Wallace Run?" *Harper's Magazine*, February 29, 1948, 241–48.

20. Hale, "What Makes Wallace Run?" 241–48.

21. Hale, "What Makes Wallace Run?" 241–48; interview of Robert W. Kenny, UCLA, transcript, accessed November 1, 2022, https://static.library.ucla.edu/oralhistory/text/masters/21198-zz0008zbrd-3-master.html#chapter29; MacDougall, *Gideon's Army*, 114.

Chapter 4

1. "P. C. A. Merger Authorized to Back Wallace," *Los Angeles Times*, January 19, 1948, 1.

2. "New Political Group Goes to Bat for Labor, Minorities," *California Eagle*, January 16, 1947, 7.

3. "Hollywood Fete Nets $15,110 for Red Probe Defense," *Evening Sun* (Baltimore), March 6, 1948, 2.

4. "My father was the king of obfuscation," Sloane's son explains, "and it was obviously in his interest to do so at that point. Obfuscation and misdirection. Note the mention of the Almanac Singers [in his 'admission']. I think he was proudest of having sung with them on occasion, although apparently many people did through their various iterations." Email, Jonathan Sloane, December 30, 2022.

5. "American Business Consultants: Counter Attack NYC," Ernie Lazar FOIA Collection, retrieved March 25, 2022, https://archive.org/details/AmericanBusinessConsulta ntsCounterattackNYC629189/page/n49/mode/2up.

6. George Mills, "Former FBI Men 'Spied' on 3rd Party," *Des Moines (IA) Register*, August 1, 1948, 1.

7. Devine, *Henry Wallace's 1948 Presidential Campaign*, 198–99.

8. Terry Klefstad, "Shostakovice and the Peace Conference," *Music & Politics* 6, no. 2 (Summer 2012), online journal, https://journals.publishing.umich.edu/mp/site/about/.

9. Phillip Deery, *Red Apple: Communism and McCarthyism in Cold War New York* (New York: Fordham University Press, 2014), 114.

10. Klefstad, "Shostakovice and the Peace Conference."

11. Central Intelligence Agency, Information Report.

12. Central Intelligence Agency, Information Report.

13. Central Intelligence Agency, Information Report.

14. Billy Rose, "Pitching Horseshoes" column, "Of Mice and Marx," *Ithaca Journal*, February 24, 1950, 16.

15. Lester Cole, *Hollywood Red: The Autobiography of Lester Cole* (Palo Alto, CA: Ramparts Press, 1981), 333–34.

16. FBI file 100–371293, Hannah Dorner Weinstein.

17. FBI file 100–371293, Hannah Dorner Weinstein.

18. Robert P. Newman, *Owen P. Lattimore and the "Loss" of China* (Berkeley: University of California Press, 1992), 265–66.

19. Ken Zurski, "A Saintly Supper: Fulton Sheen and the Turning of a Communist," *The Peorian*, April 4, 2014, accessed February 19, 2020, http://www.peorian.com/history/ history-news/local-history/1611-a-saintly-supper.

20. Zurski, "A Saintly Supper."

21. It is important to note that Sheen always maintained—privately and publicly—that his only concern for Communists and Communist sympathizers was the forced atheism dictated by Stalin and the Soviet Union's attempt at a utopian society. In other words, he was not concerned about politics but rather the souls of human beings.

22. Robert M. Lichtman, "Louis Budenz, the FBI, and the 'List of 400 Concealed Communists': An Extended Tale of McCarthy-Era Informing," *American Communist History* 3, no. 1 (June 2004): 25–54.

23. FBI file 100–371293, Hannah Dorner Weinstein.

24. For a good summary, read "Truman's Loyalty Program," Harry S. Truman Library and Museum, https://www.trumanlibrary.gov/education/presidential-inquiries/trumans -loyalty-program.

25. See, for example, "Executive Orders Disposition Tables," Federal Register, National Archives, https://www.archives.gov/federal-register/executive-orders/1947.html; Robert Justin Goldstein, "Prelude to McCarthyism: The Making of a Blacklist," *Prologue Magazine* 38, no. 3 (2006), https://www.archives.gov/publications/prologue/2006/fall/agloso.html.

26. United States Commission on Government Security, *Report of the Commission on Government Security, Pursuant to Public Law 304, 84th Congress, as Amended* (US Government Printing Office, January 1, 1957), 657–58.

27. FBI file 100–371293, Hannah Dorner Weinstein.

28. FBI file 100–371293, Hannah Dorner Weinstein.

29. FBI file 100–371293, Hannah Dorner Weinstein. If T-3 remained the same designation over the years, Harwood was used as an informant at least through 1952.

30. FBI file 100–371293, Hannah Dorner Weinstein; "Committee of One Thousand Formed to Ban Thomas Group," *York (PA) Daily Record*, January 19, 1948, 1.

31. David J. Garrow, "FBI Political Harassment and the FBI Historiography: Analyzing Informants and Measuring the Effects," *Public Historian* 10, no. 4 (Autumn 1988): 10.

32. Correspondence with Ileene Heiman Simon's daughter, Gale Simon-Biernbaum, March 2, 2020, email in possession of the author.

33. See Carol Stabile, "Red Networks: Women Writers and the Broadcast Blacklist" Morris Fromkin Memorial Lecture, October 2, 2008, 4, retrieved November 1, 2021, https://minds.wisconsin.edu/bitstream/handle/1793/46194/Stabile%20Fromkin%20Final.pdf?sequence=1.

34. John Crosby, "He's Agin' Firing of Miss Muir," *Miami Herald*, September 9, 1950, 25.

35. "CBS Asks Staff Sign Loyalty Vow," *New York Daily News*, December 21, 1950, 36.

36. See Carol Stabile, "Red Networks: Women Writers and the Broadcast Blacklist" Morris Fromkin Memorial Lecture October 2, 2008, 6, retrieved November 1, 2021, https://minds.wisconsin.edu/bitstream/handle/1793/46194/Stabile%20Fromkin%20Final.pdf?sequence=1.

37. Peggy Phillips, *My Brother's Keeper* (Lincoln, NE: iUniverse, Inc., 2002), 146.

38. Abramowitz, *Is That a Gun in Your Pocket?*, 16–18.

39. The Dodds and Dodd-Sterns are the inspiration for Erik Larson's *Love, Terror, and an American Family in Hitler's Berlin* (New York: Crown, 2011); FBI file 100–371293, Hannah Dorner Weinstein.

CHAPTER 5

1. New York *Daily News*, December 17, 1950, 95.

2. *Washington (D.C.) Evening Star*, December 17, 1950, 6.

3. "Vishinsky Says Russia Ready to Sign Trade Pacts," *Gazette and Daily* (York, PA), December 3, 1946, 38; FBI file 100-HQ-371293, Hannah Weinstein.

4. Barzman, *The Red and the Blacklist*, 259–60; FBI file 100-HQ-371293, Hannah Weinstein.

5. Rebecca Prime, "'The Old Bogey': The Hollywood Blacklist in Europe." *Film History* 20, no. 4 (2008): 477.

6. Barzman, *The Red and the Blacklist*, 259–60.

7. Barzman, *The Red and the Blacklist*, 259–60; interview, Norma Barzman, by author, September 30, 2019.

8. Dave Mann, "Epicurean Disdain and the Rhetoric of Defiance: Colonel March of Scotland Yard," *Scope: An Online Journal of Film and Television Studies* 11 (June 2008), retrieved July 11, 2021, https://www.nottingham.ac.uk/scope/issues/2008/june-issue-11.aspx.

9. Mann, "Epicurean Disdain and the Rhetoric of Defiance"; "The Return of the Ghost—That's Me, Says Boris," (UK) *Daily Mirror*, July 12, 1952, 12; Lillian Gerard and Gordon Hitchens, "Boris Karloff: The Man Behind the Myth," *Film Comment* 6, no. 1 (Spring 1970): 46–51.

10. Clyde Haberman, "Recalling a Cheerful Man Made Angry by Hypocrisy," *New York Times*, July 11, 2008, B1.

11. Andrew Paul, "Reassessing Blacklist Era Television: Civil Libertarianism in *You Are There*, *The Adventures of Robin Hood*, and *The Buccaneers*," *American Studies* 54, no. 1 (2015): 29–33.

12. For example, in "The Emergence of Jazz," an episode written by Polonsky, *You Are There* turns to a depiction of the closing of the Storyville district in New Orleans during the First World War. The show centered on the debate over whether or not Storyville was a hive of moral depravity or the birthplace of a modern art form. The majority of screen time was taken up by African American jazz musicians, delivering thoughtful monologues about the origins of jazz. This episode aired November 5, 1954, during an era when most depictions of Blacks in America were of minstrel caricatures or other derogatory forms.

13. Jeff Kisseloff, *The Box: An Oral History of Television 1920–1961* (Golden, CO: ReAnimus Press, 1995), 389–391; Paul, "Reassessing Blacklist Era Television," 29–33.

14. The National Archives at Washington, D.C., Washington, D.C., Series Title: Passenger and Crew Lists of Vessels and Airplanes Departing from New York, New York, 07/01/1948-12/31/1956, NAI Number: 3335533, Record Group Title: Records of the Immigration and Naturalization Service, 1787–2004, Record Group Number: 85, Series Number: A4169, NARA Roll Number: 164, retrieved via Ancestry.com, July 16, 2021; FBI file 100–371293, Hannah Dorner Weinstein.

15. Mann, "Epicurean Disdain and the Rhetoric of Defiance"; Walter Bernstein, *Inside Out: A Memoir of the Blacklist* (Boston, MA: Da Capo Press), 248. In fact, Carr had no idea that his book had been made into filmed entertainment until his mother told him she'd seen it on television more than a year later.

16. "The Return of the Ghost—That's Me, Says Boris," 1.

17. Brain Neve, *The Many Lives of Cy Endfield: Film Noir, the Blacklist, and Zulu* (Madison, WI: University of Wisconsin Press), 2015.

18. Bernstein, *Inside Out: A Memoir of the Blacklist*, 248.

19. "New Telepix Shows," *Daily Variety*, December 9, 1953, 28.

20. A special thanks to Dr. James Chapman for explaining this to me.

21. Mann, "Epicurean Disdain and the Rhetoric of Defiance."

22. Douglas G. Greene, *John Dickson Carr: The Man Who Explained Miracles* (Cincinnati, OH: Crippen & Landru, Publishers), 376–77; Steve Chibnall, *The British 'B' Film* (British Film Institute, 2019), 223–25.

23. Neve, *The Many Lives of Cy Endfield*, 104.

24. Kisseloff, *The Box*, 420–21.

25. Kisseloff, *The Box*, 420–21.

26. Kisseloff, *The Box*, 420–21.

27. Jeff Kisseloff, *The Box*, 420–21; Slote's sister Helen Slote Levitt was also a gifted screenwriter. She and husband Al Levitt were blacklisted in the early 1950s. "I assume their blacklisting had something to do with my father's decision to be a front. . . . I always found this an odd detail in the history of blacklisting," recalls Slote's son. "Although my uncle was blacklisted as a writer, he served for a time as the front for a blacklisted composer. He told me the story because of the humour involved in him not knowing anything about music and fronting as a composer. But I was amazed at the incongruity of him fronting when he was himself blacklisted and he said that there was no consolidation of the blacklists: a blacklisted writer was still kosher for other jobs in Hollywood." Email interview with Sam Slote, dated July 27, 2021, in possession of the author.

CHAPTER 6

1. "Letters to the Editor" column, the *Indianapolis Star*, November 9, 1952, 28.

2. "Letters to the Editor" column, the *Indianapolis Star*, April 20, 1953, 8.

3. "Official Will Re-Read Story to Decide if It's Subversive," *Terre Haute Tribune*, November 13, 1953, 1.

4. It's not clear whether White provided this information or not, but in any case, MacLeod died in 1914 and her name does not appear anywhere in this report. She may have been confused by reports about party membership by educator and civil rights activist Mary McLeod Bethune, who was not a member of the Communist Party but was a member of the Independent Citizens Committee for the Arts, Sciences and Professions.

5. Fremont Power, "Foe of Robin Hood Hides Bow and Arrow," *Indianapolis News*, November 13, 1953, 1.

6. "Robin Hood Called Red, Pre-Marx," *Fort Worth Star-Telegram*, November 15, 1953, 34; Dawn Mitchell, "Textbook Group Member Saw Problems with Robin Hood," *Indianapolis Star*, October 21, 2018, A2.

7. "It's Official: Changes and Growth Feature Story of This Film Distributor," *Television Age*, April 1955, 53.

8. "Levy Bros. After Stanton's Scalp?," *Weekly Variety*, August 16, 1950, 25; "It's Official," 53.

9. For a tidy summary, see PBS So Cal, "Make 'Em Laugh: The Funny Business of America, History, Cable Television," December 1, 2008, https://www.pbs.org/wnet/makeemlaugh/featured/history-cable-television/33/, retrieved November 2, 2021.

10. Michele Hilmes, *Hollywood and Broadcasting: From Radio to Cable* (Champaign: University of Illinois Press, 1990), 150.

11. "Television Reigns: Broadcasting Queen Elizabeth's Coronation," Science Museum, October 29, 2018, retrieved November 15, 2021, https://www.sciencemuseum.org.uk/objects-and-stories/television-reigns-broadcasting-queen-elizabeths-coronation.

12. Catherine Johnson and Rob Turnock, eds., *ITV Cultures: Independent Television over Fifty Years* (Berkshire, England: Open University Press, 2005), 16–17.

13. Johnson and Turnock, eds., *ITV Cultures*, 17.

14. Johnson and Turnock, eds., *ITV Cultures*, 17.

15. "The History of ITV, Part 8," Teletronic, n.d., retrieved November 15, 2021, https://www.teletronic.co.uk/pages/history_of_itv_8.html; Lew Grade, *Still Dancing: My Story* (London: HarperCollins, 1987).

16. For example, Doug McIntire and Rob Kamensky, "The Right Angle" column, "WDTV Premier," *Morning Herald* (Uniontown, PA), January 27, 1954, 4.

17. Douglas G. Greene, *John Dickson Carr: The Man Who Explained Miracles* (Cincinnati, OH: Crippen & Landru Publishers), 376.

18. Sid Cole: BFI Screen Online, BECTU Interview, Part 3 (1987), retrieved July 4, 2021, http://www.screenonline.org.uk/audio/id/838166/index.html.

19. Paul, "Reassessing Blacklist Era Television," 39.

CHAPTER 7

1. Marjory Adams, "Handsome Richard Greene Likes the Theatre Better Than Films," *Boston Globe*, January 4, 1953, 82.

2. "Richard Greene Biography," IMDb, retrieved August 22, 2021, https://www.imdb.com/name/nm0338901/bio?ref_=nm_ov_bio_sm.

3. "Richard Greene: Hair-do Made, Broke Career," *Newcastle Sun* (New South Wales, AU), January 14, 1954, 20.

4. Dan Van Neste, *They Coulda Been Contenders: Twelve Actors Who Should Have Become Cinematic Superstars* (Orlando, FL: BearManor Media, 2020), 121.

5. Adams, "Handsome Richard Greene Likes the Theatre Better Than Films," 82.

6. Bob Thomas, "Davy Crockett, Robin Hood Meet in Hollywood Eatery," syndicated column, AP, *Corpus Christi (TX) Caller-Times*, March 31, 1956, 7.

7. Thomas, "Davy Crockett, Robin Hood Meet in Hollywood Eatery," 7.

8. Grade, *Still Dancing*, 158.

9. Grade, *Still Dancing*, 158.

10. Tony Gruner, "'Television Outlook,' Grade Discusses the U.S. and the Future," *Kinematograph Weekly*, January 23, 1958, 22.

11. For example, "Pearl and Dean Over at Southall," *Kinematograph Weekly*, January 27, 1955, 7.

12. *Kinematograph Weekly*, December 23, 1954, 5.

13. Email from Victor Stone to author, dated August 17, 2021, in possession of the author.

14. "Oldest Studio Looks Ahead," *Kinematograph Weekly*, April 14, 1955, 42.

15. A special thank you to John Cimperman Jr. for helping me better understand his father's role in overseas intelligence. Interview, September 3, 2021, notes in possession of the author.

16. A special thank you to John Cimperman Jr.

17. To be sure, the United Kingdom was at this time consolidating a lot of immigration policies owing to wartime resettlements and increased tourism due to the Queen's coronation in 1953. However, Weinstein fell under special purview owing to her reputation as a Communist, or at least a Communist sympathizer.

18. FBI file 100–371293, Hannah Dorner Weinstein.

19. For more about Peter Proud's wartime experiences, read Rick Stroud's *The Phantom Army of Alamein: The Men Who Hoodwinked Rommel* (New York: Bloomsbury, 2012).

20. Peter Proud: BECTU Interview Part 2 (1987), http://www.screenonline.org.uk/audio/id/837682/.

21. Proud: BECTU Interview.

22. "Marquess and Miss Bartok Walk Out as They Are Recognized," *Evening Standard* (London), February 14, 1955, 5.

23. Louis Marks, "Hood Winked," *The Listener* 123, no. 3148 (January 18, 1990): 9.

24. Interview with Helena de Crespo, July 9, 2021, notes in possession of the author.

25. Margaret Cowan, "Ralph Smart Works Alone . . . and Prefers It That Way, *Television Today*, February 19, 1959, 16.

26. Interview with Robert Crabtree, son of Arthur Crabtree, February 22, 2021, notes in possession of the author.

27. Anderson, "Notes from Sherwood," 159–60.

28. Anderson, "Notes from Sherwood," 159–60.

29. Anderson, "Notes from Sherwood," 159–60.

30. Gavin Lambert, *Mainly About Lindsay Anderson* (New York: Alfred A. Knopf, 2000), 79.

31. Christen Kelley, "Retired Flagler Professor Celebrates Oscar-Winning Father, Ring Lardner Jr.," *St. Augustine Record*, February 8, 2020, retrieved October 3, 2021, https://www.staugustine.com/news/20200208/retired-flagler-professor-celebrates-oscar-winning-father-ring-lardner-jr.

32. Ring Lardner Jr. and Victor Navasky, *I'd Hate Myself in the Morning: A Memoir* (Westport and New York: Prospecta Press, 2017); Richard Severo, "Ring Lardner Jr., Wry Screenwriter and Last of the Hollywood 10, Dies at 85," *New York Times*, November 2, 2000, Section C, 23.

CHAPTER 8

1. Lardner Jr. and Navasky, *I'd Hate Myself in the Morning*.

2. Lardner Jr. and Navasky, *I'd Hate Myself in the Morning*.

3. Special thanks to Dr. Amy Zimet for her insight into the legal practice of her father, and to Molly Sandomire and Ivan Sandomire for their insights into the legal practice of their grandfather.

4. Letter from Ian McLellan Hunter and Ring Lardner Jr. to Hannah Weinstein, dated December 16, 1954, Ian McLellan Hunter Papers, 1938–1989, Margaret Herrick Library, Academy of Motion Picture Arts and Sciences (hereafter Hunter Papers).

5. See https://www.bard.edu/archives/voices/koch/koch.php (retrieved October 18, 2021) and "Howard Koch," *Film Comment* 4, no. 4 (July–August 1978): 38. Interview with Peter Koch, March 3, 2021, notes in possession of the author.

6. In 1977, Brown's acting career revived somewhat when he appeared in a film in what he then thought a "minor role, in a film going nowhere." This role was Luke Skywalker's uncle in *Star Wars*.

7. Howard Koch, *As Time Goes By: Memoirs of a Writer* (New York: Harcourt, Brace, Jovanovich), 1979, 201–6; Peter Koch interview.

8. Interview with Kevin Brown, November 8, 2021, notes in possession of the author. Aloha, Kevin.

9. Koch, *As Time Goes By*, 200.

10. Koch, *As Time Goes By*, 203–5.

11. Koch, *As Time Goes By*, 200–201.

12. Letter from Howard Koch to Ian McLellan Hunter and Ring Lardner Jr., January 26, 1955, Hunter Papers.

13. Letter from Howard Koch to Ian McLellan Hunter and Ring Lardner, Jr., dated January 26, 1955, 1, Hunter Papers.

14. Letter from Hannah Weinstein to Ian McLellan Hunter and Ring Lardner Jr., dated January 10, 1955, Hunter Papers.

15. Letter from Hannah Weinstein to Ian McLellan Hunter and Ring Lardner Jr., dated February 9, 1955, Hunter Papers.

16. Phone interview with Albert G. Ruben, November 14, 2019, notes in possession of author.

17. Letter from Howard Koch to Ian McLellan Hunter and Ring Lardner Jr., dated January 26, 1955, 2, Hunter Papers.

18. Letter from Sidney Cole to Hannah Weinstein, dated January 20, 1955, enclosed with Koch letter to Ian McLellan Hunter and Ring Lardner Jr., dated January 26, 1955, Hunter Papers.

19. Letter from Albert Ruben to Ring Lardner Jr. and Ian McLellan Hunter, dated July 20, 1955, Hunter Papers.

20. Letter from Ian McLellan Hunter and Ring Lardner Jr, dated November 20, 1954, Hunter Papers.

21. Letter from Ian McLellan Hunter and Ring Lardner Jr, dated November 20, 1954, Hunter Papers.

22. Ring Lardner Jr., "My Life on the Blacklist," *Saturday Evening Post*, October 14, 1961, 38–44.

23. Lardner Jr., "My Life on the Blacklist," 38–44.

24. Lardner Jr., "My Life on the Blacklist," 38–44.

25. Marks, "Hood Winked," 8–9.

26. Marks, "Hood Winked," 8–9.

27. Hazel Rowley, *Christina Stead: A Biography* (New York: Henry Holt & Co., 1994), 423.

28. Anne Edwards, *Leaving Home: A Hollywood Writer's Years Abroad* (Lanham, MD: Scarecrow Press, 2012), 39; email from Anne Edwards to author, dated December 14, 2021, in possession of the author.

CHAPTER 9

1. Letter from Hannah Weinstein to Ring Lardner Jr. and Ian McLellan Hunter, dated February 9, 1955, Box 283, Hunter Papers.

2. Letter from Albert Ruben to Ring Lardner Jr. and Ian McLellan Hunter, dated April 13, 1955, Box 283, Hunter Papers.

3. Telegram from Hannah Weinstein to Daniel Sandomire, dated February 11, 1955, Box 283, Hunter Papers.

4. Letter from Daniel Sandomire to Sy Fischer, dated February 16, 1955; letter from Sy Fischer to Ian McLellan Hunter, dated February 17, 1955, Box 283, Hunter Papers.

5. Phone interview with Albert G. Ruben.

6. Phone interview with Albert G. Ruben; "An Interview with Albert Ruben," *Film Studies* 7, no. 1 (Winter 2005): 104–15.

7. Special thanks to the family of Marie Malkus (Miles).

8. Albert Ruben, [interviewed by] David Marc, New York City, March 9, 1998, Steven H. Scheuer Television History Interviews, Syracuse University Special Collections Research Center, New York.

9. Letter from Albert Ruben to Ring Lardner Jr. and Ian McLellan Hunter, dated March 3, 1955, Box 283, Hunter Papers.

10. Letter from Hannah Weinstein to Ring Lardner Jr. and Ian McLellan Hunter, dated March 14, 1955, Hunter Papers.

11. Steven H. Scheuer, "TV Keynotes," *Times* (Munster, IN), March 21, 1955, 7.

12. Tom Clavin, "Fast Forward Through 30 Years of TV," *New York Times*, April 19, 1992, L12.

13. David Colker, "First TV Critic to Give Advance Reviews," *Los Angeles Times*, June 9, 2014, 12; Clavin, "Fast Forward Through 30 Years of TV."

14. Interview with Alida Brill-Scheuer, December 1, 2021, notes in possession of the author; Scheuer, "TV Keynotes," 7.

15. Steven H. Scheuer, "TV Keynotes," *Times*, March 22, 1955, 3.

16. Scheuer, "TV Keynotes," 3.

17. Letter from Ring Lardner Jr. and Ian McLellan Hunter to Albert Ruben, dated April 9, 1955, Hunter Papers.

18. Letter from Albert Ruben to Ring Lardner Jr. and Ian McLelland Hunter, dated March 18, 1955, Hunter Papers.

19. Letter from Ring Lardner Jr. and Ian McLellan Hunter to Albert Ruben, dated April 9, 1955, Hunter Papers.

20. Anderson, "Notes from Sherwood," 159–60.

21. For his trouble, Duncan received a commendation of bravery from Queen Elizabeth II.

22. Letter from Albert Ruben to Ring Lardner Jr. and Ian McLellan Hunter, dated June 11, 1955, Box 283, Hunter Papers.

23. Letter from Hannah Weinstein to Ring Lardner Jr. and Ian McLellan Hunter, dated April 12, 1955, Hunter Papers.

24. Monopoly Problems in Regulated Industries, Part II—The Television Industry, Thursday, September 20, 1956, House of Representatives, Antitrust Subcommittee of the Committee on the Judiciary, New York, NY, 3993–94.

25. As other producers and distributors were doing at this time, Official Films first made a deal with several large "flagship" stations, such as KTTV in Los Angeles, with an "escape clause" that let it cancel the deal if a national advertiser decided to pick up

the rights, which it did, sowing continued ill will between independent stations and the networks.

26. Letter from Ring Lardner Jr. and Ian McLellan Hunter to Hannah Weinstein, dated June 6, 1955; letter from Albert Ruben to Ring Lardner Jr. and Ian McLellan Hunter, dated June 23, 1955; letter from Hannah Weinstein to Ring Lardner Jr. and Ian McLellan Hunter, dated June 24, 1955, Box 283, Hunter Papers.

27. Letter from Ring Lardner Jr. and Ian McLellan Hunter to Albert Ruben, dated May 5, 1955, Box 283, Hunter Papers.

28. Letter from Albert Ruben to Ian McLellan Hunter, dated May 9, 1955, Box 283, Hunter Papers.

29. Letter from Albert Ruben to Ian McLellan Hunter, dated May 9, 1955, Box 283, Hunter Papers.

30. Letter from Ring Lardner Jr. and Ian McLellan Hunter to Hannah Weinstein, dated May 18, 1955, Box 283, Hunter Papers.

31. Letter from Ring Lardner Jr. and Ian McLellan Hunter to Hannah Weinstein, dated May 18, 1955, Box 283, Hunter Papers.

32. Marks, "Hood Winked," 9.

33. Anderson, "Notes from Sherwood," 159–60.

34. Anderson, "Notes from Sherwood," 159–60.

CHAPTER 10

1. Jack E. Anderson, "TV Commercials Make British Laugh," *Miami Herald*, September 11, 1955, 106; Ancestry.com, US Departing Passenger and Crew Lists, 1914–1966, database on-line, Provo, UT, USA: Ancestry.com Operations, Inc., 2016.

2. Herb Rau, "Off to London Via Martinis," *Miami News*, September 4, 1955, 16.

3. Letter from Hannah Weinstein to Ring Lardner Jr. and Ian McLellan Hunter, dated June 29, 1955, Box 283, Hunter Papers.

4. "Old World Brought to New," *Raleigh Register and Beckley* (WV) *Post-Herald*, January 14, 1956, 11.

5. Dwight Newton, "Day and Night with Radio and Television" column, "Sherwood Forest," *San Francisco Examiner*, September 12, 1955, 27.

6. Mary Wood, *Just Lucky I Guess* (Garden City, NY: Doubleday, 1962), 83–84. Thank you to Sally Wood Thomson for providing me with a copy of these pages from her mother's book.

7. Fairfax Nesbit, "Britisher Becomes Deputy of Texas," *Dallas Morning News*, September 9, 1955, 13.

8. Will Jones, "Jones Visits Robin Hood's Haunts and Wonders Why," *Minneapolis (MN) Tribune*, September 11, 1955, 59.

9. William Keough, "TV Writers' Safari to Britain Heralds New Era," Section VI: Amusements and the Arts, *Providence Journal*, September 18, 1955, 171.

10. Ernie Hill, "Liberace and Roy Rogers Descend on British Sets," *Oakland (CA) Tribune*, September 11, 1955, 78.

11. Anderson, "TV Commercials Make British Laugh," 106.

12. Merrill Pannett, "Advertisers Don't Miss Trick with Robin Hood Show," *TV Guide*, as reprinted in the *Philadelphia Inquirer*, September 7, 1955, 35.

13. Hal Humphrey, "Banished to Siberia," *Mirror News* (Los Angeles), September 9, 1955, 26.

14. Keough, "TV Writers' Safari to Britain Heralds New Era," 171.

15. Art Cullison, "'Robin Hood' Sword Play Draws Blood," *Akron Beach Journal*, September 9, 1955, 42; Herb Rau, "Egad! Served by Wenches," *Miami News*, September 8, 1955, 25; Peg Simpson, "TV Writers Dine at 12th Century Feast in London," *Syracuse (NY) Post-Standard*, September 10, 1955, 7; "Ye Ed Eats Boars Head and Quaffs Mead on TV Exploration of Britain," *New York Daily News*, September 25, 1955, 401.

16. Robert L. Sokolsky, "Looking and Listening," *Syracuse Herald Journal*, September 10, 1955, 9; Anderson, "TV Commercials Make British Laugh," 106.

17. Dwight Newton, *San Francisco Examiner*, September 23, 1957, 67. As many television writers did in the 1950s, Newton resurrected notes he didn't use from his coverage stemming from the September 1955 junket, which he attended. And as others did, he bolstered that with information gleaned from other reporters and by viewing more recent episodes. Newton mentions Patricia Driscoll as the new Marian, for example.

CHAPTER 11

1. "On the International Scene," *Advertising Age*, April 30, 1956, 89.

2. Chapman, *Swashbucklers*, 25.

3. Chapman, *Swashbucklers*, 25.

4. Chapman, *Swashbucklers*, 25–26; "When Knighthood Was in Flower on TV Film," *Variety*, January 9, 1957, 103.

5. Clifford Davis, "Maid Marian Is Quitting the TV Forest," *Daily Mirror*, January 31, 1957, 1.

6. Mel Heimer, "John Bull Trains Big Guns on TV," *Miami Herald*, October 28, 1956, 9.

7. Chapman, *Swashbucklers*, 23–25.

8. Margaret McManus, "'Robin Hood' Plans Tour of America," *Fort Worth Star-Telegram*, October 17, 1956, 29.

9. Email from Christopher Toyne to author, dated November 14, 2020, in possession of the author.

10. Interview with Oliver Hansard, September 23, 2021, notes in possession of the author; email with Maggie McLean, dated October 21, 2020, in possession of the author.

11. "Official Blueprints 'Slade of Lancers,'" *Billboard*, July 23, 1955, 12.

12. "Sapphire's Big Sea-Going 'Studio,'" *Variety*, November 9, 1955, 7.

13. "'Pirate' Vessel: Falmouth Mayor Pays an Official Visit," *West Briton and Cornwall Advertiser*," June 21, 1956, 6.

14. Andrew Paul, "The Roots of Post-Racial Neoliberalism in Blacklist Era Hollywood" (diss., University of Minnesota, March 2014), 213–24.

15. "Newest Two-man Set-up in the Business," *Kinematograph Weekly*, September 13, 1956, 22.

16. https://historyproject.org.uk/interview/c-m-cyril-pennington-richards.

17. Email from Jennifer Risner Read to author, August 7, 2021, and email from Roger Seifert to author, November 16, 2021, both in possession of the author.

18. Phillips, *My Brother's Keeper*; phone and email discussions with Jon Bucci, son of Phillips, in possession of the author.

19. Phillips, *My Brother's Keeper*, 87.

20. Phillips, *My Brother's Keeper*, 144–46.

21. Frank Launder, "Obituary: Thelma Connell," *Film & TV Technician* 41, no. 390 (June 1976): 5; Melanie Bell, *Movie Workers: The Women Who Made British Cinema* (Urbana: University of Illinois Press, 2021), 87–93.

22. Thank you, Jim Kahn, for the funnier version of this story. Phone interview with Jim Kahn, December 2, 2020, notes in possession of the author.

23. Letter from Hannah Weinstein to Lillian Hellman, dated January 23, 1956; letter from Lillian Hellman to Hannah Weinstein, dated January 30, 1956, Lillian Hellman Papers, Box 84.10, Harry Ransom Humanities Research Center, University of Texas at Austin.

24. "TV Turpin," *Sunday Mirror* (UK), February 10, 1957, 16; "British TV Film Exports Bring in the Dollars," *Kinematograph Weekly*, February 28, 1957, 34.

25. $42,000,000 Yield Thus Far on Robin Hood Merchandising," *Variety*, October 30, 1957, 33.

26. "A Problem Faces Robin's Girl Friend," *Leicester (UK) Evening Mail*, March 15, 1957, 7; as related by Sean Hogan, in his obituary for O'Farrell: "Robin Hood's courageous sweetheart," *Irish Times*, November 6, 1999, retrieved November 15, 2021, https://www.irishtimes.com/news/robin-hood-s-courageous-sweetheart-1.247231.

27. Tom Valance, "Obituary: George Baxt," *Independent* (UK), July 10, 2003, https://www.independent.co.uk/news/obituaries/george-baxt-36736.html.

28. "Syndication Review," *Variety*, November 15, 1957, 54; "'In Vision': Ideals and a Wall," *The Stage*, January 16, 1958, 5; "Margaret Cowan's Stage View," *The Stage*, September 11, 1958, 7.

29. "Television Outlook, by Tony Gruner: 'A Lusty Baby, but It Needs a Careful Diet,'" *Kinematograph Weekly*, September 25, 1958, 18.

30. "Margaret Cowan Writes on The Four Just Men: A TV Series Which Makes TV History," *The Stage*, February 19, 1959, 10.

31. American Broadcasting Company was still building its identity after its merger with Paramount Theaters. Weinstein most likely had meetings with the company, but until about 1962, its lineups typically included Disney fare and programming purchased from Warner Bros. Dramatic series did not become a staple until the first half of 1960.

32. Cowen, "The Four Just Men," 18.

33. Ramsden Greig, "Mr. Hawkins Joined the Serial Brigade," *Evening Standard*, September 12, 1959, 10.

34. Thanks to Larry Ceplair for explaining this blacklist gray area to me.

35. Tise Vahimagi, "Obituary: Edwin Astley," BFI Screenonline, retrieved November 22, 2021, http://www.screenonline.org.uk/people/id/771888/.

36. "Zero Is British Short Entry for Venice," *Kinematograph Weekly*, June 30, 1960, 6. The author respectfully requests that anyone who has a copy of this eight-minute film to get in touch!

37. "Sapphire Films Buy Conan Doyle Film Rights," *Coventry Evening Telegraph*, February 24, 1960, 37.

38. Bill Edwards, "Production," *Kinematograph Weekly*, March 3, 1960, 18.

CHAPTER 12

1. Cathryn Rose, "The Quiet Woman," *Leicester Evening Mail*, January 16, 1959, 5.

2. Interview with Jill Langley, April 20, 2022, British Entertainment History Project, https://historyproject.org.uk/interview/jill-langley.

3. Abramowitz, *Is That A Gun in Your Pocket?*, 19.

4. Interview with Angela Babin, July 15, 2021, notes in possession of the author; email with Angela Babin, December 20, 2022, in possession of the author.

5. Interview with Angela Babin; Abramowitz, *Is That a Gun in Your Pocket?*, 21.

6. Interview with Angela Babin; email with Angela Babin.

7. Email between author and Victor Stone, dated August 17, 2021, in possession of the author.

8. FBI file 100–371293, Hannah Dorner Weinstein.

9. Margaret Cowan, *The Stage*, June 23, 1960, 11.

10. "Elizabeth Taylor: She Is Filming Cleopatra," *Evening Standard*, August 22, 1960, 10; "Film Star Changes Her Mind," *Esher (UK) News and Mail*, August 26, 1960, 7; Henry Fielding, "Homeless Liz," *Daily Herald* (London), August 23, 1960, 2.

11. Interview with Cyril Pennington-Richards, January 9, 1990, British Entertainment History Project, retrieved December 15, 2021, https://historyproject.org.uk/interview/c-m-cyril-pennington-richards.

12. Abramowitz, *Is That A Gun in Your Pocket?*, 18; Rebecca Prime, *Hollywood Exiles in Europe: The Blacklist and Cold War Film* (New Brunswick: Rutgers Press, 2014), 173.

13. "'Robin Hood' Film Studios Lost £78,000 in Year," *Evening Standard*, April 24, 1961, 17.

14. FBI file 100-HQ-371293, Hannah Dorner Weinstein.

15. FBI file 100-HQ-371293, Hannah Dorner Weinstein.

16. "Weinstein was kind to my grandmother and quite lovely to my mother," Fisher's granddaughter noted.

17. Abramowitz, *Is That A Gun in Your Pocket?*, 18.

CHAPTER 13

1. Rowley, *Christina Stead*, 422.

2. Frank Krutnik, Steve Neale, Brian Neve, and Peter Stanfield, eds., *"Un-American" Hollywood: Politics and Film in the Blacklist Era* (New Jersey: Rutgers University Press, 2007).

3. At age ninety-one, Lees declared that the speech he delivered in 1951 to the House Committee on Un-American Activities was the best thing he ever wrote.

4. Interview with Shirl Hendryx, December 10, 2020, notes in possession of the author; interview with Nancy Flanagan, December 18, 2020, notes in possession of the author.

5. Len Scher, *The Un-Canadians: True Stories of the Blacklist Era* (Toronto: Lester Publishing, 1992), 40–41.

6. Gene Spagnoli, "22 Thousand Cheer Gene & Peace Here," *New York Daily News*, August 16, 1968, 2.

7. See, for example, Robert Sklar's *Movie-Made America: A Cultural History of American Movies* (New York: Vintage Books, 2012).

AFTERWORD

1. Mollie Gregory, *Women Who Run the Show: How a Brilliant and Creative New Generation of Women Stormed Hollywood* (New York: St. Martin's Press, 2002), 113.

2. Carol A. Stabile, *The Broadcast 41: Women and the Anti-Communist Blacklist* (University of London: Goldsmiths Press, 2018), 158.

3. Stabile, *The Broadcast 41*, 158.

4. For example, Central Intelligence Agency, Information Report, 3; Cyril Pennington-Richards interview.

5. Phone interview with Joseph Stevenson, July 9, 2021, notes in possession of the author.

6. Patricia Eliot Tobias, "A Shadow over the Town," *Writers Guild of America, West* 6, no. 2 (February 2002): 53.

7. Sara Weber, email to author, January 12, 2023, in possession of the author.

8. Marks, "Hood Winked," 9.

9. Ring Lardner Jr. papers, "Speeches," Margaret Herrick Library, Academy of Motion Picture Arts and Sciences; Ray Loynd, "Liberty Hill Salutes Weinstein," *Daily Variety*, April 18, 1984, 4.

10. Douglas Boyd, "Richard the Lionheart May Not Have Spoken English—Plus 7 More Surprising Facts," History Extra, April 8, 2020, https://www.historyextra.com/period/medieval/8-things-you-probably-didnt-know-about-richard-the-lionheart/.

Index